2/2012

WITH ...

YOUR MUSICIANSHIP AND YOUR
WILLINGNESS TO GENEROUSLY SHARE
YOUR KNOWLEDGE AND INSPIRE OTHERS.
YOU HAVE BROUGHT MUCH JOY
TO MANY MUSICIANS AND AUDIENCES

Warmest best wishes,

Within the Sphere
of
The Master

Within the Sphere of The Master

My Recollections as a Student and Long Time Colleague of Adolph Herseth, Trumpeter Supreme of the Chicago Symphony Orchestra

Timothy J. Kent

Silver Fox Enterprises
Ossineke, Michigan
2006

Copyright © 2006 by Timothy J. Kent
Published by Silver Fox Enterprises
P.O. Box 176
11504 U.S. 23 South
Ossineke, Michigan, 49766

All photographs by Timothy or Dorothy Kent unless otherwise noted
All drawings by Richard Kanter unless otherwise noted
Printed by Thomson-Shore Inc., Dexter, Michigan

Publishers Cataloging-in-Publications Data
Kent, Timothy J.
Within the Sphere of the Master; My Recollections as a Student and Long Time Colleague of Adolph Herseth, Trumpeter Supreme of the Chicago Symphony Orchestra
260 pp., 6 x 9 inches.
Contents:
1. Music. 2. Symphonic Music. 3. Musicians. 4. The Art of Playing Trumpet. 5. Trumpet Players. 6. The Art of Playing Brass Instruments. 7. Brass Players. 8. Chicago Symphony Orchestra. 9. Biography of Adolph S. Herseth. 10. Autobiography of Timothy J. Kent.

Library of Congress Number 2006900584
International Standard Book Number 9780965723053

Front Cover: Tim Kent and Bud Herseth at Orchestra Hall in November of 1996, on the occasion of Tim's official retirement party, after they had performed the Mozart 92nd and Beethoven 7th together. Tim is sporting the Chicago Symphony Orchestra Theodore Thomas Medallion for Distinguished Service, which Bud presented to him at the festivities (photo by Avis Herseth).

Other Books by Timothy J. Kent:

Birchbark Canoes of the Fur Trade, Volumes I and II

Tahquamenon Tales; Experiences of an Early French Trader and His Native Family

Ft. Pontchartrain at Detroit; A Guide to the Daily Lives of Fur Trade and Military Personnel, Settlers, and Missionaries at French Posts, Volumes I and II

Paddling Across the Peninsula; An Important Cross-Michigan Canoe Route During the French Regime

Rendezvous at the Straits; Fur Trade and Military Activities at Fort de Buade and Fort Michilimackinac, 1669-1781, Volumes I and II

Acknowledgements

Numerous individuals assisted me in various ways in my development as a musician. The most obvious and direct input was generously offered by my trumpet teachers, including my father George Kent, Cliff Lillya at the University of Michigan, and Bud Herseth. In addition, the many fellow players with whom I worked over the span of nearly four decades all contributed to my advancement and my deep love of music, as also did Archie Best and Charlie Lenz, directors of the Alpena High School Band and the Alpena City Band, respectively, and certain of the other conductors under whom I performed over the years.

Finally, my wife Doree, who has been my dear friend since we first met at the age of fourteen, was absolutely vital to my successes. I simply could not have thrived without her constant encouragement and support during all of my years of development, as well as during the decades of professional work. She also scoured the manuscript of these memoirs, made many valuable suggestions, and reminded me of numerous events from my years as a musician.

To Doree and all the other individuals who helped and encouraged me along the way, I express my heartfelt gratitude.

Timothy J. Kent

For Doree, Kevin, and Ben, my family,

Whose understanding, patience, and wholehearted support have made both of my careers possible.

Obstacles
are those frightful things you see
when you take your eyes off your goal.

Henry Ford

Table of Contents

List of Illustrations

1. Tim Kent at age 16, with his combo of fellow students called The Blue Notes.

2. Bud Herseth at U of M on October 1, 1967, the day Tim first met him and first heard symphonic music in a live performance.

3. Caricature of Tim after his freshman year of college.

4. Bud demonstrating a passage in his basement studio, during one of Tim's lessons ca. 1970.

5. Two very supportive spouses, Doree Kent and Avis Herseth at the Herseth home in July of 1973, as the Kents were about to depart for their life in Germany.

6. Bud with Kevin Kent, 1976.

7. Tim prepared for a trip to his practice studio at a distant church, loaded with Kevin, four trumpets, and diaper bag.

8. The Chicago Symphony Orchestra, of which Tim was a member for nearly eighteen years.

9-10. Two impressions by Richard Kanter, CSO oboist, after listening to 140 candidates audition for the trumpet position in the Symphony which Tim won in January of 1979.

11-12. Two impressions by Richard Kanter, CSO oboist, after listening to 140 candidates audition for the trumpet position in the Symphony which Tim won in January of 1979.

13. The longest-running unchanged trumpet section in the history of the Chicago Symphony, together for thirteen years:

Bud Herseth, Tim Kent, George Vosburgh, and Will Scarlett (with former section member Phil Smith, visiting from New York), during summer of 1980.

14. Tim, George, and Phil paddling during the same summer gathering.

15. Poster for program of trumpet duets and solos by Bud and Tim in 1984.

16. CSO brass section rehearsing in Orchestra Hall during fall of 1982: trumpets Tim Kent, George Vosburgh, and Bud Herseth, trombones Jay Friedman, Frank Crisafulli, and Ed Kleinhammer, tuba Arnold Jacobs, and horns Dick Oldberg, Norm Schweikert, and Dale Clevenger.

17. Tim keeping his chops in shape, while paddling the Mattawa River in Ontario with Doree and their sons Kevin and Ben, June of 1984.

18. Tim reading backstage amid CSO steamer trunks during a European tour, before a concert in Amsterdam in January of 1985.

19. Bud demonstrating for Doree how his chops feel after a concert, during 1986 tour of Japan.

20. Visiting Maestro Solti at his home in London at the conclusion of another European tour, September 19, 1989: Tim, Solti, George Vosburgh, and Bud.

21. Colleagues enjoying brunch outside of the Maestro's poolside music room: Sando Shia, Betty Lambert, Frank Fiatarone, Sam Magad, and Tim.

22. Bud and Maestro Solti, at the farewell party hosted by the Maestro in Tokyo on April 18, 1990, at the end of another Japan tour.

23. Tim and Doree at the Chicago Symphony 100th anniversary festivities in October of 1991.

24. Arrival of the Kent family at Ft. Chipewyan in northern Alberta, at the northwestern end of the 3,000 mile fur trade canoe route from Montreal, in August of 1995.

25. Artwork presented to Bud by Tim and Doree for his 75th birthday in July of 1996.

26. Bud preparing to drape Tim with the CSO Theodore Thomas Medallion for Distinguished Service, at the official retirement party for Tim in November of 1996.

27. With Henry Fogel, President of the CSO, listening, Bud recounting his 27 years of association with Tim, including nine years of mentoring and then eighteen years as colleagues together in the section.

28. The CSO trumpet section at Tim's retirement festivities: Mark Ridenour, John Hagstrom (who replaced Tim), Tim, and Bud. Doree was made an honorary section member for the day.

29. Bud celebrating with Doree and the Kent sons Ben and Kevin.

30. Tim as the newest member of the CSO, in January of 1979 (in the author section).

31. Tim after his retirement from the Orchestra, as a living history presenter (in the author section).

Preface

For more than a half-century, Adolph "Bud" Herseth has been a living legend in the music world. Having served as the principal trumpet of the Chicago Symphony Orchestra for fifty-three years, he is acknowledged as the greatest symphonic trumpet player of all time. In fact, he is generally regarded as the very finest orchestral player among all brass instrumentalists who have ever practiced the art (although Bud is too modest and self-effacing to admit to these worldwide assessments of his artistry). Under his leadership and guidance, the entire brass section of the Chicago Symphony became the most distinguished in the world.

This book presents a comprehensive memoir of the musical life of Timothy Kent, one of Adolph Herseth's finest students. It includes a detailed description of the many years of training which Tim received from Bud (providing an extensive discussion of the master's musical concepts and teaching methods), as well as an account of Tim's professional career that followed, including eighteen years as a member of the Chicago Symphony trumpet section. His account is truly an insider's perspective on the musical life of Bud Herseth and the phenomenal brass section which he led. It will be of great interest to professional and avocational musicians, teachers, audiophiles, and music enthusiasts everywhere.

Chapter One

Prelude
1949-1967

I have had the privilege and good fortune of being probably the only trumpet player who was taught and transformed by Bud Herseth from an absolute greenhorn in symphonic music into a high-level performer over the course of a very extended, long-term period. In addition, I eventually became his colleague in the Chicago Symphony Orchestra, in which we worked together for eighteen years. These two experiences have given me a unique double perspective on his artistry, his genius, and his work ethic.

During the previous half-century or more, extremely few trumpet players in the world have had ready access to Bud's personal guidance and leadership, as either a student much less as a colleague. My intent in writing this memoir is to relate many of the personal experiences that I had with the master, first as a protegé and later as a member of his section, as well as to share many of the lessons that he passed on to me, both by directive and by example. These recollections are intended to inform and inspire not only brass players, but also other inter- ested individuals.

I first met Adolph Herseth in Ann Arbor, Michigan on October 1, 1967, when I was a brand new freshman at the University of Michigan. On that day, I heard for the very first time symphonic music played live; it was only a few weeks ear- lier that I had been first introduced to such music on record- ings, in music literature/history class. That sunny Sunday afternoon in October, I heard the Chicago Symphony play "Ciaconna" by Buxtehude (arranged by Chavez), the world premiere of the *Seventh Symphony* of Roger Sessions (which had been commissioned by the University for its sesquicentennial year of 1967), *Nobilissima Visione Suite* by Hindemith, and Ravel's *La Valse*. In addition, the second piece on the program was the *Concerto for Trumpet in D Major* by Teleman, featuring Mr. Herseth. (To this day, I am still awed by the tape recording I have of the live performance of this piece which he and the orchestra did two weeks later back in Orchestra Hall in Chicago.) After the heavenly rush of the concert, I eagerly made my way to the stage door to meet the trumpet master, get his autograph, and take his picture with my Polariod camera. When I framed and hung those two treasured mementos on the wall in my dorm room the next day, I could never have imagined that, eleven years and three months later, I would be one of Bud's colleagues in that trumpet section. In fact, until that fateful Sunday afternoon, I had not even imagined that I would become a professional player.

I was born one month premature in May of 1949. My parents, who had been married near the end of the war in 1945, had moved to the tiny crossroads community of Ossineke (population ca. 300) in the northeastern Lower Peninsula of Michigan during the summer of 1948. They had moved after having had minimal success making ends meet in Oak Park, my father's home town, the first suburb west of Chicago. During high school, Dad had studied trumpet with the commercial players who were part of the NBC staff at the Merchandise Mart in downtown Chicago, before the network moved to New York City. He had long held dreams of becoming a professional musician, hoping to begin after his stint in various dance bands and concert bands in the Army was completed. However, hundreds of other players had similar goals, so there was not enough work to go around when the many GI musicians returned home after the war. Even with Dad working as a sales clerk at a music store and selling Fuller brushes door-to-door on the side, and Mom doing piecework secretarial tasks at home, their expenses totaled more than their income. So they moved to Ossineke with their toddler son (my older brother), to the area where my mother had been born and raised on a pioneer farm. In this region, housing costs and living expenses were much cheaper, so they purchased from one of the relatives a very small, two-bedroom log house beside the highway.

In Alpena, the town ten miles from Ossineke with a population of 10,000, the solitary music store had no employment offerings for my father. So he utilized his GI Bill to attend cosmetology school in Alpena, and then rented an upstairs office space in the downtown area there, to operate his modest hairdressing shop by himself. During that first year up north, Dad sold his trumpet to generate the cash to buy a set of chicks to raise in the chicken coop behind the house, for the eventual production of eggs and meat. My parents also raised rabbits for a time in the rabbit pen in the yard, as food items. The winter after I was born, in 1950, they began baking bread in their kitchen to sell to neighbors, and also to deliver to grocery stores in Alpena. Summer tourists also stopped at the house to buy bread, and eventually other baked goods as well. A few years later, my parents also became the managers of the tiny credit union of the Catholic church in Ossineke. In time, this business expanded enough that they held open hours at the living room table in our home two evenings a week; by the time I was of high school age, the credit union had developed into a part-time business, with limited daytime and evening hours in an office in the church hall. After my younger brother and sister joined our family in 1953 and 1956, an addition was built onto our 20 by 22 foot log home; this necessary expansion was financed by the meager combined income from the beauty shop, the home bakery, and the credit union.

My first decade was filled with attending the area-wide elementary school, a half-mile walk from home, and creating my own simple fun with my older brother Mike. With very few other people around, we played catch outdoors with each other for hundreds of hours, and generally entertained ourselves. In time, we grew old enough to romp in the adjacent fallow field and woods, go fishing in the nearby Devil River, and ride our bikes to Lake Huron a mile and a half away, where we spent many warm summer days at the white sand beach. The roofless basement of an abandoned uncompleted house served as a court for our handball games. This was a generally carefree existence in an insulated environment, with no television, little music, and few books in our lives, except the school texts that were used during the school year.

However, the activities that were available to us certainly increased just before I turned ten. That spring, Dad called Mike and me together and asked us if we would like to learn to play the trumpet from him. When we answered in the affirmative, he got out his old mouthpiece, and showed us how to buzz it to produce what would eventually be trumpet sounds. He then ordered from a buddy from the Army band days, who lived in a Chicago suburb, an Olds student-line trumpet plus an Olds mouthpiece for me (when it would arrive, the older mouth-piece would belong to Mike), as well as the two standard etude books which Dad had been trained with during his own youth, the Arban and St. Jacome books. While we waited for a month for these wonderful packages to arrive, we practiced daily under our father's direction on the single mouthpiece. That summer, Little League baseball and Boy Scouts were also intro-duced into our little community, both of which we avidly enjoyed for years. Our world was expanding somewhat, although it would continue to be a quiet, backwater place right out of Norman Rockwell Americana.

My route of progress on the trumpet from these earliest beginnings to my first lesson in Bud's basement studio ten years later was rather unusual, compared to the organized musical upbringing of most of the other players who ultimate-ly became members of the Chicago Symphony. The zig-zag course of my non-traditional training also permeated my later outlook and approach, compared to the approach of most typ-ically trained symphonic musicians.

With the arrival of the single Olds trumpet for us to share, plus my own personal mouthpiece and the two etude books, my brother Mike and I started our lessons, at about the time of my tenth birthday. These training sessions took place officially once each week; the insistent tapping of my father's slippered foot on the oak floorboards, helping to solidify my rhythms, is indelibly fixed in my brain cells. However, much of his coaching was delivered informally through the wall, from the hallway or the bathroom, while we were practicing in our bedroom. "Slow down the tempo a little." "Make those articulations clearer." "Don't rush the rhythm."

The solid foundations of technical brass playing that my father developed in me, over the course of eight years of lessons, served me very well during the following years of higher training and during my entire professional career. Not a single aspect of his fundamentals ever required alteration. Dad was entirely unacquainted with symphonic playing and its literature; however, his understanding of the technical aspects of playing the instrument was excellent, as well as the use of those techniques within the context of concert band, jazz band, and combo performance. Later lessons with Clifford Lillya at U of M and Bud in Chicago added many further dimensions, as well as multiple layers of refinement and knowledge, to Dad's original foundations; however, these additions were supplemental to the solid grounding of his home training. Our father helped to develop the same degree of aptitude on the trumpet in each of his four children, although he had never taught any students before us, nor did he ever teach anyone after his fifteen years of instructing us. All of my siblings played through their high school years; afterward, my younger brother Chris earned a University of Michigan degree in trumpet performance but pursued a career in real estate development and community planning; Mike became an engineer and then a housing administrator; and Elyse became a veterinarian specializing in cats and, beginnning from scratch at the age of 45, a top-notch competitive body-builder.

Strange as it may seem, during the course of my many years of lessons with Dad, he never once demonstrated on the horn, and we had no recordings of his playing. However, from his Army friend in Chicago we soon began receiving trumpet albums in the mail. These 33 r.p.m. platters from the outside world would serve as my only aural role models until I first heard legit music as a freshman at U of M (legit music is a term used by jazz and commercial musicians to refer to symphonic music). Over my years of growth as a young player, until I entered college, I listened for many hundreds of hours to these thrilling albums of Rafael Mendez, Maynard Ferguson, Al Hirt (his playing on his very earliest recordings, before he became highly commercialized, was absolutely mind-blowing), Doc Severinsen, and Harry James. The artistry of these expressive, dramatic, extroverted musicians would color my tastes and approach to playing all genres of music for the rest of my life.

My introduction to ensemble playing occured after Mike and I had each been practicing solitarily for about a year. A family of friends from downstate who spent summers at their cottage nearby on Lake Huron included two boys about our age, one of whom had also begun playing trumpet at about this time. He brought his instrument along for the summer, but seldom practiced it; this lack of discipline on his part was our good fortune. We Kent brothers now had a second horn on hand, so that we could play short duets together from the Arban book. We were now able to experience for the first time the harmonies of ensemble playing, and enjoy the sensations of playing with accompaniment. I still remember crying bitterly into my pillow that first night after our friends had left at the end of the summer, since we no longer had a second instrument available for playing duos such as *Red River Valley*. However, the seeds of harmony had been planted, and before long a second Olds trumpet arrived from Chicago. We brothers were now equipped to play duets whenever we liked; we were soon performing various duos at home when friends and relatives visited, and in local and regional talent competitions of the 4-H organization. I still have a treasured photo of the two of us at the conclusion of one such contest, proudly holding our horns and the first-place blue ribbon that we had just earned for our rendition of *The Fox Hunt*. There I stand, at the ripe old age of twelve, decked out in white shirt, tie, and striped sport coat, with my pants zipper fully down. Brotherly duets would remain my sole exposure to ensemble playing during my first four years of playing, until the summer before I entered high school, when I joined the Alpena City Band.

From the time I had first begun playing trumpet at the age of ten, I had decided that I would pursue a career in music. However, this plan entailed becoming a music teacher, since this was the only fulltime musical profession that I knew existed. This was a belief that continued throughout my high school days, since I could not connect the solo artists whose recordings I avidly devoured to any known occupation in my world. The musicians of whom I was aware played only part-time or sporadic jobs, in bars and at weddings and parties.

On a related theme, when Mike entered high school and I was age twelve, our parents made it very clear that they would not be able to pay for any of the costs of our college education. We would have to finance this advanced study ourselves, from our own savings and also by achieving excellent academic grades in high school, from which we would receive university scholarships. We eventually did just that.

Shortly before I turned fourteen, I was forced to make a few physical adjustments in my playing. During the previous seven years, including the four years of playing the horn, the lower half of my right front tooth had been missing. It had been broken off when I was six years old, when I had fallen face down on the ice at school and another student had fallen atop my head. When my parents were finally able to afford to have a dentist install a crown on the damaged tooth, I was frustrated to discover that the huge opening through which my air had previously flowed when I played was now blocked by the crown. At the same time, the dentist also ground off two corners of my two lower front teeth, the corners which projected outward considerably due to serious overcrowding. Until then, these sharp points had sometimes pierced the skin inside my lower lip when I would play extended demanding passages. In addition, during an earlier year, I had once attempted to execute a running hurdle through a backyard swing. Due to a miscalculation, I had instead kicked the seat board of the swing upward into my mouth, driving my upper front teeth completely through my lower lip. However, the minor alterations that were wrought on my embouchure by these various incidents were miniscule compared to the devastating damage which had been inflicted on Bud's teeth and mouth in his automobile accident during the spring of 1952. (I had been nearly three years old when that had happened to him at the age of nearly 31.)

When I became a member of the Alpena City Band, three months before entering high school, I occupied the second chair position, next to my older brother, who served as the lead player of the group. This ensemble, composed of a motley crew of musicians who rehearsed one evening per week year-round, played one concert each week during the summer, outdoors on an elevated open stage adjacent to the City Hall parking lot. The audience, listening from their cars through unrolled windows, honked their horns as applause after each number. Since the band had been founded in 1918, much of its library dated from that period, particularly the marches and concert pieces; these were interspersed with medleys of show tunes, plus various trumpet solos and duets featuring the Kent brothers. I happily performed with this group for five summers, until I departed for college. I remember one particularly memorable July day in which Mike and I pedaled our bikes several miles from our house to a farm, hefted bales of hay onto a wagon all day in the stifling heat and then unloaded them into a barn loft, pedaled home, showered, ate supper, drove to town, and played a concert program that featured one of our duets.

The high school in Alpena, which served the widespread populace of the entire county, had a band which was of moderate quality, but no orchestra until a beginning ensemble was established in my junior year. The new young band director was seriously hampered by several realities: an instrumental music program was only just then being established in the elementary grades as an eventual feeder system, virtually none of the band students at the high school received private lessons, and there was no available source of recordings to instill refined sounds in young ears. Public radio and public television broadcasts were still a thing of the future; the only radio signal that was readily available emanated from the Alpena station, which featured primarily polka and country western bands, birth announcements, and obituaries. The solitary music store in town dealt mainly in polka and rock-and-roll records, along with a stock of guitars, banjos, accordians, drums, and a few student-level band instruments. Although the televised Lawrence Welk Show was very popular throughout the county, this region was by no means one of musical sophistication. (To my chagrin, some years later when I successfully auditioned for the principal trumpet position in the Radio Orchestra in Stuttgart, the local newspaper ran an article entitled "Kent Joins German Band.") The high school experience did, however, offer me four years of ensemble and solo experiences in concert band and big band jazz playing.

Equally helpful to my musical development was the combo work that I did during my latter three years of high school. On the first day of sophomore year, I enlisted three friends to form the group we called The Blue Notes. With a rhythm section that consisted of piano, upright bass, and drums, Terry, Mike, Jerry, and I played many Saturday night wedding and anniversary dances throughout the county. That same year, I also began working with several different adult combos in bars; during this period while I was age fifteen to eighteen, I would occasionally spend time in the back room of a tavern where I was playing, when a liquor inspector would make an unannounced visit. My very first experience at a bar job entailed improvising polkas for four hours straight on a Saturday night at the Hideaway Inn, with an accordian player and a drummer. A year or two later, whenever I would work with that same drummer, I would have to take my pay in cash from his pocket when we would finish at one o'clock in the morning; he would be too smashed to pack up his drum set until the following day. A much more sophisticated quartet that I thoroughly enjoyed working with included Dennie on chordovox (an accordian from which the sound was altered by an amplifier into that of an electric organ), Burl on amplified acoustic guitar, and Scoobie-Doo on drums. The latter player, a recovering junkie, had long been a member of the house band at the Sands Hotel in Las Vegas; he was now a born-again Christian leading a new life in the north woods. Although he had changed his lifestyle, Scoobie still opened my eyes about various facets of his previous existence on the wild side.

While working in the bars, I often strolled around the tables while playing, serenading the patrons, and sometimes when the night wore on and the eyes of the crowd glazed over with drink, I would lie on my back on an unoccupied table while playing. Invariably, someone would pretend to pour a mixed drink or a pitcher of beer down that apparently inviting vertical brass funnel, to the delight of the other patrons. Four hours a night of ballads, Latin numbers, blues, and uptempo tunes, all played by ear with ad lib variations, did wonders for my endurance, ear training (both my perfect pitch and relative pitch), and familiarity with a wide range of styles.

Sometimes these bar gigs, which often ran three nights a week, took us out of town a couple hours drive away. Packing up after the one o'clock finish and then driving back to Alpena would leave me only a few hours to sleep at a friend's house in town, before returning to morning classes at the high school. To this day, whenever I hear on an oldies radio station certain tunes that were played on the juke boxes in the bars during those high school years, I experience a flood of interesting memories of this shadowy "second life" that I experienced for three years.

All the while, I kept practicing heavily, playing in the school ensembles and City Band, excelling in my classes, saving money for college, and aiming for scholarships. At the age of sixteen, I vowed to myself that I would practice three hours every day. Theoretically, this was an admirable goal, reflecting how badly I wanted to achieve my goals. However, later musical maturity showed me that it was a senseless approach for a brass player. Practicing less and conceptualizing my playing more by singing the music would have been much better; but I was not yet aware of this more mature approach to music-making. To find enough time for all of these activities, I slept only five hours a night year-round for seven years straight, from age fourteen on (again, later maturity would change that approach as well).

The first opportunity that I ever had to hear a live performance by one of my role models presented itself during the summer when I was fifteen, when I enjoyed a concert by Al Hirt with his Dixieland combo in Cincinnati. This occurred while my brother Mike and I were spending the summer working at our Uncle Jim's chain of Hitching Post restaurants in that city. Al Hirt was amazing in the way he used his immense technical mastery of the trumpet within the context of complicated, improvised Dixieland music, a talent that has never been matched. Three years later, I was able to hear Rafael Mendez present a clinic and an evening solo performance with a high school band in southern Michigan. My blood sizzled when exposed to the live sounds of his masterful technique and his exciting musicianship, and my passion for his recordings of flashy Spanish pieces and opera aria transcriptions soared all the more. I did not realize until years later that many of his expressive trumpet solos had actually been composed as vocal music for an opera house setting. During my first semester of college, I was also inspired by a live performance that Doc Severinsen played with the U of M Symphony Band. His risk-taking in the demanding, jazzy Werle Concerto was a wonderful learning experience for me, and I was thrilled by the manner in which he applied his thorough technical control and expressive artistry to various types of commercial music.

Always intent upon earning money to pay for my future university training, I felt that I could not take time out during my high school years to attend summer music programs. I reasoned that it would be a double financial setback for me to attend such a program, considering both the costs of the session and the concurrent loss of income. As a younger boy, I had earned cash by picking strawberries commercially on local farms and by making bakery items in our kitchen to sell to the tourist traffic; as a high schooler, I labored summers bringing in hay and painting houses, and also worked year-round in a fifteen-cent hamburger restaurant. Later, from age eighteen through college, I was hired each summer to work at Abitibi, the wallboard factory in Alpena.

During my high school period, I would order each year the literature from the Interlochen Arts Academy. In these materials, I noted the programs of the concerts that were being performed there, during both the school year and the summer session, and learned the names of those who played trumpet in the various ensembles. (Some years later, a number of these individuals would be fellow students at U of M, and I would eventually meet others as fellow competitors on the orchestra audition trail.) The single week that I did spend at a summer music program, at Michigan State University during my sixteenth summer, was only moderately helpful to my development as a player. Although I did play lead in the concert band and the jazz big band, the single private lesson that I received from the University professor offered me virtually nothing. That week, I did not hear any symphonic music, although there was an orchestra included among the ensembles.

At the time of my graduation from high school, my official-ly stated goal was "to earn a Master's degree in trumpet and teach at the university level." I was still totally unaware of the beauties of symphonic music, and was oblivious to the fact that certain musicians actually made their living playing it. I was extremely deficient in many areas for entrance into a high-level university music curriculum. Compared to the majority of those musicians of my generation who would eventually attain high levels of proficiency on their various symphonic instru-ments, I had never played piano; I had not been exposed to any theory or music literature/history training; and I had neither heard nor performed symphonic music, either in the format of a full orchestra or chamber ensembles.

During the autumn of my senior year, oblivious to the defi-ciencies in my background, I had applied for admission to the University of Michigan's School of Music. Opting to send a recorded sample of my playing rather than audition in person,

I cast about for a piece to present my best attributes. The closest thing that I could find to legit music was the lead part from the old-fashioned cornet duet entitled *Ida and Dottie Polka*. This I recorded, with the clumping accompaniment of a friend on a very out-of-tune upright piano, onto a small tape with a cheap portable machine at the high school. Although Clifford Lillya, the trumpet professor at U of M, must have smiled to himself at my offering, he apparently recognized on the tape enough raw talent and solid foundations of training to grant me admission into the prestigious school. This was the first of many generosities that he would extend to me.

I departed for the University of Michigan on a full scholarship, which covered room and board, tuition, and even some spending money. Thus, the considerable savings that I had accumulated could be applied toward the purchase of horns, mouthpieces, mutes, music, stereo components, and records. My musical world was about to burst brilliantly open, illuminated by Adolph Herseth and the Chicago Symphony Orchestra.

Chapter Two

University of Michigan, CSO Recordings, and Early Adolph Herseth Lessons 1967-1970

In September of 1967, the University of Michigan School of Music had about one thousand enrolled music majors. Located on a new, separate campus north of the town and the main campus, the music building complex operated as a conservatory, in which all classes were offered centrally. The only exceptions were the physical education course which was required for one year, and the single non-music academic class which was required each semester in residence; these latter courses were taught on the main campus.

The program at this school emphasized primarily its music education curriculum, which had trained for many decades legions of high quality directors of bands and student orchestras. Although numerous graduates of the year-round high school at the Interlochen Arts Academy attended the U of M music school, often in the performance degree program, the main focus of the University was not on such degrees, nor particularly on its symphony orchestras. However, this emphasis began to change with my class; the increasing interest of students wishing to earn a degree in instrumental performance, especially in orchestral performance, soon led to the development of a double major in both music education and performance. I began my training in the straight music ed program, and switched after two years to the double major curriculum.

Based upon my entrance audition, I was assigned to study not with Clifford Lillya but instead with the doctoral student who was working toward a degree in trumpet performance. This individual had virtually nothing to offer me during two full semesters of weekly private lessons. He mostly listened silently while I ran through etudes that I had worked on for years under my father's guidance. Later, after completing his degree, this individual would go on to a career teaching and playing in the hinterlands, in Texas.

At the start of my freshman year, I was placed as the lead trumpet in the Concert Band, the second-level ensemble. There were numerous players less advanced than me in the lower positions within the first ensemble, the Symphony Band; however, I was placed in the Concert Band so that this group would have a strong and secure lead player. According to the band director track in which I was enrolled, I also signed up for the marching band. As the football season progressed, my chops became more and more brutalized from the simultaneous high-step marching and playing (what a lousy combination of activities!). As a result, I was gradually moved down to second and then third position in the Concert Band, superseded by two players who were not enduring the rigors of marching band.

After my chops had recuperated during the holiday break, I arranged to audition privately for William Revelli, who was known nationwide as the dean of band directors. Since he liked what he heard in the audition, I was elevated to the Symphony Band for the second semester, as the lead player in the third trumpet group. After I had completed my presentation for Revelli, he asked with whom had I studied previously; I answered, "Just with my father." Revelli: "Really! He must be a professional teacher." Kent: "No, he runs a little credit union and a home bakery with my mother." Revelli: "Oh. Then he must have earlier been a professional teacher." Kent: "No, previously he was a hair dresser."

During my very first day at U of M, I had met Orlando Cora, a warm-hearted Puerto Rican who had been personally sent by Pablo Casals to earn a double master's degree in trumpet and piano performance. Although his command of the English language was minimal, we soon became fast friends.

One of our favorite activities was to go to pizza joints near the main campus, at which I would pretend to speak no English and Orlando would manage to communicate for both of us with his very fractured language. It was fascinating to note how co-ed waitresses seemed to be particularly drawn to dark-complectioned (Orlando was mahogany and I was olive), black-haired guys who spoke little or no English.

I was first introduced to legit music during my first week of college, when I began attending music theory and music litera-ture/history classes. At first, the content was mostly an incom-prehensible blur, particularly due to the pace of the course-work. Nearly all of the other students in the music school had already received much exposure to a wide range of musical genres; in addition, the vast majority of them had spent many of their youthful years studying piano. Thus, the pace of the college-level classes was generally geared to their considerable degree of pre-knowledge and musical competency. My fellow students in beginning piano class only needed a short refresh-er course, after years of playing as youngsters. In stark contrast, I was hard-pressed to memorize during the first week which of those eighty-eight white and black keys were associated with which notes on the printed page. In addition, after eight years of reading only a single line of music, reading multiple lines of a piano score while locating the notes on the keyboard was an excruciating feat. My nemesis that entire year was piano class, which I passed only due to the sympathy and extra assistance of a very charitable teacher. The one strong suit that I possessed for music theory was my gift of both perfect pitch and relative pitch, which made aural dictation a breeze. In music litera-ture/history, I was totally unfamiliar with both the names and the characteristic sounds of the standard composers, while most of my student colleagues could already identify by ear specific compositions. I remember how excited I was in the lis-tening lab when I was finally able to identify by ear the piece *Till Eulenspiegel's Merry Pranks*, and to know that it had been written by Richard Strauss. Now, there was a remedial music student! My sensations of unfamiliarity were further accentuat-

ed as I participated in the various beginning instrumental classes during my years at U of M, acquiring a very basic command
of many of the band and orchestra instruments in preparation
for a career as an ensemble conductor.

As an antedote to this avalanche of unfamiliar musical and
academic content while a freshman, I sometimes played quietly along with the radio in my dorm room, improvising variations to the tunes as I had done for years on gigs with combos.
Those former long nights of playing dance tunes under dim
lights in a smoky haze, with the associated lovely female
scenery passing by, now seemed very distant in the past.

After my introduction to how thrilling symphonic music
could be, at the Chicago Symphony concert on the first of
October that featured Adolph Herseth playing the Teleman
concerto, I began avidly buying CSO records. At the time, I did
not have stereo equipment of my own to play those platters, so
I spent many hours savoring them on the communal stereo in
the lounge at the end of the hall in my dorm. During this same
period, I became friends with Stanley Szymko, an upper class-
man bass trombonist who for many years had been an avid
CSO fan, a student of Ed Kleinhammer of CSO fame, and a
rabid record collector. Many nights after the music building
closed at 10:30, he and I would listen to records at his apartment of "Bud and the Boys," as Stan dubbed the Chicago brass
section. He owned all of the Orchestra's recordings from the
earliest Kubelik years forward, and he could knowledgeably
conduct most of the pieces, in many cases without a score.

While working my way through Stan's massive record collection, it became very clear that the CSO brass section, with
Bud at its helm, represented the absolute cream of the crop in
the symphonic world, and the only one that I felt was worth
emulating. Even though I had only met Bud once, after the
runout concert in October, I was already seriously studying
with him, at a distance, by absorbing the orchestra's recordings.
I did not realize at the time that, within a year and a half of that
concert, I would have access to in-person lessons with the master. At this point, I was learning, with the resources that were

then available to me, how to emulate as best I could his sound, his style, and his manner of playing lead on legit music. At the end of that school year, when I heard the Philadelphia Orchestra under Ormandy playing its traditional week of May Festival concerts in Ann Arbor, I realized all the more clearly how far in front of the rest of the pack were Bud Herseth and his colleagues in the Chicago brass section.

All my life, I had admired trumpet soloists whose styles, although played in various different genres, were emotional, dramatic, well-disciplined, extroverted, and virtuosic. Thus, I was drawn to Bud's artistry from the very first time that I heard it. His playing possessed all of the traits that I loved, yet he applied them within the genre of symphonic music, which was entirely new to me.

Every aspect of Adolph Herseth's music-making was astounding. His magnificent tone was so rich and concentrated, with loads of overtones and plenty of air flowing, that it could be heard within the orchestral texture no matter how softly or in whatever register he played. His intonation was impeccable, as was also his disciplined precision, execution, and rhythm. His complete mastery of all technical aspects of trumpet playing in all registers, as well as his fantastic dynamic range, power, and endurance, resulted in music that was always clearly articulated, rhythmic, and energetic. Bud's immense musicality, involving a constant pulse and forward motion as well as an acute sensitivity and attention to the slightest of nuances, was so communicative that it caused visceral reactions in everyone who heard it, including me. These reactions would range from tears brought about by a simple six-note lyrical passage in *Pictures at an Exhibition* to exhaltation from a bombastic and glorious ending of a piece like Mahler's *Symphony Number 5*, as well as myriad other sensations in between. The degree of artistry that he consistently maintained created an indelible impact on all listeners. When this pillar of self-confidence played his horn, Gabriel himself likely stood in awe, and I was next in line. I was determined to do whatever it took to some day play with at least some semblance of that style and degree of quality.

After finishing my freshman year with a university band tour to Carnegie Hall and several cities in Pennsylvania, I returned home, commenced my summer job at the wallboard factory, and practiced and listened a lot. However, one day my upper front tooth that bore a crown broke apart, which then required converting three of my upper front teeth into a single bridge. This procedure entailed several weeks of having no front teeth at all, which meant no practicing during those weeks.

At the conclusion of the summer, which had been filled with factory work, eventually much practicing, and bar gigs with combos, I returned to Ann Arbor for my sophomore year, more intensely inspired than ever to learn to play with the Chicago style and quality. This year, having a single room in the dorm equipped with my own stereo, the instructional listening sessions with Stan Szymko were even more regular, including a weekly rendezvous with the CSO live broadcasts on Public Radio. In these sessions, I was enthralled by the entire brass section, since they had decades earlier acquired most of Bud's musical attributes, under his leadership and direction. By this time, I had acquired a set of thirteen volumes of trumpet orchestral excerpts; now, I could visually follow along with the most important passages. However, at this point I had no clue as to how to transpose the keys of any of those parts; this was a handicap which, in symphonic trumpet work, was nearly equivalent to not being able to read music.

During this school year, I benefitted very much from private lessons with Clifford Lillya, although I had access to his guidance for only four months during the fall semester. Cliff did not have an orchestral background, but he did have a great deal of knowledge to impart concerning solo literature, etudes, ensemble playing, and overall musicianship. He was also extremely adept at the psychology of teaching and playing, being very gifted at discerning the appropriate guidance that each particular student needed. He often said, "A trumpet player plays as much on his ego as he does on his chops."

To encourage progress and generate performance opportunities for his students, Cliff sponsored a monthly noon-time recital featuring trumpet solos with piano accompaniment. Some of the students participated in only one or two of these shows, but I enthusiastically played a different solo in each one; I was elated to have so many chances to incorporate Cliff's valuable guidance, and to become familiar for the first time with some of the standard solo literature. To promote a variety of musical styles within a given student's repertoire, he would wisely alternate old-fashioned cornet virtuoso solos between the legit pieces during the course of a semester. Cliff also put me in touch with Glenn Bridges of Detroit, who made tape recordings upon request from his huge collection of early cylinder and thick platter recordings of famous cornet soloists. The tapes that I received from him, which included performances by such early masters as Herbert L. Clarke and Allesandro Liberati, were very inspiring to me. I had played this style of virtuoso solos and duets throughout my years in the City Band, but I had rarely heard recordings of such pieces.

During the fall semester of 1968, I traveled to Chicago to purchase from the Schilke Company a B flat and a C trumpet and a Schilke mouthpiece (until then, I had always played an Olds B flat and an Olds mouthpiece), after which I began to become familiar with playing the horn in the key of C. It was during this period that my perfect pitch became a bit confused. Since the age of ten, I had always played a B flat instrument, and had interpreted whatever I heard on recordings in this key. However, as I became more and more familiar with the C trumpet, my brain for a time was sometimes in one key and sometimes in the other when I listened to recordings; finally, extensive usage of the C horn finally converted my brain permanently into the key of C.

Since my interest in playing symphonic music had become salient by this point, I enrolled in both the band and the orchestra this year, playing lead in the group of second trumpets in the band. However, in the orchestra there were very few opportunities for me to actually play anything, since the upper classmen had been previously ensconced there and I was the newcomer.

√

In the band, Revelli enjoyed intimidating and demeaning most of the students, except his few obvious favorites; a legend in his own mind, he attempted to model himself after his Italian counterpart Toscanini. I did not appreciate this condescending approach to conducting, particularly in a student setting in which these younger and developing players ought to have been encouraged rather then discouraged. Likewise, I felt that those students who intended to become conductors ought to be presented with a positive role model to emulate, instead of a grotesquely negative one who delighted in beating players down. Therefore, on the first day of the second semester, I visited Revelli in his office to tell him that I was resigning immediately from his band, intending to focus instead on orchestra playing. Fixing me in his famous blistering gaze, he indicated that he had been grooming me to become his lead player the following year. He then declared that I would never have a successful career in music, shouted "You damned skunk!" and ordered me out of his office. (I never did report back to him in later years, to happily indicate that, in spite of his angry hex, I had actually had an excellent career in music.)

Cliff Lillya was absent during the second semester, on a sabbatical leave. Leonard Smith, the cornet soloist and conductor of the Detroit Concert Band, was scheduled to teach each of Cliff's students for the semester. However, as a punishment for my mutinous behavior, Revelli arranged that I would instead receive lessons from the doctoral student teacher. The individual in the doctoral position at this time, a friend of mine, was chagrined at the prospect of having to give me lessons. He privately indicated that I should not bother coming to the studio during my assigned lesson time; he would simply register for me an A grade for the semester, and I could better use the time practicing on my own. Thus, the entire second half of this year of college offered me no private lessons, no noon-time solo outlets (those recitals had been temporarily suspended during Cliff's leave of absence), no band playing, and minimal orchestra participation. So I practiced heartily, and also listened intently to CSO recordings and live broadcasts with excerpt books in hand.

At the end of the semester in early May, I traveled to Chicago to have the Schilke technicians do a couple of minor repairs on my two horns. Afterward, I slept overnight at my Greek grandmother's apartment in the suburb of Oak Park, and then stopped in to see my aunt a few blocks away, before beginning the long drive to northern Michigan to spend the summer. During the course of the conversation at my aunt's home, she happened to show me a newspaper clipping which described a soloist who had played the Hummel *Concerto for Trumpet* with the Civic Orchestra of Chicago the previous Sunday evening. She asked, "Have you ever heard of this cornet player? He lives just down the street, in the next block. [Our son] Bob has been good friends with his daughter Christine ever since they were little." I was stunned when I read the headline of the article: "Herseth Triumphs in Trumpet Concerto."

"He lives here?! He's the greatest trumpet player in the world!" I exclaimed. I could see from the look on her face that she was not convinced that the guy down the street with the southward-slouching porch steps had international stature in any field. And she did not have time to be convinced, since she was leaving for work.

Pulling away from the curb of South Clarence Avenue, I suddenly had the impulse to stop at house number 1044 and say hello to the master. So I first headed for the nearest gas station, a few blocks away, to brush my teeth and hair for the momentous occasion. Returning to the house, my heart pounding in my chest, I excitedly mounted those slanting green steps and rang the bell. When the door swung open, I said, "Hello, Mr. Herseth, I'm Tim Kent, a nephew of the Neumanns just down the street. When my aunt mentioned that you lived here, I thought I would stop by, to say hello and tell you how much I admire your playing. I'm a trumpet student at U of M in Ann Arbor, and I met you when you played there a year and a half ago." Although I had interrupted his practicing in the basement, Mr. Herseth was very gracious and cordial. Encouraged by this, I suddenly had the thought of asking him if he might occasionally give me lessons, if I drove there from Michigan. Without the slightest hesitation, he agreed! At that time, I was totally unaware that the master very rarely taught anyone, except the trumpet players in the Civic Orchestra. That specific moment on the porch signalled the very beginning of many years of generosity, encouragement, and in-depth training by Bud Herseth directed toward me. It is certainly food for thought to consider how my life might have played out quite differently if my aunt had not shown me the Hummel review clipping, or if Bud had not been home on that particular morning, or if he had chosen to not answer the doorbell and had instead continued his practice session in the basement, or if he had not decided on the spot to teach me. When I descended those five porch steps, the direction of my life had improved considerably. And, thinking back all these years later, there were very few times thereafter when I would come down those steps without my chops being absolutely wiped out and my mind being thrilled from all of the improvements that Bud had just wrought in my playing.

En route from Oak Park to Ossineke, where I would spend the summer working at the Abitibi wallboard factory and practicing, I stopped at Michigan State University in East Lansing, to share the wonderful news with my long time friend Doree Minton. She had been my first girlfriend in high school, when we had been fourteen, and we had remained good friends ever since. In the course of telling her about my exciting encounter with the master and his agreeing to give me private lessons, I neglected to relate to her that I had already decided to marry her. She had a serious long-term boyfriend at the time, but both of those issues would be sorted out by the end of the summer.

During the next year and a half, each of my monthly lessons with Bud entailed a round trip of one thousand miles by car from Ossineke during the two summers, and a round trip of five hundred miles from U of M during the 1969-1970 school year. On several occasions during those two summers, I drove the five hundred miles from Ossineke, immediately took the lesson, and then drove directly back without sleeping, in order to squeeze the trip into my work schedule at the factory. During nearly all of the trips during that school year, I also heard a concert by the CSO in Orchestra Hall, using a ticket that Bud would purchase in advance for me at the box office. Hearing the master and the orchestra live and in person was even more thrilling than listening to those fabulous sounds on recordings. After each of those live performances, the brass passages would replay continuously in my head throughout the long drive back to Michigan.

Previous to my first training sesson with Bud, I had taken lessons in the fundamentals of playing from my father for eight years at home, and had received four months of training from Cliff Lillya on a very few pieces from the legit solo repertoire. I had not played any of the standard orchestral literature, I did not know how to transpose in any key, and I had become only moderately familiar with the C trumpet, but not with any of the high horns.

My first lesson in Bud's basement studio took place on June 19, 1969. On the way there from Michigan, after eight hours of driving, I missed the expressway intersection near downtown Chicago which would have directed me westward to Oak Park. When I finally realized that I was well off the track, I stopped and learned that I had driven to the northern suburbs. Calling Bud from a pay phone, I received directions on how to reach his home from there; he told me not to hurry. When I finally arrived, well after the scheduled time, he offered me an iced tea and allowed me to relax and then warm up a bit, before we started a training program that would be continued for years. During the course of that time, I would be given open access to the master's encyclopedic knowledge of music and its interpretation, of trumpets, mouthpieces, and mutes, and of conductors and concert halls. Several years later, I asked him why he had agreed to teach that complete stranger who had appeared on his porch in May of 1969. He explained that if I had not played well during the first lesson, it would have been my last one as well.

Since I felt so terribly deficient in the standard orchestral literature, I requested that we focus on that particular aspect of playing at first, which we did for about the first two years of my instruction. Learning to play the passages from each piece which appeared in the excerpt books also involved mastering each of the transpositions, as well as becoming totally familiar with each of the high horns. In addition, I was expected to acquire an understanding of the appropriate style of each piece and how the excerpted passages fit into the total orchestra texture, by listening to recordings as well as live concerts and broadcasts. For this training program, I purchased a Schilke D-E flat trumpet, a Selmer four-valve piccolo trumpet in A-B flat, and appropriate Bach mouthpieces for each of them, as well as Bach mouthpieces for the Schilke B flat and C horns that I had previously bought.

During the course of each lesson, in discussing the excerpts that I played, Bud would note how they fit into the complete orchestra context, and while I played he would sometimes sing an important countermelody with which my part was to fit. In addition, he sometimes played the second trumpet part, to provide accompaniment and harmony, and he occasionally demonstrated passages for me. I vividly remember him once playing for me, without a single note of warmup and with great beauty, the slow and sustained lyrical solo from *Parsifal* that soars up to high C. Now that was inspiring! In our sessions, he also described and tried out on me the varying requests that certain conductors had made concerning those passages over his many years on the job. In addition, he talked about the various horns, mouthpieces, and mutes that he had used for the pieces, the venues in which the orchestra had performed them, and the work schedules that had been involved. I was intrigued to learn that, in spite of his many decades of experience, he still continued to experiment on a regular basis with both equipment and interpretations, constantly expanding his knowledge base. This wealth of knowledge that he was passing on to me in the lessons was invaluable, teaching me about all aspects of handling an orchestral position. In addition, these interesting discussions also allowed me some time to recover during the course of those strenuous sessions, before launching into the next set of excerpted passages. The lessons would usually continue for two or three hours; it was clear that Bud was not the least concerned about the extensive amount of time that he was investing in me and my advancement.

Even before the first lesson, I had been acutely aware of Bud's degree of dedication to excellence and the highest musical standards, from the CSO recordings. However, the private lessons afforded me a much deeper glimpse into his total commitment to performing at the highest level possible, and the extent of his passion for music-making. His demands on me mirrored the rigorous program that he had carried out himself for many decades. These sessions allowed me to share in his inspiration, gave me a chance to absorb some of his vast store of knowledge, and eventually enabled me to acquire at least a moderate amount of his abilities.

Besides all of the musical aspects of my training, Bud also advised me on the benefits to be derived from a regular physical exercise program, such as the Royal Canadian Air Force exercises that he did, as well as appropriate eating regimens on rehearsal and concert days. He also stressed the value of having avid non-musical interests, which helped greatly in keeping one's interest in music fresh. In Bud's case, he loved to play golf, as well as to contemplate art. Between rehearsals at Orchestra Hall, he frequently crossed Michigan Avenue to the Art Institute of Chicago; there, he was particularly drawn to the Impressionists, one of the strongest collections in the museum. He also loved to travel and cook, as well as study Viking history and culture, which represented his own Norwegian ancestry. In addition, he was deeply interested in the ancient art, religious shrines, foods, and lifestyles of Japan.

In order to retain as much as possible of the content of our sessions, I made copious notations on the music itself during the course of each lesson. In addition, beginning with the very first visit to Bud's basement studio, I would leave his house, drive around the corner of the block, park, and immediately write in my notebook as much as I could remember of what he had related to me. Later, I would reread those notations many times, and thus continually reabsorb this wealth of information between lessons.

One of the categories of interesting information that I recorded in my notebook was a list of each of the many instruments that Bud had in his studio, which he would occasionally show me during the lessons. To keep track of the 35 or more horns plus the many bells, I kept a running list of them over the years, separating them according to the key in which they were pitched.

B flat: Besson trumpet, Couesnon trumpet, an engraved cornet, Monke rotary trumpet, Schmidt rotary trumpet, Kunzel rotary trumpet, Bohm rotary trumpet, and a combination A-B flat rotary trumpet.

C: Bach large bore trumpets with 229 bells and various lead pipes (both his own horns plus the one belonging to the CSO), Schilke C5 trumpet, Schilke C5 trumpet with huge bell, two Holton trumpets, Heckel rotary trumpet, Honorka rotary trumpet, and Altridater rotary trumpet.

D: Bach trumpet, Holton trumpet, and Schilke combination D-E flat trumpet (E3L) with four different changeable bells.

E flat: Conn cornet, and Boston rotary trumpet (besides the Schilke E3L trumpet listed above).

E: Two changeable bells for the Schilke E3L frame, and two changeable bells for the Schilke F-G frame listed below.

F-G combination: Schilke trumpet.

G: Bach trumpet.

Piccolo combination A-B flat: Monke rotary trumpet with three valves, Monke rotary trumpet with four valves, Yamaha prototype trumpet with three valves (valve section from a medium large C trumpet fitted with short pipes and bell section), and Yamaha standard trumpet with four valves.

Piccolo B flat: Couesnon trumpet, and Schilke trumpet.

Bass trumpet: Kruspe combination C-D-E flat rotary trumpet.

Modern reproductions of natural Baroque trumpets in various keys: one round coiled version, and one coiled version and two long versions by Tarr.

During the course of the lessons, Bud would occasionally bring out some of these hidden treasures, tell me their histories, play a little on them, and encourage me to play them as well. He also sometimes had me play passages with the horns, mouthpieces, and mutes that he used on a regular basis at home and on the job. As added inspiration, he occasionally made for me copies of tapes of certain of his live performances of solo pieces. In one instance, after we had begun focusing on piccolo playing, he produced for me a copy of a performance of the Bach *Brandenburg Concerto Number 2* that he had done with members of the orchestra. On the same tape, he also included a recording from the 1930s of the same piece by members of the Ecole Normale Orchestra of Paris, with Eugene Foveau playing a Besson F trumpet. For me, this tape illustrated just how far the development of modern instruments had advanced since the days of Bud's youth, and how extremely far he had personally raised the bar on the quality of playing.

Although I had passed muster enough with Bud at my very first lesson to be kept on as his student, that lesson was nearly my last one for another reason. In July, while working the night shift at the factory, I fell asleep at the wheel one early morning while driving home after work. I did not wake up until I had drifted across the oncoming lane and struck the ditch at 70 miles per hour. Rolling repeatedly end over end and sideways, the car was finally brought to a stop on its side by a stand of trees. Climbing out through the opening that had shortly before been the windshield area, I thought I had escaped undamaged. However, this accident signalled the beginning of serious pain at L-5, the lowest vertebra of my spine, which would ultimately be a contributing factor in my choosing to give up a successful career as an orchestral player several decades later.

During my junior year at Michigan, I continued my monthly treks to Oak Park to study with Bud and to hear Chicago Symphony concerts. During those jaunts, it was a real pleasure feasting on home-cooked Greek meals at the apartment of my eighty-year-old Gram Kapantais, since I was subsisting at school on canned food that I warmed in my room on an electric griddle. At the University, I received lessons from Cliff Lillya, performed a different solo each month at the noon-time trumpet recital (including my first experiences with the Haydn and Hummel concertos), and played in the school orchestra (only one performance of each of two different programs during the course of the year). In addition, I played fifth trumpet on three performances of one program with the Toledo Symphony, all of which did not yield a great deal of orchestral playing experiences. All the while, I continued to inculcate my brain with the sounds of Bud and the CSO, via recordings and live concert broadcasts.

During the fall semester, I took both oboe and saxophone classes, as part of my music education curriculum. Those classes, coupled with the necessary private practice sessions on the two reed instruments, tended to wreak havoc with my trumpet · chops. However, this was accentuated all the more by the fact that my oboe class finished just ten minutes before the orchestra rehearsal commenced. Another factor during this entire school year that distracted me to a certain degree from maximum musical progress was my courtship of Doree at Michigan State. My weekly lesson with Cliff was scheduled for ten o'clock each Monday morning. When I would blearily knock on his studio door, having just arrived after the sixty-mile drive from East Lansing, he would assess my unsteady condition with an appraising glance from beneath his bushy white eyebrows. Then he would shuffle toward me and say, "Let's sit and chat for a while, before we start playing." He also had the wisdom to have me sit to play during our lessons, even though I customarily stood to both practice and take lessons at the school. Besides his musical knowledge, Cliff also knew a great deal about young students, life, and love.

By mid-winter, after our official engagement, I had decided to leave the University at the end of the semester, with only three years completed toward a degree. In that era of the Vietnam War, this action would mean losing my college deferment and being drafted into the Army. So I subjected myself to a haircut from a barber (the very last barber cut of my life), flew to the West Point Military Academy, auditioned for the band there, and arranged to spend the next four years safely out of combat in upstate New York. During the spring, the first televised draft lottery was held, in which each of the 365 days of the year were individually chosen in random order from a hopper, to determine the order by birthdate in which eligible candidates would be drafted. Doree and I paid close attention to the T.V. in the basement of her dorm at MSU, our future uncertain. My birthday, May 22, was chosen as number 329, so the likelihood of my being drafted that year after leaving college seemed to be considerably reduced. However, immediately after the lottery, a high-ranking general announced that even those individuals with higher numbers, such as mine, would probably not escape the draft. So I proceeded with my plans for West Point, by taking the required tests and physical exam, after which I was assigned a date in late September to report for basic training. According to our plans, Doree would complete the final semester for her degree during my months of training, and then join me at West Point in December.

The Chicago Symphony made its first triumphant trip with Maestro Solti to Carnegie Hall during the spring of 1970, near the end of Solti's first season as Music Director of the orchestra. En route to New York, the ensemble performed Mahler's *Fifth Symphony* in Toledo, which was an easy drive for both Doree and me. After the thrilling concert, I introduced her to Bud backstage. Two decades later, during a CSO tour of Japan, he would observe, "You guys were holding hands when I first met you, and you're still holding hands!"

By this point in 1970, I realized that my Schilke B flat and C trumpets were simply not putting out as much as I was putting into them. This fact had become very apparent whenever I played on Bud's Bach horns during lessons. So I asked him if he would choose for me Bach replacements for my two Schilke big horns, at a downtown Chicago music store. In June, after a considerable number of C trumpets had been shipped from the Bach factory to that dealer, Bud chose the best one out of the batch, purchased it at a discount, and sent it to me in Michigan. He later located a good B flat and sent it to me the following October.

After my summer filled with practicing, laboring at the wallboard factory, and making a number of thousand-mile trips for lessons, Doree and I celebrated our wedding on September 5, and soon departed for our honeymoon in Puerto Rico. (However, in the true spirit of an avid developing trumpet player and his very supportive spouse, we postponed our honeymoon for a week so that we could attend a tour concert by Maurice André in southern Michigan.) Staying in San Juan, Puerto Rico with my old college friend Orlando Cora and his wife Betsy, we witnessed the birth of their first child, after which I played as Orlando's substitute on a number of recording sessions for radio and television commercials, as well as on several rehearsals of the musical *The Man of La Mancha*. In the process, I was offered the job of playing the entire run of the show; this gig would have been fun, but at this point I was still intending to report for basic training at Fort Knox, Kentucky at the end of the month.

However, back on the mainland, it soon became apparent that I would not face the Army draft. So I simply neglected to show up on the assigned reporting date, and abandoned my plans for a four-year stint with the band at the West Point Academy. Instead, with a very generous cash gift from Orlando and Betsy Cora, we rented a small apartment in an old converted motel, and I spent the fall practicing, listening to recordings, and keeping the household running during Doree's last semester at Michigan State. In early October, Bud sent me the new Bach B flat trumpet, which facilitated my progress all the more.

It was during the summer and fall of 1970 that I developed a mental hangup in my playing which would plague me considerably for the next couple of years. Each time I would put the horn up to my face, I would become fixated on the actual start of the first tone, instead of focusing on the music that I wished to produce. This attention to the physical aspects of playing hindered my carrying out the natural steps that would create the envisioned musical product. This mental mis-focus distracted me considerably from a healthy approach to playing, and eroded my self-confidence a great deal. If I had had numerous playing outlets at the time, either solos or ensembles, I would have had many opportunities to focus on the proper aspects of music-making and thus bypass this distortion in my thinking. For example, during my monthly lessons with Bud, I did not have the problem, since my mind was entirely attuned to the music during those sessions. However, all of my other playing at this time consisted of only my own private practice sessions, during which I focused on my recalcitrant tongue instead of on the desired musical product. Over the course of the following couple of years, as I became involved in more and more healthy playing outlets, my focus gradually returned to musical goals rather than the physical activities of playing.

On November 4, 1970, the Chicago Symphony played a runout concert at Michigan State, with Daniel Barenboim making his conducting debut with the orchestra and Jacqueline du Pré, age 22, his wife of three years, performing the Dvorak *Concerto for Cello*. The following week, Ms. du Pré recorded the concerto with the orchestra and Barenboim in Orchestra Hall, which represented the young conductor's first recording with the CSO. Noone could have imagined at the time that the gifted cellist's career would be cut short three years later, when she would be stricken with multiple sclerosis, a disease which would finally claim her life sixteen years later. After the Michigan State concert, Bud took Doree and me out for dinner and an inspiring personal chat in Lansing. In the process, we learned that Bud and Avis' wedding anniversary, September 5, was the same date as ours, just a few decades earlier.

In late November, we traveled to Oak Park to locate an apartment, in anticipation of our move to the Chicago area late in the following month. My paternal grandparents had had a large home built for themselves in Oak Park in 1918, and my father had been born and raised in that suburb. It was a familiar place, since I had made occasional trips there with my family all of my life to visit relatives, and it was thus a logical location for us to set up our residence.

Chapter Three

The Training Period in Chicago
1971-1973

Within three weeks of our move from Michigan to Oak Park, Doree had begun working as a counselor on an adolescent unit of a nearby psychiatric hospital. Her income (and our careful budgeting) would sustain our household as long as it would take for me to complete my years of training and eventually secure a playing job.

What a pleasure it was to now be able to take lessons with the master every two weeks, and to have those lessons involve a journey of only a few blocks within the same suburb, instead of a round trip of either five hundred or one thousand miles from two states away! In addition, hearing the CSO in live performances now required only a twenty-minute ride downtown on the elevated train.

Since I had become very dissatisfied with the small, toy-like sound of my Selmer piccolo, Bud offered to me, on a long-term loan basis, the use of the prototype Yamaha combination A-B flat piccolo that he had earlier shown me. He had assisted considerably in the development of this large-toned instrument, which had a valve section from a medium-large C trumpet with short pipes and a miniature bell section. This horn, which was not yet even in production in Japan, was equipped with a standard third slide, as well as a replacement elongated third slide which could be installed as needed for the low F tone which sometimes appeared in the Baroque literature. Along with this horn, he also loaned me various Bach mouthpieces to try with it; after I had chosen from the batch the 1D and 7E models, each with a 117 piccolo backbore, and had bought new versions of them, he loaned me a tapered jeweler's reamer. I used this handy tool to slightly open the throat on the new piccolo mouthpieces, as well as the throat on each of the Bach mouthpieces that I used on my large horns. Each of these consisted of a model 1 interchangable screw-off rim, a 1C cup, a 25 throat, and either a standard or an enlarged 24 Schmidt orchestra backbore. Bud also advised me on another improvement in my equipment, for playing the Haydn and Hummel concertos. I purchased from the Schilke company a large E flat sliding bell in raw brass for my Schilke D-E flat horn; this was actually the Type A bell that was usually built for installation on certain B flat trumpets.

In addition to providing lessons, equipment, and advice, Bud also assisted me in arranging some playing outlets in the Chicago region. On his recommendation, I was immediately taken into the Oak Park Symphony as the lead player, by its conductor Perry Crafton, a violinist in the CSO. This proved to be an excellent turn of events, since Bette Dasaro-Eilers, a long time fixture on the Chicago scene who had been the first trumpet in the Oak Park ensemble before I arrived, generously began sending gigs my way; she also turned over a number of her young trumpet students to me.

For the next two years, I would travel weekly to the homes of a handful of young students in the Oak Park area, to give them lessons. The few dollars that these sessons brought in contributed little to our meager family coffer, but they did allow for regular purchase of CSO recordings. More important-ly, this very limited amount of teaching helped me to fix the concepts of the master all the more clearly in my head, by explaining and passing on those concepts to the students. On one memorable occasion, when a young boy was absent at the time of my arrival, his father took the lesson in his place, although the man had not played since high school. One of the students whom Bette Dasaro turned over to me, the son of a United Church of Christ minister, would prove to be a particu-larly important contact in the following months and years.

Another arrangement by Bud, this time with his colleague Gordon Peters, head percussionist of the CSO, led to my playing lead with the Elmhurst Symphony, which Gordon conducted. When I traveled to Elmhurst for the spring concert, I shared a ride with a pianist whose husband was the principal of a Lutheran school in Oak Park. Again, this particular contact would become one of considerable importance to me that spring.

The crucial subject to which I refer was my quest for an appropriate place to practice each day. There was no chance of my practicing in our apartment building, a large multi-unit structure with poor sound insulation between the units and between the floors. During our first two weeks in Oak Park, I practiced for a couple hours each afternoon in the unheated basement of Gram Kapantais' four-unit apartment building. None of the other tenants were home during the daytime hours to hear me; however, when the janitor finally discovered me hard at work there one day, he insisted that I find somewhere else to practice, since I was not an official resident.

Seeking a remedy for this problem, I visited all of the Catholic churches in the entire area, asking each pastor if I could practice in their school building each day after the students had departed, in return for my playing at church services as often as requested, at no charge. All of the priests summarily turned down my offered exchange, except for one. However, in the arrangements with this particular parish, St. Edmonds, I had to be ready to enter the school the moment the last of the students departed, since the doors automatically locked behind them. In addition, the parish would not grant me access to the building on weekends; on Saturdays and Sundays, I was obliged to practice as best I could in our apartment, with a cup mute.

After enduring this unacceptable situation for a few months, I happened to ride to an Elmhurst Symphony concert with the wife of a Lutheran school principal. The following day, at her instigation, we made arrangements for me to practice in their building after school hours on weekdays and anytime on weekends, letting myself in with a key, in return for my playing at their church services on all major occasions. Entirely by coincidence, this school was located directly across the alley from the garage and back yard of Bud and Avis Herseth. This situation led to one of the most treasured compliments of my entire career. One day when I arrived for a lesson with Bud, Avis told me that she had been working in the kitchen one day earlier that week, and had thought that she was hearing her husband practicing downstairs in the basement. However, she eventually realized that he was not even home, and that those familiar trumpet sounds were emanating from the school building across the alley! I thoroughly enjoyed the excellent arrangements at this school for several months, until one hot and steamy summer evening when I was practicing with a window open for ventilation. A band of neighbors suddenly burst in, confiscated my key to the building, and announced that my practicing days there were over.

By coincidence, while I had been teaching the son of a United Church of Christ minister earlier that very week, the young man had passed on a piece of information from his father: the church board would be pleased to offer me a key to the function rooms attached to their church, so that I could practice there anytime I wished. Lo and behold, I was very much in need of such a place just a few days later, after the Lutherans had had enough, and was elated to accept their kind offer. I would practice at this church, and play for them on important occasions free of charge, during the following two years until my departure for Germany, and again for another $3^1/_4$ years after my return from Germany, until I would eventually become a member of the Chicago Symphony and purchase a home in Oak Park. Again by complete coincidence, this home of ours would be located directly across the street from that picturesque stone church and my practice room there.

During the spring of 1971, the three-tooth bridge at the front of my mouth broke, which required a repair and reinstallation of the unit. Unfortunately, the dentist installed it at a slightly different angle within my mouth compared to its former position; this required some slight readjustments in my playing, to accomodate the new position of the three teeth.

These adaptations were accomplished in time for me to perform a number of solos with organ accompaniment at the graduation ceremonies of the Illinois Insititute of Technology in May. This gig, which took place in Orchestra Hall, was my first playing experience in that famous building, in which I would soon spend much of my training time, and later the bulk of my professional career as well.

As my schedule of gigs as a free-lance player began to become busier, I developed a standard check-list that I went through upon leaving the apartment each time: horn, mouthpiece, glasses, mutes, music, stand, reading material, clothing, traveling directions, etc. Often when Doree saw me at the exit door, running through my mental list and checking the contents of my pockets, she would deliver the punch line from an old joke about an elderly priest and his long time housekeeper. (The woman commented to the priest one day that it was so touching to see him making the Sign of the Cross so reverently with his hand each time before he departed from the rectory, praying for a safe return. He responded, "Oh, no, I'm just checking to make sure that I have my spectacles, testicles, wallet, and watch.")

That May, I began my own study of the archaeology of the prehistoric period of the northeastern woodlands region of North America on a fulltime schedule, as if I were enrolled in a university doctoral program. While doing this over the course of the following decade, I assembled an extensive research library of books and site excavation reports. In addition, I gradually studied the collections at virtually all of the primary museums, large and small, within the northeast and midwest regions of the U.S. During this decade, I also assembled a considerable private collection of prehistoric artifacts. Later, I would switch my focus of study and collecting to the historic era, and eventually develop and expand this interest into a completely new career as a historical researcher and writer. Just as Bud had indicated, these non-musical interests would help a great deal in keeping my musical activities fresh over the years; however, neither he nor I could have foreseen that these avid interests would eventually draw me entirely away from my trumpet playing career.

In June of 1971, I passed the audition for membership in the summer program of the Civic Orchestra of Chicago. This was a four-nights-per-week regimen of sight reading, spanning six weeks, which was designed to introduce developing players to a wide array of orchestral literature. This summer program, which also entailed many rehearsals and two different concert performances, provided free passes to the members for lawn admission to CSO concerts at Ravinia Park, the summer home of the orchestra. I also began at this time playing a series of outdoor concerts with the Oak Park Band. Marches were certainly never high on my list of favorite compositions, but the band did add one more ensemble experience to my total training regimen.

The absolute high point of the summer was my first opportunity to perform with the Chicago Symphony, at Ravinia. Those rehearsals and finally the performance of Mahler's *Second Symphony* on June 24, which represented James Levine's conducting debut with the CSO (he would soon become Ravinia's music director), were absolutely mind-boggling. Even though I had been avidly listening to recordings, live concerts, and radio broadcasts of live concerts by the group for four years, it was an entirely different experience hearing those fabulous sounds at close range from the vantage point of the stage, and actually joining in with them as one of the offstage band players. The breadth and depth of the sound, the solidity of the intonation and the rhythm, and the musicality were amazing at close range, and so very easy to fit into, compared to the free-lance ensembles in which I was accustomed to playing. Aside from being composed of less advanced players, these latter groups typically assembled only to do a single rehearsal and concert, or a limited series of such services. Thus, there was never an opportunity for the musicians to play together on a daily basis over an extended period of time, and to thus forge a unity of sound, intonation, and style. When I went downstairs to the locker room to change clothes after the

Mahler concert, Ed Kleinhammer, the eminent bass trombonist who would later become my good friend, said, "Look at him, he looks dazed." I had similar personal reactions three weeks later, when I performed as one of the offstage players on a performance of Verdi's *Rigoletto* under Kertesz.

From this summer on, Doree and I had a standing agreement about scheduling services as an extra player with the CSO. Whenever Radi Lah, the personnel manager and bass player, would phone while I was away practicing or on a gig and offer me a chance to play with the orchestra, Doree would accept the job, no matter what I already had on my schedule. I would then arrange a substitute player as needed for any conflicting free-lance engagements. Playing with the Chicago Symphony, which I liked to call "the last big band in the Loop," took precedence over any and all other gigs in town. There were few more exciting messages from Doree during that period than "Radi called today."

When he had called to hire me for the Mahler concert, I had only one day to purchase a formal white coat for the performance. On such short notice, I was only able to find one for sale at a distant rental store, and that particular one had rather dramatic lapels trimmed with fancy white lace. For sentimental and humorous reasons, I continued to use that same white coat during my two years as an extra player with the orchestra and later during my entire eighteen year tenure as a member. Whenever any of the colleagues commented on it, I explained that it was left over from my earlier days of playing with the Latin Lizards.

Shortly after Bud played the Hummel concerto with the orchestra at Ravinia on July 8 (Doree and I heard both the rehearsal and the concert, sitting with Avis at the performance), he produced for me a copy of a pirated tape recording that an avid fan of his had made on a cassette machine during the concert. On the tape, Bud also included performances of the Purcell *Sonata* and the Hadyn *Concerto* that he had done with the Lake Forest Symphony the previous January, as well as the Vivaldi *Concerto for Two Trumpets* that he and his colleague

Vince Cichowicz had played with the CSO in May. These informal recordings were wonderfully inspirational teaching tools for me, which I played repeatedly at our apartment. I was tickled to note that, during the Hummel performance at Ravinia, the rumble of the scheduled evening diesel train cruising through the park sounded like a long tympani roll in the background, which was perfectly timed and crescendoed to accompany the segue between the second and third movements of the piece and the exposition of the third movement.

The Symphony made its first European tour in the fall of 1971, led by Solti, playing twenty-five concerts in fifteen cities. During those several weeks, Doree and I house-sat for Bud and Avis, giving their home a daily inspection, watering the flowers, etc. During the welcome-home ticker-tape parade along LaSalle and State Streets downtown, we were pleased to receive and record on film Bud's personal wave of acknowledgement as the vehicles passed by us.

In October, after the return of the orchestra, I passed the audition for membership in the Civic Orchestra of Chicago during its 1971-72 season. This ensemble had been founded in 1919 by Frederick Stock, music director of the CSO, to free his orchestra from the uncertainty of relying on European replacements, by training American musicians in orchestral literature and discipline. It is the only training ensemble that is affiliated with a major American symphony orchestra. The well-rounded program of the Civic entailed two rehearsals each week in Orchestra Hall, plus weekly sectional rehearsals coached by the principal players of the CSO, along with providing tickets costing only one dollar apiece for each Friday afternoon concert of the Symphony. Six performances of the Civic were presented in Orchestra Hall each season, and various chamber ensembles from its membership played concerts regularly in schools throughout the Chicago region.

The Civic trumpet sectional rehearsals, which Bud expertly conducted with a pencil for a baton, were extremely educational, since all of the parts were being played and heard by each of us in the section. As he had done in my private lessons,

Bud explained how our passages were to fit into the total orchestral picture, and he also discussed the various requests that many conductors had made concerning those passages over the years.

Since I was now working on orchestral playing in these sessions within an entire trumpet section, Bud expanded the content of my private lessons at this time to also focus on etudes (Charlier *36 Etudes*, Walter Smith *Top Tones*, and Sachse *100 Etudes*) and a wide range of solo literature. The fees for these lessons during the regular season were paid by the Civic Orchestra, and Bud customarily taught the members of the Civic section only during that season, between October and May. However, from the time I moved to Oak Park until I departed for Germany, he taught me every two weeks without interruption in all seasons. During the summers, when the Civic scholarship was not in effect, he and Avis gave me opportunities to work off the lesson fees, along with Doree's assistance. However, those work sessions at their house, which entailed such jobs as painting interior trim, scrubbing kitchen areas, and cleaning cupboards, were instead wonderful opportunities for me to hear the master doing his daily practice routines in the basement. In addition, the Herseths provided us with generous gifts for our services (such as fine wines, dinner at their home, etc.), so there actually was no working off of any lesson fees at all, in spite of our protests.

The brass quintet that five of us members of the Civic Orchestra formed, called the Chicago Brass Consort, was the first brass ensemble in which I had ever played. Over the course of the next two years, we rehearsed heavily and played myriad school performances, gigs at churches and other venues, and public concerts. Our programs, including trumpet solos and duets, quartets, and quintets, were presented both unaccompanied and with organ accompaniment. This was a wonderful developmental experience for me, made all the richer by the coaching that both Bud and Ed Kleinhammer gave us occasionally. Neither the venues in which the Consort performed nor the meager attendance at certain of the concerts hindered our musical growth. On one bitterly cold Sunday evening in January of 1972, after many weeks of diligent rehearsing, we performed an excellent program at a cozy greenhouse in Chicago. The entire audience consisted of the proprietor and his plants along with one young woman from around the corner who had seen the posted fliers. Later inquiries revealed that we had unwittingly chosen Super Bowl Sunday as the date for this particular concert.

In September of 1971, I began taking classes to complete the remainder of my undergraduate degree, at De Paul University in its high-rise building in downtown Chicago (the new campus on the near north side had not been constructed at this point). Shortly after moving from Michigan, I had visited the admissions and scholarship office at each of the major universities in the Chicago region, to discuss the transfer of my three years worth of credits from the University of Michigan and the availability of scholarship funds for completing my degree. De Paul had made the most generous offer, the complete coverage of all tuition and fees, in return for my playing lead in the school orchestra; so I accepted their offer. The drawback of attending this institution was that their program required a number of courses each year in the philosopy and religion department, which had not been part of my program at U of M. Thus, I was required to take a total of five classes within this department to make up for this lacking during my Michigan years, plus the usual music theory and literature classes, to earn a music degree from De Paul. The trumpet instructor there at the time, a third-rate player of summer band concerts and occasional musicals, seemed intimidated at the prospect of giving me lessons. He indicated that I would not need to attend the scheduled sessions, and he would simply submit an A grade for me for each quarter. I must say that the quality of the De Paul music program has soared since my time there; first Ross Beacraft, my colleague in the Civic Orchestra trumpet section, and now John Hagstrom from the Chicago Symphony, have both elevated the level of the offerings of the school immensely.

During this time, I continued to listen a great deal to the

playing of Bud and his colleagues, both live and on recordings, as my aural role models. Devouring the music on CSO records was a very typical form of evening entertainment for Doree and me. In addition, we were present virtually every time Bud played solos with the various community orchestras in the Chicago region. On one such occasion with the Oak Park Symphony, he announced to the audience before commencing a piece, "O.K., start your tape recorders now; and don't touch them again until the piece is over." He was a little irked by the commotion of listeners fiddling with their miniature machines, turning them on and off and changing cassette tapes, during the course of his performances. After his solos, he was always gracious and modest in accepting compliments. In one instance, when Doree and I complimented him on his playing, he noted, "Even a blind pig finds an acorn occasionally."

In addition to avidly listening to the local stars, I also made it a point to hear the concerts of visiting orchestras from the U.S. and abroad, to note various other styles of playing and differing approaches to music-making. On one occasion, during a performance by the Cleveland Orchestra, I was amazed at how very much the rather young lead trumpet was aided by his assistant on decidedly non-strenuous pieces. In addition, when the Los Angeles Philharmonic played in Orchestra Hall, I was amused at the excessively casual behavior of the trumpet players, with legs crossed and an arm draped across the back of the adjacent vacant chair while counting rests. They were apparently signalling to all listeners that they were very relaxed, in spite of their playing in the home hall of the celebrated Chicago Symphony. It was also during this time that I heard Maynard Ferguson present a daytime clinic followed by an evening concert with his band; it was very exciting for me to finally hear a live performance by one of the prominent role models of my youthful days.

One important aspect of the training that was offered to Civic Orchestra personnel was the chance to perform with the CSO when extra players were needed. In March of 1972, I was thrilled to play a week of rehearsals and concerts with the ensemble in Orchestra Hall, doing the world premiere of a new work by Moderna. This was my very first opportunity to play with the group in its downtown venue, and it was as inspiring as the Ravinia experiences had been during the previous summer.

That spring, I also performed the Haydn concerto with the De Paul Symphony in Orchestra Hall, and did the same piece with the Chicago City Symphony, as well as playing a program of solos with piano accompaniment at the Chicago Cultural Center (all with coaching from the master). During the course of the summer, I played in the summer program of the Civic Orchestra, and performed onstage as an extra player at two CSO concerts at Ravinia. I also presented my degree recital at De Paul with piano accompaniment on a very steamy July day, for which Bud coached me on the solos, and supportively attended both the gig and the celebration party afterward at our apartment on his day off from Ravinia. The following month, I played an opera festival in Beloit, with colleagues from the Civic Orchestra.

On the first day of the 1972-73 school year, the dean of the School of Music at De Paul informed me that my tuition scholarship had been rescinded, to be given instead to a new entering freshman. So I paid the tuition myself for the remaining two quarters, and refused to play in the school orchestra, since my participation in that ensemble had been contingent upon my receiving a full tuition scholarship. Thus, I was receiving no private lessons from the staff there, and was not performing in any school ensemble, yet I was finishing a degree in trumpet performance at that institution.

During the fall, Gordon Peters, the conductor and administrator of the Civic Orchestra, held auditions behind a screen to determine which members of the ensemble would play the solo parts in Martin's *Concerto for Seven Winds, Tympani, Percussion, and String Orchestra* on the upcoming program. Based on these auditions, I was chosen from the trumpet section. In preparing to play the part for Bud in a lesson, I studied a tape of the live concert radio broadcast and the associated commercial recording of the piece that Bud and his colleagues had done under Jean Martinon some years earlier. In the process, I noticed that a triplet marking had been omitted from a figure of three thirty-second notes in the printed part, in a complex passage in the second movement. In the CSO rehearsals, concerts, and recording session, Bud had read that particular figure, along with the sixteenth note rest that preceded it, as four sixteenths, and Martinon had not noticed this slight mis-reading. In my lesson, we chuckled about that minute oversight, and I thought to myself, "What a track record, to have missed one tiny item due to a printing error during the course of several decades of music-making!"

From November to May during the 1972-73 season, while playing with the Civic, I was elated to receive the call to be an extra player with the Chicago Symphony on a number of occasions. These included a pops concert conducted by Fiedler, and four memorable performances as an offstage player on Berlioz' *Damnation of Faust* with Solti, including one concert in Carnegie Hall. Later, it was a real thrill to be part of the section while Bud wailed on the solos in Scriabin's *Poem of Ecstasy* in Chicago and Milwaukee, and later to play a pops concert and a Saturday Night Special performance. Near the end of the season, it was also a fine experience to play with the orchestra on two programs, doing *Balshazzer's Feast* and Respighi's *Roman Festivals*.

In each instance, the rehearsals and concerts offered me an opportunity to see and hear from the inside how the members of the Chicago brass section did their job, both at home and on the road. This aspect of the training that was afforded to the members of the Civic Orchestra was invaluable for my development. Unfortunately for later members of the Civic, the door to such experiences closed very shortly after my time in the training ensemble. The following year, while certain members of the Civic trumpet section were performing as offstage players on a Mahler Symphony recording with Solti, their playing required a number of re-takes. In frustration, the Maestro privately instructed Bud, "Please, no more students." Thus, the calls for extra musicians were thereafter directed to older established players in Chicago, instead of the younger developing ones in the Civic Orchestra.

My experiences in auditioning for professional positions began in January of 1973. At that time, there were some thirty-three symphony orchestras and six opera or ballet orchestras paying professional salaries in the U.S. However, a considerable number of these ensembles had short seasons and low pay scales, requiring considerable teaching to supplement the income, and many of them had less than stellar musical attributes. I had already decided that I would not leave the free-lancing opportunities in Chicago to play and teach in a backwater locale. As a result, various of the openings which were advertised in the *International Musician,* the union paper, were not of interest. However, I was interested when the National Symphony in Washington, D.C. announced a vacancy for the assistant first/third position.

In early January, each of the members of the Civic section made our way to the Capitol for the audition. Feeling like a racehorse primed to run, I did not get much sleep the night before the event, while staying at the apartment of my old college roommate, who was now a school band director in a nearby Virginia suburb. None of the large number of candidates at the audition was pre-assigned a playing time; instead, we were each assigned our order of playing in the order in which we arrived at the Kennedy Center. Likewise, no small rooms were made available to the candidates; we each staked out our individual place in one or two large rooms, in which cacophony reigned as the players warmed up and some foolishly ran through much of their solo and all of the excerpts on the list. As the day progressed, my Civic colleague John DeWitt and I became two of the finalists, and he eventually won the job in the final round. Although I did not get the position, I was pleased to have become a finalist on my first time out.

A few weeks later, auditions were held in Boston for the assistant first/third slot there. Again, all of the myriad candidates were instructed to arrive at Symphony Hall at the same time on the same day, and we were assigned our sequence of playing based upon the order in which we checked in. And once again, the assemblage of noisy trumpet players were all amassed in a large offstage room and in the adjacent hallways, with no access to smaller rooms or any semblance of quiet for preparation. Near the end of the very long day of auditions, the personnel manager announced the names of the six candidates who had been chosen as finalists, including Tim Kent. However, he indicated that there were still about ten candidates remaining to be heard. During the following couple of hours, two facts became very clear. First, the audition committee had predetermined the maximum number of finalists who would be invited to return at a later date for the second round. Second, a very favored student of the lead trumpet in the Boston Symphony was among the group of individuals who had not yet played when the list of finalists was announced. As a result, after the latter group of players had completed their auditions, the roster of finalists was revised so that Tim Kent was eliminated, having been replaced by a player from the last group of candidates. Although I was bitterly disappointed by this amateurish approach to holding auditions in the supposed big league, I was again pleased that I had been deemed finalist material.

The following month, auditions were held in Milwaukee for a slot in the trumpet section there. In this case, the number of applicants was much reduced, due to the lesser stature of the orchestra; but the same cattle-call procedures were carried out, with all of the candidates handled in herd fashion. During the course of the day, various of the players indicated to me that I was obviously the most advanced among the group of finalists. However, the outcome of the entire audition procedure there had apparently been pre-arranged, giving the job to the individual who had already been playing the position for some time in an informal substitute arrangement.

There were no more openings of interest looming on the horizon, but I was determined to seek a full-time playing position. So I turned my attention to orchestras in Europe. The office of the Civic Orchestra received each month an issue of *Das Orchester*, the publication of the German musicians' union.

In it appeared announcements of orchestra openings in Germany, as well as in certain other European countries, particularly France, Luxembourg, and Belgium. In late April, I applied to twelve German orchestras for an invitation to audition for their advertised trumpet opening. I did this by sending a letter of application, a resume, and various recommendations from Bud, the Civic Orchestra, and the Chicago Symphony, all translated into German by the Austrian-born parents of one of my students. Since it took considerable time for the magazine *Das Orchester* to arrive in Chicago by surface mail (and I was dealing with a number of old issues), and auditions in Germany were typically held about six weeks after the opening had been advertised, most of the auditions for which I was applying had already taken place. Three of the orchestras sent me a letter reporting that the position had been filled, two indicated that I would be contacted at a later date (meaning if they did not hire a German player in the first audition), and five did not bother to respond. I was invited to attend an audition of the Nordmark Orchestra in Flensburg; however, since this small ensemble did not pay well, I simply sent a tape recording of my playing to them. The one orchestra that did pay rather well and which invited me to audition was in Gelsenkirchen. In advance of my trip there, Bud coached me on the list of orchestral and operatic works that were to be prepared for the audition.

After flying from Chicago to Luxembourg City via Icelandic Airlines at the end of May, with a short stopover en route in Iceland, I made my way to Gelsenkirchen by train. Without any skills in the German language, the activities of locating a hotel for the night, arranging transportation to the opera house, and playing the audition presented a bit of a challenge. In contrast to the large number of candidates at American trumpet auditions, there were only six of us present on this occasion, one each from six different countries, including one German; I was the only non-European there. It was on this day that I learned that, in nearly all instances, orchestras in Germany fill their vacancies whenever possible with German musicians. If a German candidate within the field of applicants is at all qualified to do the job, he or she will almost always be hired, irregardless of whether various of the foreign candidates are much more skilled as players.

After the audition, I made my way to Kassel, Germany, where Rod Miller, my colleague from the Civic trumpet section, had taken a pre-arranged position in the opera house a few months earlier. While waiting for the next issue of *Das Orchester* to be released, with its new slate of openings, and for those auditions to take place, Rod and his family generously took me into their home for a month. During that time, I studied regularly with the bass trombonist of the Kassel opera, who played each year in the orchestra at the Wagner Festival in Bayreuth. He was very familiar with the manner in which German brass auditions were conducted, so he taught me how to win a position there using their ground rules. The entire preliminary audition for trumpets usually consisted of only the first portion of the first movement of the Haydn concerto, through the high D flat, and within this context a player had to demonstrate as many of his or her attributes as possible, including a strong lead trumpet orchestral style. The Germans played with and listened for a heavy tongue, so it would be advantageous to show this aspect of playing in the concerto, whether it was musically appropriate or not. Most of the listeners at an audition would be looking for a player who could produce all of the notes strictly as written, with minimal individualism or musical liberties. They would be interested in a candidate who played with strict rhythms, good dynamic contrasts, and only minute amounts of musical expression. Final audition material would include both orchestral and operatic excerpts, but it would be mostly drawn from the opera literature.

The new issue of the German union publication advertised open trumpet slots in four German orchestras, to which I applied at the beginning of June. Three of the four sent me invitations, with the first of these auditions scheduled to take place in Trier on July 3. On this occasion, there were again about five or six of us participating, with each candidate being from a different country. Since there were no German players present, the judging would be based this time on musical attributes rather than on nationality; thus, I won the audition. After indicating that I had been chosen for the position, the management hired me to sight-read the lead trumpet part on the opera performance that evening (this was not a final stage of the audition procedure, however, since I had already signed my official employment contract for the next season).

At dusk on the following evening, during the low-altitude approach of my plane to O'Hare Airport in Chicago, I was convinced that all those fireworks being blasted skyward from myriad communities below were in celebration of my having won my first professional position. After passing through the airport customs inspections with only a moderate amount of searching of my various horns and luggage, I excitedly met Doree at street level with a hearty embrace, and placed my baggage into the trunk of the car. Immediately, two plainclothes agents took me by the arms and escorted me back into the building and downstairs to a small office. One asked, "Before you empty your pockets and get searched, is there anything you'd like to tell us?" After responding in the negative, I endured their rather personal search, and was finally released. Apparently, I fit various of the profiles that such agents utilized in their work. This kind of treatment would become rather routine for me during the rest of my playing career in the U.S., and with each incident I would be reminded of what brown and black individuals experience in our country on a daily basis.

Two days later, Bud and Avis had us over for dinner at their home, to hear the stories of my German adventures and to celebrate the outcome. Bud was very pleased with my success on the audition trail, which, from my perspective, indicated that many of the lessons that he had generously offered to me over the span of four years had been absorbed. However, he would be the first to assert that, in spite of an individual having considerable natural talent and plenty of guidance along the way, that individual has to put out massive and ongoing effort and have considerable self-confidence, to develop that talent into artistry and to continue to maintain and improve that artistry over the course of many years.

Thinking that we were moving permanently to Europe, Doree and I sold many of our possessions and packed the remainder for shipment to Germany. We then traveled to Ravinia to hear Bud and his colleagues in the CSO brass quintet play a concert for a young audience, which included a concerto for garden hose featuring Bud. From Ravinia, we headed directly to Michigan for final goodbyes and a sight-seeing tour through our home state.

On August 15, we finally departed for Europe. Just as our plane lifted off the runway at J.F.K. International Airport in New York, I instantly thought of myself as a professional player rather than as a student. At that specific moment, at the age of 24, I had finally completed the initial stage of my development as a player, having been very heavily influenced and molded by Bud Herseth and the Chicago Symphony brass section during the previous six years. Their strong influence would also continue to steer my ongoing development over the course of many years into the future.

Chapter Four

European Adventures
1973-1975

Trier, Germany, which would be our home base for the next two years, is an ancient city dating back to pre-Roman times. Located on the Mosel River in west central Germany, it is positioned six miles from the border of Luxembourg and twenty-two miles from the border of France. During the era of the Roman Empire, this community served as the western capitol of that empire, ruling the entire region that stretched from Britain to Spain; Emperor Constantine the Great moved from his palace in Trier to establish Constantinople as the eastern capitol of the empire. Due to its prominence in ancient times, Trier still boasts from the Roman era a massive throne room building, a coliseum, a set of baths, a huge gateway remnant from the original city walls, and a massive bridge spanning the river, while the central core of its ancient cathedral was once a Roman temple. Many buildings representing later eras of history also survive in the compact city of 90,000 inhabitants, including Renaissance homes surrounding the ancient market place, an elaborate Baroque palace, and the modest birthplace of Karl Marx, who was descended from a long line of Trier rabbis. The white wine industry for which the city and the entire Mosel Valley have become world famous was initiated during the Roman era.

Heinz Rose, the former lead trumpet of the Trier orchestra who had just moved down to the second position, very kindly and generously assisted Doree and me during our entire stay there. Although there was no common language between us until we gradually learned enough German, Heinz made us feel very welcome, helped us to rent an apartment overlooking the Roman bridge, aided our purchase of a Volkswagon beetle, and familiarized us with the places to shop and obtain various services. He also guided us though miles of red tape and myriad rubber stampings during such activities as filling out payroll deduction forms and acquiring international driver's licenses, and generally made our lives as comfortable as possible. This applied on the job as well, as he guided me through the daily details of life in an opera pit orchestra that also played monthly symphonic concerts on stage. In addition, he and various of the other wind players patiently served as my language coaches, speaking clearly and slowly as I made my way through this musical, cultural, and linguistic adventure. A definite sign of my language progress came just ten weeks after we had arrived in Germany, when I was able to discuss details of our insurance policy with an insurance agent, on the phone in an outdoor phone booth at a very noisy intersection. The orchestra's first flute Rikio Arai, his wife Shoko, and their toddler daughter Sayaka, who became our closest friends in Trier, spoke no English, and we spoke no Japanese; the Germans thought it was amusing to hear us communicating with each other in German, our only common language.

Beginning with our very first week in Trier, Doree and I took full advantage of the touristic opportunities that were available to us as year-round residents of Europe. Starting with the area of the city itself, and then expanding outward in ever-widening circles, we thoroughly studied the historical, artistic, musical, and architectural aspects of each country. Every time my work schedule offered two or more days off in a row, we were on the road, learning about and absorbing the cultural aspects of European life. And during the days when we were at home and I was on the job, we were continually studying and planning our future jaunts. Compared to American tourists who have a limited number of days in which to squeeze in as many activities as possible, we had few time constraints on our travels. When our available time came to an end on any given trip, we returned home to Trier for me to do my job, and then drove back to our previous stopping point some days or weeks later, to continue our traveling. We seldom had to depart from a country without enjoying each aspect of that particular land which interested us. It was during this period that I worked out a system of keeping in excellent shape by practicing three times a day in our parked Volkswagon, while living as a tourist at the same time. I continued to utilize this practice system throughout my entire playing career, which enabled me to simultaneously keep my chops in shape and enjoy traveling and studying.

In the opera house, the monthly symphonic concerts on stage represented the job that I had been training for over the course of many years, and the scheduled literature was excellent. The seven programs that particular season included such pieces as Berlioz' *Symphony Fantastique*, Handel's *Water Music*, Richard Strauss' *Bourgeoisie Gentilhomme*, Prokofiev's *Classical Symphony*, Stravinsky's *Firebird Suite*, Schumann's *Second Symphony*, and Beethoven's *Ninth Symphony*.

In contrast, playing opera accompaniments provided more of a challenge psychologically. The literature was fine, including such works as Verdi's *La Traviata*, Humperdinck's *Hänsel und Gretel*, Mozart's *La Clemenza de Tito*, and the German operetta *Vogelhändler* (The Bird Seller), which was filled with interesting trumpet solos that I enjoyed playing during each of its twenty-eight performances. However, the accompaniment role of the orchestra in an opera house, nearly always subservient to the vocalists on the stage, was in decided contrast to the extroverted and emotive style of playing that I had emulated all my life, and I found it rather difficult to perform this background role on a steady daily basis. Since the majority of German orchestral players are brought up listening to such performances and studying with opera-playing teachers, they readily accept this subdued mentality of an anonymous pit musician. As a result, they find the occasional symphonic concerts on stage much more of a challenge, since they have not spent their lives developing the more extroverted style of music-making which much of this literature requires to be played properly. Even those relatively few German musicians who perform exclusively symphonic pieces tend to play in a very non-individualistic style, nearly always subservient to the combined ensemble sound. This non-virtuosic approach tends to produce very lackluster performances, especially when it is applied to works of the Romantic and Modern periods.

My first introduction to the more casual, subdued, and hidden approach of German playing came when we opened the season in Trier with a series of performances of Mozart's opera *La Clemenza de Tito,* presented on an outdoor stage amid the picturesque ruins of the ancient Roman baths. I was rather taken aback when the other members of the trumpet section and the entire trombone section headed off down the street during their tacet movements of each performance, to have a beer at the nearby tavern. From long experience, they knew exactly how many minutes the score allowed them to be absent; so they timed their return accordingly, and then played in their usual subdued and barely-noticed fashion. Later, when we moved into the theatre for the main season, it was not unusual for many of the colleagues to drink beers in the musicians' canteen downstairs during both tacet movements and intermissions of performances. In fact, during our opera presentation on New Year's Eve, the music director himself provided an entire case of champagne for the orchestra members to imbibe during the intermission. That evening, since it was actually condoned and promoted by the boss, who was conducting that particular performance, I figured I would join in the conviviality. My playing during the second half certainly did not match the standards that I had observed among the Chicago brass section. Having had that experience one time, I never again drank while on any job.

A couple months after first arriving in Trier, I mentioned in a letter to Bud and Avis that I had been booked to play a number of performances of Handel's *Messiah* in the region during December, as well as a presentation of Bach's *Christmas Oratorio* with Ed Tarr (the latter contact was due to Bud's recommending me to Ed). I would later also play another set of Baroque gigs with the Edward Tarr Trompeten Ensemble in Munich, during the following year. Shortly after my letter went out, I received a return missive from Bud with some welcome news:

"I just sent you today by air mail your favorite Yamaha piccolo trpt. I figured if you haven't run into a decent one over there, you might need it. So it should arrive almost with this letter. I included both of the third valve slides also." I certainly was elated to have that original experimental horn available to me again, since I had returned it to Bud before moving to Germany, and had been relegated ever since to using my lesser-grade Selmer. The master again wrote some weeks later, "I'm glad the little piccolo trpt. got there O.K. I figured you might as well be using it, since I have others here to use, and I know you like that one."

On the subject of the development of new horns and bells, Bud again wrote me in January: "I'm doing the Hummel with Solti next week, in Ed Tarr's Universal Edition in the key of E. Schilke made several bells, both for my E flat frame and the F-G frame, and one in red brass worked really well on the F-G frame, so I'll be using that one." A couple weeks later, he reported on the response of the horn during the solo events, and also revealed his mental outlook concerning the extremely heavy demands of the Chicago Symphony's schedule: "The Hummel went very well. I have several pirate tapes, and will run off some copies so you friends can have one. The trumpet was excellent. Arno Lange [from the Berlin Opera] thought it sounded like a German B flat!... I will do the Brandenburg in Carnegie Hall next year, I think. Solti has asked me several times before, but it's always on with Mahler 6th or something else very strenuous. But I have a little Martin piccolo that laid around Schilke's shop for years. I finally tried it, and it is a sensational Brandenburg horn. So I think I will play it there next year, along with some Schoenberg and the Tchaikowsky 5th. 'Take a lot of beer to cool my chops after that concert, I imagine!! But since Solti has been quite anxious that I should play it in New York, I really want to. So I told him if this Martin trpt. is as good as I think, and if he doesn't care if I pop a couple on the Tchaikowsky, I'll do it. And of course, it keeps me practicing." This private glimpse into Bud's outlook illustrated the degree of mastery that he had developed over the decades, as

well as his extraordinary level of confidence. The following season, he did perform the Brandenburg in New York, as well as
in Boston and Washington on the same tour, along with the
Tchaikowsky *Fifth Symphony* on each performance.

In the early winter of 1974, Bud began searching for a good
Bach C trumpet to send to me for my Trier colleague. In the
process, he reported a couple of discoveries: "I have just recently gotten some interesting information about the Bach trumpets. You know, they have been using the #25 leadpipe for
many years now. That's what we all have on our horns here.
And you remember how we discussed why your horn and
some others were brighter in sound than others of the same 229
model large bore? Well, it has just come to my attention from
several sources that they make a different #25 pipe now for a
standard pipe, but make the older type such as we have and
call it the 'Herseth pipe.' And all of this unbeknown to me all
this time!! The horns I have here now [to choose from for your
German colleague] all have the new 25 pipe, and while they
tune very well and play free and open, they are a little bit
brighter and more raw sounding than mine, so it has to be the
pipe. Look at the pipe on yours, and if it is flared out a little just
before it goes to the tuning slide tube, it is a new 25 pipe. So,
that is some new information to think about...These 239 bells
are now identical to [the former] 229 bells, which they were not
some years ago. So that is not a concern. They all play well, but
are brighter than my own, but also easier to play and tune a little better than mine." Bud had an encyclopedic understanding
of horns and mouthpieces, and he could thoroughly judge their
various qualities after a very short amount of playing.
However, he nearly always focused on musical subjects in his
playing and teaching, rather than on technical and physical
aspects and on equipment.

Among the features of various European museums that
were of particular interest to us during our travels were their
extensive musical instrument collections. During this period
while Baroque trumpets and music were a special focus for me,
we thoroughly enjoyed a major collection of early instruments

at a museum in Brussels. However, one of our Kent family jokes thereafter was based upon the incident that took place when I reached over the velvet rope to check out with my fingertip the cup of the mouthpiece on an eighteenth century long trumpet that was displayed on the wall. Just then, a guard stepped into the room, causing me to quickly retract my arm and, in the process, jar the mouthpiece from the horn and send it clanking to the floorboards. That guard followed us rather closely during the following several hours while we continued our study of those precious instruments.

Ever since arriving in Germany, I had been corresponding with the Yamaha office in Hamburg, which oversaw the importation of all Yamaha instruments for the entirety of Europe. The officials at the firm kept me posted concerning the production of their new piccolo trumpet, which, unbeknown to them, Bud had helped to create with Mr. Kaji, the chief of Yamaha's brass development department near Tokyo. Finally, the officials wrote in the early spring, to inform me that the very first shipment of the production model of this horn was due to arrive shortly. As soon as I had several days off in a row, we departed for northern Germany, taking about three days en route for touristic stops. When we finally arrived at the Yamaha offices in Hamburg, I was grubby, disheveled, and unshaven after several days of camping and touristing in very rainy weather (one of my favorite disguises for concealing my occupations as a dignified symphonic musician and scholar). At first, the Japanese office staff seemed to be a little put off by the appearance of this apparent resident of the street. However, they artfully retained their polite demeanor, and the manager soon escorted me to a large room that had several rows of new piccolos laid out on tables. I pulled from my old torn gig bag the original prototype version in raw brass, and began playing back and forth between it and the production versions. Curious about the horn that I had brought for making comparisons, the very quiet manager and his colleague politely asked to see it. When I showed it to them, I pointed out its serial number of 001, and mentioned that it had come directly from the workbench of Mr. Yoshihiro Kaji, the head of the company's brass instrument development department in Hamamatsu. With wide eyes, they exclaimed, "Ah, so!" and whisked it off to a back room to examine it in detail. After trying out the entire series of production horns, I happily departed with the best of the batch, as well as with the original developmental version, which the Yamaha people were a little reluctant to release to me. I would have loved to have heard the behind-the-scenes conversations in their suite of offices that day!

In early April, I traveled to Stuttgart to audition for the solo trumpet position in the Radio Orchestra, an ensemble of the Sud Deutche Rundfunk, the South German Radio Company. There were eight broadcasting companies in Germany, and each of these companies except the one in Berlin had two fulltime orchestras on its staff. Each of the eight so-called Symphony Orchestras, which employed from 56 to 114 core players, taped symphonic programs for later broadcast, typically doing one program every two weeks. The seven so-called Radio Orchestras (the broadcasting company in Berlin did not have such a group), each employing 45 to 89 core musicians, likewise taped a program every two weeks for later broadcast; however, these latter ensembles tended to record somewhat lighter music, including overtures and pop tunes. At this time, a total of ninety-seven fulltime professional orchestras operated in Germany, all of which were supported by the state. These opera companies and symphonic ensembles were generously funded by a usage tax that was levied each year on every radio and television set operating in the country. Among all of these musicians, the members of the fifteen staff orchestras of the broadcasting companies were paid the highest salaries. The only exception was the Berlin Philharmonic, whose 120 members earned an even more generous income. In addition to their high salary, the staff musicians in the broadcasting orchestras typically prepared only one program for taping every two weeks, which allowed considerable time off between programs for doing outside performances and teaching. Thus, in the world of German musicians, the radio orchestra positions were the absolutely best ones to have.

I suspected that the audition procedure for the Radio Orchestra job would be out of the ordinary when my invitation did not include a list of operatic and symphonic excerpts to prepare for the final round. The reason for this omission became apparent after all of the candidates had completed the customary preliminary round, using the first movement of the Hadyn concerto. After the elimination of most of the players in this first round, we semi-finalists then each played through the second and third movements of the Haydn. Finally, with the field of candidates now very much reduced, each of us finalists played a series of five or six orchestral excerpts. However, we could not have prepared to play these specific passages in advance, since each of them had been transcribed from little-known music for other instruments; in addition, they had been written out so that a different key of transposition was required for each excerpt. In this final round, all of my years of heavy emphasis on practicing the various transpositions, by both singing and playing, really paid off. After I had finished playing on stage, I could hear a male German voice out in the dimly lit hall asserting that my use of a C trumpet on the excerpts, instead of the customary B flat of German players, gave me an unfair advantage in the transpositions. Another voice countered that statement, explaining that I had to transpose just as much as any of the other players, including all passages in the key of B flat. With little further discussion, I was chosen as the new solo trumpet, after which I signed my employment contract. At the time, I did not realize the significance of my signing that routine document.

Happily returning to Trier, I gave notice of my imminent departure to the management of the opera house. Knowing the specific end date of my opera accompaniment career made my heart soar like a hawk! After finishing the last two months of operas and symphonic concerts, Doree and I then enjoyed a wonderful trip of eight weeks through France, Spain, and Portugal. During our five days in the Pyrenées, we spent more time underground in the painted caves of ancient man than on the surface. Later, on the Pic du Midi, we were awakened in the middle of the night by the arrival of hundreds of French people; they were excitedly awaiting the cyclists in the Grand Tour de France, who would soon be coming through the mountain pass on which our little tent was pitched!

Upon our return to Trier, intending to leave shortly for Stuttgart to locate an apartment, I found a letter from the broadcasting company waiting for me. Some three months after my audition and contract-signing in April, the management had decided to combine the personnel of the two staff orchestras into a single oversized ensemble, in order to reduce costs. In the process, some of the members of each group had taken an early retirement, while certain others had been fired; in time, the number of members in the large combined ensemble would be gradually reduced by further retirements. Since a young solo trumpeter had been hired for the Symphony Orchestra in recent years, I was offered the fourth position in this ensemble, although my employment contract, based upon my audition, had specified the position of solo trumpet.

By German standards, the fourth trumpet chair in a radio orchestra was the absolute dream position to have. There was a very widespread custom, practiced among nearly all symphonic wind players in this country, of moving down within the section as a person aged, leaving the work of the lead position to the younger, less experienced individuals. This seemingly odd practice allowed the older, more experienced musicians to have more time for both playing outside performances and teaching. I was being offered the enviable opportunity to move directly to the fourth slot, while I was still a very young man, without having to put in my time playing lead. "How could you possibly refuse such an offer?" they wondered.

However, I did refuse to join the orchestra under those conditions. In my best German, across the table from the Radio Company's lawyer, I asserted that I had auditioned for and had signed a contract to play a solo trumpet position, and that was the position in which I was interested. When it became clear that I intended to hold firm on this decision, the management worked out a compromise agreement with me, by which I would be paid one year's salary without having to play a note. They even agreed to split the lump sum of the salary between two different tax years, so I could avoid paying the higher rate of taxation that would be levied on a single large payment.

Obviously, it would have been utter folly for me to have turned down the offered fourth position if Doree and I had intended to remain in Europe on a long-term basis. However, we had already decided that we would return to the States after completing all of our travels in Europe. I had trained most of my life to be a lead player, and I did not want to accept a section position at this point, especially among German players. In addition, I did not wish to spend my entire career among musicians of lesser quality than those who played in the major orchestras in the U.S. Besides, at age 26, we had begun making plans to start our family and raise our children in the States.

Not knowing that I had made this personal decision, the staff of the magazine *Bild und Funk* (the national television and radio guide for Germany, which was also distributed in Austria, Switzerland, and France) published the following account (here translated):

Out of Work on the First Day? Bad Prospects for Trumpeter Timothy Kent

Willy Matthes, the head of the Radio Orchestra of the South German Radio Company, was enraptured. "The young man is brilliant! Let's hire him!" The enthusiasm of the Stuttgart music boss concerned an American who had auditioned for him several months earlier, Timothy Kent, the outstanding solo trumpeter from Chicago. "Such a talent," said Matthes at the time, "one simply cannot let escape."

But in the meantime, it appears that this talent nevertheless is slipping from him. Not because the American has done something to break the contract, but because Matthes' Radio Orchestra of the South German Radio Company appears to face dissolution. The time for this planned orchestra-exodus: that month in which Timothy Kent should have begun in Stuttgart— September.

South German Radio director Bausch is as unhappy about this development as the musicians. "But our plans really do not rise out of wantonness, but rather only out of the necessity to save money." The Radio Company hopes to save some two million marks annually through the dissolution, partly through moving musicians to the Symphony Orchestra, partly through early retirements, and partly through dismissals. Enough to justify so massive a step?

Yet the Radio Company meets with strong trade-union opposition because of its action. One musician said: "If at first an orchestra dissolution is carried out here, then the other radio-television orchestras in Germany will also go."

Therefore, there is still one tiny hope for solo trumpeter Timothy Kent if he arrives unsuspecting in Stuttgart at the beginning of September: namely, that perhaps at the last minute the dissolution of the Stuttgart orchestra has been called off.

During the previous March, Bud had written to inform me that Vince Cichowicz would be retiring from the CSO trumpet section in the fall. On September 4, 1974, he updated me on the situation: "The opening in the trumpet section has now been announced in the union magazine, and the auditions are for 4th (Charlie G. is moving to 2nd), and are planned for late October and November, no specific dates yet. For the arrangements and the list of requirements (to be really fair, I think the excerpt list should come from the office, not from me), write to the personnel manager of the Symphony." After applying to play for the audition, I was assigned a time slot on October 16, 1974.

Before we flew to the States for me to take the audition, the orchestra made an extended tour of Europe in September, including a concert in the Frankfurt suburb of Höchst. Doree and I met Bud and Avis there, to have a brief get-together and to hear the performance.

On the sixteenth of October, I witnessed in Chicago for the first time how a classy audition would be conducted by a top-flight orchestra in the big league, in contrast to all of the previous auditions that I had ever played before going to Germany. First of all, each and every applicant was allowed to audition, irregardless of his or her background, training, and experience. Only five candidates were scheduled to be heard each hour by the audition committee, whose nine members represented a cross section of the orchestra's instrumentation. Upon the arrival of each applicant at Orchestra Hall, he or she was ushered to a private room downstairs, to warm up and quietly prepare to offer the best possible performance. An orchestra staff member kept each one posted on their approaching playing time, and when that time arrived, Mr. Williams, the dignified and fatherly African-American who was the head of Orchestra Hall security, ushered the applicant into the elevator and up to the offstage area. From there, the audition proctor led the candidate out onto the stage, where they both walked on a long strip of carpet to conceal any telltale heel sounds. A long row of folding screens was stretched across the front of the stage, concealing the applicant from the listeners in the ground-floor seats. The proctor, setting a relaxed mood, instructed the player concerning the pieces that he or she was expected to perform, which included first a portion of the Haydn or Hummel concerto (the candidate's choice) followed by a series of orchestral excerpts. In some cases, Bud, sitting in the audience area, would request that a player repeat a given passage, with certain alterations. Each applicant was guaranteed a minimum of five minutes of performance time; however, all qualified ones played for at least ten minutes.

After a given set of five candidates had completed this preliminary audition, the committee voted silently, with no discussion of any kind being allowed. By this method, no influencing or vote-peddling could be done by a member to promote his or her students or friends. The voting was not a comparison of the various candidates to each other; instead, it was simply a straight assessment of whether any of them was definitely of Chicago Symphony quality. An applicant was required to receive six or more committee votes to be advanced to the finals. If someone received five votes, he or she played again, anonymously, in a later round, to give them another chance to garner the required six votes. After the votes had all been tabulated, a staff member announced the results to the five candidates downstairs, so that there was no interminable period of waiting and hoping. No limit was placed on the total number of applicants who could be advanced to the finals. In this orderly, calm, and dignified procedure, every effort was made by the CSO to help each candidate to play as well as the situation of a high-stakes audition would allow.

Three such days were spent in hearing the preliminary round of applicants, on October 12, 16, and 25. My "hour in the barrel" took place between ten and eleven o'clock in the morning on the sixteenth. This was not the greatest time of day to show one's best attributes, but someone had to be assigned to those early time slots, and I happened to be one of those less fortunate souls. From the field of eighty candidates who played over the three days (an equally large number of individuals had eliminated themselves in advance, after receiving the list of the expected repertoire), five finalists were chosen. They included Phil Smith from the Master's degree program at Julliard and Tim Kent on a temporary visit from Germany. These five individuals were invited to return for the final audition on November 23, traveling at the orchestra's expense.

For the latter audition, which took place between 4:30 and 7 P.M., each of us was again given excellent treatment, with a private dressing room in which to warm up and prepare, and to spend the time between the solo round and the excerpts round. In this case, there was no carpet strip or concealing row of screens across the front of the stage. We could be clearly seen by the audition committee members, Bud, and Maestro Solti, in their ground-floor seats. First, each of us played a major portion of the Haydn or Hummel concerto, with piano accompaniment, while the other candidates remained in their respective rooms downstairs. Then, we each returned, one at a time, to play a number of excerpts. Thus, the playing time of each individual applicant totaled about half an hour.

For the first round, the solo, I was in excellent form; however, during the interval while each of the others played their solo, I allowed myself to cool off, so that my playing in the excerpts round did not represent my best abilities. A deserving Phil Smith won the position, and I was given time to learn from the experience and develop my playing further.

The following day, which was the last day on our six-week round trip airline tickets from Germany, Doree and I visited Bud and Avis at home in Oak Park. There, Bud said that I had definitely played the best among the five candidates in the solo round. And he agreed that I had not played my usual on the orchestral excerpts in the final round. He was very supportive, and we both knew that other opportunities would likely unfold in due time. Before we departed, Bud and Avis presented us with a signed copy of the book entitled *The Chicago Symphony Orchestra*, a wonderful photographic study of life in the CSO.

After returning to Trier, I spent the winter and early spring doing free-lance gigs, including Bach oratorio performances with Ed Tarr, while we awaited the arrival of warmer weather so that we could resume our long-range travels. In late February, Bud wrote me about an open position that he thought I might want to audition for: "You may have heard about the opening in Detroit. Frank Kaderabek is going [from Detroit] to Phila. on 1st —Gil Johnson quit to go to Miami U. to teach. They offered me the job [in Philadelphia], but I turned it down, of course, so they had a small invitational audition and Frank got it, so his old job is open. The ad just came out in the International Musician, and it says the audition will be late March...I don't know the repertoire for Detroit, but if I can find out soon, I'll send it, although they should send that to you soon." I was not interested in playing in the Motor City at that time, considering the serious financial instability of the orchestra. However, when the lead job soon opened up in both Cincinnati and Edmonton, Alberta, I thought that this pair of auditions would be worth a trip back to the States, before Doree and I set out on the road again.

After packing all of our belongings and shipping them to friends in Oak Park, to be stored until our return in the fall,

Doree set up temporary residence with friends in Trier, and I departed across the Atlantic. By coincidence, the two auditions were scheduled to take place within the span of two days. I first traveled to Cincinnati, where I played on each piece exactly as I wanted, in both the preliminary round and the finals later in the day. Various of the other candidates in the final round indicated to me that I had clearly swept the competition and had certainly won the job. Thus, we were all very surprised when the personnel manager announced that noone had been chosen for the position. This outcome was only explained some time later, when a player who had not even auditioned for the position was simply appointed to fill it. It seemed clear that this had been a pre-arranged situation, and that the public audition had apparently been a sham, held so that the orchestra would appear to be following the norms of the above-board audition procedures that were becoming more common by then.

Within hours of the Cincinnati audition, I had made my way to the airport there, had caught a flight to Toronto (where the Edmonton Symphony audition was to be held at the University the following day), and was ensconced in a small airport office with three Canadian immigration and customs officials. In addition to my appearance, which fit perfectly the profile of both a terrorist and a drug runner, my story definitely sounded concocted: I was an American musician, living in Germany but without a permanent address or employer there, flying from the U.S. into Canada to audition for an orchestra job. I bore an invitation from the Edmonton Symphony, and was laden with four trumpets and plenty of music. However, in their eyes I was either a terrorist, a mule smuggling in drugs, or someone who intended to sell those instruments in Canada and slip out without paying sales tax to the government (why would a suspicious-looking guy have four trumpets with him, unless he was going to sell them?). Finally, after a very thorough search of both my possessions and my personhood, I was released into the Toronto night, to find a hotel for a few hours sleep and then to make my way to the University of Toronto for the morning audition.

The number of candidates who appeared on this occasion was rather limited, compared to the huge cattle-calls at auditions in the States, since Canadian players were not numerous and few Americans were seeking employment in orchestras north of the border. I was rather amused when one of the American applicants decided to leave without playing a single note, saying he did not stand a chance, when he heard me buzzing my mouthpiece at the beginning of my warmup. After a preliminary round on the first couple sections of the Haydn concerto, I was the only remaining candidate. The conductor then tested me for a full hour, having me play the entire Haydn, as well as all of the orchestral excerpts for which I had brought music. He then informed me in considerable detail about the ensemble, as well as the attributes of life in Edmonton. Clinching this lead trumpet position certainly appeared to be a sure bet to me. However, some time later, I was notified by the conductor that the lead player who had been poised to depart had instead decided to remain on the job, so there was, unfortunately, no place for me in the orchestra.

Returning to Germany, I rejoined Doree and we set off on a huge journey of five months, from early May through September, which took us through southern Germany, Austria, Yugoslavia, Greece, the Greek Islands, Italy, Switzerland, Denmark, Sweden, Norway, and England, before selling our car in Trier and finally departing for Chicago. Our two years in Europe had been immensely enriching for us culturally, and I had become a much more experienced player during that time.

Chapter Five

Free-lancing in Chicago 1975-1978

M y work during the next 3 1/4 years would include about
as much commercial playing as symphonic playing, a
balance that I thoroughly enjoyed. During the final couple
months of traveling in Europe, I had taken a complete vacation
from the horn, which was refreshing. Upon returning to Oak
Park, I immediately began my usual routine after a respite from
playing, a procedure that typically restored me to nearly full
capacity within ten days. However, in this instance, I had taken
a full two months off from playing, so I suspected that my
come-back this time might take a little longer than usual. As
events transpired, though, I would have no extra time to
casually return to full capacity.

Within ten days of our return from Europe, I was playing
lead on the Andrew Lloyd Weber musical *Jesus Christ Superstar*.
Its'scheduled run at the Shubert Theatre in downtown Chicago
would span about three months. I relished playing this show,
with its excellent writing for both the core rock band and the
wind players, whose licks were given extra impact by the
confines of the completely enclosed pit area. After the initial
week of rehearsals, the work schedule consisted entirely of
eight performances per week; having no rehearsals was a
feature of show playing that I found very appealing. Near the
closing date of the Chicago run, I was summoned to a private
meeting with the slender, attractive lady conductor, who did
her job wearing elegant floor-length satin dresses. (During my
later years in the CSO, I never kept that close an eye on any
conductor, not even Maestro Solti.) She had decided to add the
lead trumpet to the core of rock band players who remained
with the show as it migrated from city to city. I was pleased to
be invited to become a permanent fixture on the production,

when it would soon move on to Toronto and beyond. However, the conductor appeared to have taken a special liking to this particular lead trumpet, and it did not seem to be the wisest move to leave behind a barely-pregnant Doree in Oak Park and take on the lifestyle of a road musician. So I respectfully and wisely declined the offer.

Immediately upon our return from Europe, Doree had resumed her former employment as a counselor on an adolescent unit of a psychiatric hospital a few miles from our apartment. Her income at this institution, first as a counselor and later as the director of a 36-bed adolescent unit, would serve as the guaranteed constant support of our household, during these several years in which my work as a free-lance player would remain steady but would fluctuate considerably according to the types of music.

After the run of *J.C. Superstar* finished, I eventually became a member of the house big band at the Mill Run Theatre. This in-the-round theatre was the only venue in the entire Chicagoland region in which Las Vegas-style shows were regularly presented. During my stint there, we accompanied such acts as Tom Jones, the Beach Boys, and Mitzi Gaynor on the round, slowly rotating stage. Sometimes, two-week runs of other shows with pre-recorded backup music were interspersed between the runs of these headliner acts; during these canned-music stints, the house band was off, free to take other gigs.

The demands on me as a player while doing these shows were often very different from my legit work, and I noted that Bud had not mentioned some of these aspects of the job during my lessons over the years. For example, during the tune *Southern Nights* in Mitzi Gaynor's show, part of my role was to serve as the straight man when the star draped the huge hoop skirt of her Southern belle gown over my head and shoulders, which were conveniently located just in front of her elevated portion of the stage. In addition, during the rehearsals that preceded her two-week run, we four trumpets, situated in the back row, were specifically admonished not to glance behind us during the slinky dance routine that she performed in a flesh-colored body suit; only during the second show on closing night was a little discreet glancing to be permitted.

During most of these two-week runs, Johnny Howell and I alternated back and forth between the lead and second parts. It was a fine experience for me working beside Johnny, who had been a member of the Stan Kenton, Woody Herman, and Maynard Ferguson big bands during the 1940s and 1950s, while I had been a young boy growing up. At one point, the trumpet section in Kenton's band had included both Maynard Ferguson and Johnny Howell. I once heard a radio broadcast of a tune that had been recorded by the Kenton band in 1952 (when I was three years old), on which Johnny had played lead and Maynard had played one of the section parts! Eventually, Maynard had settled in California and Johnny in Chicago. In the latter city, Johnny had been the primary lead player in the commercial field for several decades.

Some of the highest points of my entire playing career took place well after midnight during second shows on Saturday nights at Mill Run. These events happened on those particular occasions when the headliner was good, the writing was excellent, and Johnny was inspiring me from the adjacent chair. Enthusiasm emanated from him at all times on the bandstand, through both his playing and his judicious but expressive body language. One such Saturday, as we were leaving the stage after the second show, the band leader said to my colleague, "Wow, tonight you sounded like the Johnny Howell of the old days!" Johnny smiled, pointed his thumb at me, and replied, "That wasn't me, it was him." This particular interchange rated among my most treasured compliments, almost on a par with Avis Herseth's comment to me about her mistaking the sounds of my practicing for those of her husband.

Later, I did a nine-month run of the musical *A Chorus Line* at the Shubert Theatre downtown, and I also served as the substitute player each week for the musical *Cats*, which played at the Shubert for about the same length of time. (It was during the long-running *Cats* gig that I became a member of Bud's section in the CSO; however, that is getting ahead in the story.) On one occasion when my calendar was open for a couple of weeks, I accompanied Doree and some of the residents of her adolescent unit on an out-trip, to see the splendors of the Ringling Brothers-Barnum and Bailey Circus. When I visited the bandstand during the intermission, there was Johnny Howell on the job; by the next evening's show, I had replaced him for the duration of the gig, to his immense relief, as gum disease was beginning to wreak havoc with the solidity of his teeth. The twenty minutes of continuous blowing during the opening grand promenade reminded me of my earliest days as a trumpet player: at the age of ten, my skinny arms had tired just holding up the instrument for the duration of a piece. As a boy, I had resorted to resting my elbows against my chest to help support the horn; as an adult playing the circus, I eased my pains by glancing at those lovely performers in glittering costumes riding the elephants and horses around the ring.

Sometimes, my work schedule included recording sessions to lay down the sound track of independent films. This was quite satisfying, especially those projects that involved one particular composer who wrote nice solos for me to play. One of his movie pieces consisted of an extended piccolo trumpet solo with strings accompaniment for the first and third sections, which flanked a middle section featuring the woodwinds. The day we recorded that particular piece, it was not fun having to repeat the extended solos several times due to persistent errors that were made by the woodwind players in the midsection. While a free-lancer, I also occasionally played recording sessions for television and radio commercials; however, I found these fifty-minute jingle sessions to be quite unsatisfying, especially compared to playing film scores.

One of the more memorable events for which I was hired in 1977 was the 80th birthday bash for John D. MacArthur, one of the wealthiest men in the world, who, under considerable influence from his wife Catherine, eventually became a noted philanthropist. At this celebration, which took place in the ballroom of a major hotel, I played a fanfare duet with a colleague on long herald trumpets. Immediately after we finished, the booker for the job asked me for the manuscript of the fanfare, which I had jotted down during the ride to the job on the elevated train. The booker, a rather slimy character, then added his own signature and presented the original masterpiece to the wealthy honoree as a gift, as if he had composed it himself for the birthday celebration.

Possibly the most out-of-the-ordinary gig took place in June of 1977, when I was hired to work on the Robert Altman film *A Wedding*. In the half of the movie that focused on the wedding ceremony, I appeared on camera as the lead trumpet of the eight-member brass ensemble, dressed in white cassocks, that performed at the side of the altar area. Both during and after the filming, we also laid down the sound track for the ceremony.

During these years as a free-lance musician, my legit playing was even more varied than the commercial gigs. Obviously, some of the most satisfying jobs for which I was hired were performances as a substitute or extra player with the Chicago Symphony, at both Orchestra Hall and Ravinia Park. Other established groups with which I played occasionally were Lyric Opera of Chicago, Chicago Chamber Orchestra, Chicago Opera Theatre, and Music of the Baroque. Pickup ensembles also often engaged me to perform with them, for such occasions as the spate of Handel *Messiah* gigs that took place each December. Doree accompanied me to a great many spirited presentations of this particular piece at Baptist churches in the black neighborhoods on the south side of Chicago. My work schedule also included a steady stream of weddings, anniversary celebrations, christenings, memorial services, and special liturgical occasions at which trumpet solos were wanted. On these occasions, I particularly enjoyed playing lyrical, expressive solo pieces, as well as improvising on the spot obligato parts for hymns.

In addition to these solo performances, I belonged to a number of brass chamber ensembles that rehearsed weekly and played gigs and concert presentations. These groups, which included a trio, a quartet, and two quintets over the years, provided me with a great deal of satisfaction, as well as being excellent for my musical development. One of these quintets included my colleague on trumpet who had recently played the jazz solo chair in Woody Herman's big band on the road for two years, as well as the bass trombonist who had likewise played a long stint with Woody's band on the road.

Amid all of these rehearsals and performances, I continued to practice heartily and to receive lessons from Bud about once every two or three months. These coaching sessions sometimes took place during my preparations for an important solo gig or an audition, while in other instances they were intended simply to keep my progress in symphonic playing moving steadily forward. During these sessions, Bud was now sometimes more direct in his comments about the inappropriate manner in which certain players did their job in a trumpet section. For example, he clearly stated his opinions about players who would either lay back or actually take the mouthpiece off their chops during the last page or two of a big piece, to rest a bit during the strenuous finale. Continuing on this same subject, my lesson on one occasion immediately followed the coaching session that Bud gave to a well-known player who was headed directly from Bud's house to a major International Trumpet Guild conference, where he would appear as one of the featured presenters. Bud commented to me, "He can't even play through a one-page etude without taking the horn off his face to rest at least once!"

During this time, I added a Schilke four-valve piccolo to my arsenal of horns, to augment the three-valve Yamaha with a replaceable long third slide that I had purchased in Germany. As Bud explained, the presence of the fourth valve on the Schilke horn reduced the vibrancy of the instrument somewhat, producing a more centered sound and giving the player the sensation of increased solidity. This reduced vibrancy was often a favorable trait, but the more sensitive response of a three-valve horn was more appropriate for certain pieces.

It particularly delighted me to witness Bud's degree of mastery at a brass conference that was held at Roosevelt University in downtown Chicago during this period. Shortly before his presentation, three trumpet players who did the bulk of the television and radio jingle recordings in Chicago offered a presentation on their particular line of work. First, they described in great detail how they were required to sight-read and play impeccably every single time in the recording studios, even during the very first run-through of a jingle. After all this brave talk, they then proceeded to fumble and falter considerably during the demonstrations of their supposed prowess. Then Bud delivered his talk and demonstration on symphonic playing, in which, among other excerpts, he played the high C octave call from *Zarathustra*, and then repeated the lick four times in quick succession, in four progressively higher keys.

As part of my ongoing development program, I continued to listen avidly to Bud and the CSO whenever the ensemble *orchestra* played particularly important brass literature, both in live performances and via the weekly radio broadcasts of recent live concerts. In addition, many of the premiums that were offered during the annual fundraiser of Public Radio station WFMT, the fine arts radio station in Chicago, consisted of complete works from broadcasts of earlier Chicago Symphony concerts, which had been recorded live during the 1960s and early 1970s. I taped from the radio these pieces, which were aired according to a printed schedule, and added them to my ever-expanding library of CSO live concerts. Part of my personal training program also entailed hearing radio broadcasts of the live performances of other major orchestras. I was particularly intrigued to hear the decidedly poor playing of the lead trumpet parts in concerts by the Boston Symphony. The faltering quality of those performances would never have been heard in presentations by the Civic Orchestra of Chicago, which was a training ensemble composed of developing younger players.

Doree and I continued to have a good personal relationship with Bud and Avis. Doree particularly liked phoning Bud on July 25 and playing *Happy Birthday* for him on her recorder.

In May of 1976, I was chosen through open auditions to be the lead trumpet for a new fulltime, federally-funded summer orchestra, the Chicago Festival Orchestra. During the playback at a recording session of this group, I caused a bit of a rift with its conductor, an overly confident "wannabe," when he declared to the recording engineer, "Koussevitsky [the distinguished former music director of the Boston Symphony] couldn't have done it better!" When the engineer asked, "Who's Koussevitsky?," I instantly explained, "He used ta play for da Bears." The room fell deathly silent as the conductor flushed to a deep red hue.

Near the end of the Festival Orchestra's season, as August was drawing to a close, Doree and I worked out a series of hand signs that she was prepared to use in the audience at Navy Pier concerts, to signal me if she were to go into serious labor. However, she did not have to use her sophisticated signals, since our first child, Kevin, who was nearly two weeks overdue, finally arrived just after the summer season ended, on September 4, 1976.

We soon took Kevin to meet Bud and Avis at their house, where he snoozed quietly while we enjoyed the Mexican breakfast that Avis had prepared. Then Doree and I settled into our former schedules and new duties. With Doree working her usual 3 to 11:30 P.M. shift at the hospital five or more evenings per week, I handled the child care during all of those times when I had no gigs; we needed babysitting help to cover most of my daytime rehearsals, as well as most of those evenings when I had performances. For my private practice sessions each afternoon, in addition to transporting my four horns from our third-floor apartment to the church, I now also carried an infant in a Snugli (a chest-front pouch suspended from shoulder straps), a diaper bag, and full bottles. At the church, the nursery room was handily adjacent to my practice room, so I was fully outfitted with a playpen, a windup swing, and plenty of toys for tots. When the baby was particularly fussy, I occasionally attempted to practice with him in the Snugli, and I even once played a brass quintet rehearsal with him in his pouch on my chest. However, this solution presented its own set of problems: when he was awake, Kevin liked to pull my beard and generally interfere with my playing and my concentration, and whether awake or asleep, his weight on my chest interfered with efficient breathing. Thus, during my practice sessions, he spent most of his time in either the playpen or the swing; I soon discovered that a full winding of the swing would give me sufficient time to play through a full-page etude!

When open auditions were held in August of 1977 for positions in the newly-formed Chicago Philharmonic (an attempt to establish a second orchestra in the city), I was chosen as co-principal after playing an hour-long audition. This ensemble, which only lasted through the following January, dissolved at about the same time that Doree accepted the position as director of a large adolescent unit at the psychiatric hospital, and thus increased considerably her weekly work schedule.

In addition to all of my musical activities during the years 1976-1978, I also made a considerable number of road trips to study the prehistoric archaeology and the history of Michigan, Wisconsin, Missouri, Illinois, Indiana, Ohio, and Kentucky. In some instances, I carried out the research trips by myself, but in many cases the family joined me on these camping jaunts. During this period, I also researched in depth the activities of the three generations of my French ancestors who had preceded me in Michigan: my grandfather had emigrated from central Quebec in 1884, and my grandmother had emigrated with her parents and siblings from the southeastern tip of Ontario in 1887. All of these non-musical activities kept my interest in music fresh and spirited.

Our son Ben joined the family on June 30, 1978. That particular week, I was playing with the CSO at Ravinia, as an extra trumpet onstage. Early on the morning of the 30th, I called the personnel manager to report that Doree's labor was advancing quickly, but I still might be late for the rehearsal. During the birth process, both Doree and I kept one eye on the clock in the delivery room, hoping that I would be able to make the rehearsal on time. After Ben arrived safely, I immediately left Doree in the delivery room, to commence the 45 minute drive from Oak Park to Ravinia. However, in the parking lot I discovered that I had to change a flat tire on the car before departing.

Thus, by the time I arrived at the pavilion, the rehearsal had already begun, and I learned that Radi Lah had felt the need to hire another player to replace me, for both this rehearsal and the concert to be played the following evening. So my great rush to change the tire and make the wild ride northward had not been necessary!

Now with two children to care for each day, I continued to transport them to the church every afternoon to practice. This entailed carrying infant Ben in the Snugli, and leading two-year-old Kevin with my hand that was not laden with trumpets and gear. Only years later did I learn that the aged couple who lived across the street from the church, and who watched the Kent trio arrive and depart daily, had dubbed me "Mr. Tootles."

In early June of 1978, several weeks before Ben's birth, I had been hired to play a solo recital with organ accompaniment at an Episcopal church in Chicago, to celebrate the christening of the infant son of a young couple. The new parents were very enthused about symphonic music, and had decided to make this child's public arrival a musical event, with the christening ceremony taking place during the intermission of the concert. At about this same time, I learned that the fourth/utility trumpet position in the Chicago Symphony would soon be vacant, when Phil Smith would depart to assume the lead position in the New York Philharmonic. Since Phil would be playing in the CSO through its August-September European tour, the auditions would be held shortly afterward. I decided that I would keep up the momentum that I had developed during the recital preparations of May and June, and maintain it right through the coming months until the auditions would take place in the autumn.

For the next five months, I played a solo program somewhere every week. In some cases, one or another of my organist colleagues joined me for concerts at various churches; however, utilizing an organ for a concert required considerable advance arrangements, and it limited the performance venues to churches. A much more portable combination involved a piano; in these instances, any venue that had a piano would suffice. Two different pianists and I presented many concerts, which alternated trumpet solos with piano pieces, in private homes, schools, churches, senior citizen residences, hospitals, libraries, and community centers. Some of these settings were excellent, with a well-tuned piano of high quality in a room with good acoustics; others were considerably less than ideal. However, the listeners at each locale enjoyed the offerings, and my pianist friends and I benefitted a great deal from the regular schedule of recital performances. During each concert, I incorporated discussions of the various horns that I used, since each concert involved B flat, C, E flat, and piccolo trumpets. In those weeks when no program with an accompanist was scheduled, I gave unaccompanied presentations, in the same wide variety of venues.

After the CSO vacancy and audition were officially announced in the *International Musician* and the list of orchestral excerpts to prepare was available, I added those excerpts to my solo programs. Playing them without accompaniment, I discussed my choice of horn and mute for each piece, and explained how those particular passages fit into the orchestral context.

In each instance, I recorded my presentations with a portable cassette machine, and during the following days played back the tapes, critiqued the music-making, and acted as my own teacher. During this preparation period, I did not approach Bud about any coaching sessions, thinking that any such assistance would be inappropriate. I had already received eleven years of his guidance, directly by lessons and indirectly by aural examples, and it was now time to show what I had absorbed.

In addition to heartily practicing basics and etudes to maintain and burnish the fundamentals, and playing weekly solo presentations, I also sang through many etudes, solos, and orchestral excerpts each day. When dealing with the excerpts, I focused equally on all of the trumpet parts of each piece. This singing activity was an invaluable training exercise, one which Bud had promoted since my very earliest lessons; it developed a very musical approach, since no physical instrument was involved in the process.

As with every audition for which I had prepared over the years, this one was viewed as an opportunity to make a major surge of forward progress in my music-making. It was not possible to maintain this extreme degree of effort on a permanent basis, involving this amount of practicing, performing, singing, and listening. However, an approaching audition offered the added impetus and inspiration to step up my usual program of self-improvement for a considerable number of months.

On a parallel subject, during any audition preparation period, Doree and I avoided discussing what changes might be wrought in our lives if I were to win that particular position. Our only goal was to facilitate a maximum amount of progress during that period of heavy effort. By utilizing this mental approach, there was never such a thing as an unsuccessful audition. If I did not get a certain job, either I was not yet ready to fill that position, or my style of playing was not what that particular ensemble was seeking, or I had not played my best on that particular day. Irregardless of the official outcome of any given audition, the experience was always enriching and progress-inspiring for me, never discouraging or disheartening.

Over the course of the first two weeks in November of 1978, the CSO audition committee heard 140 candidates play their preliminary auditions. Some 300 applicants had written to the personnel manager concerning the trumpet vacancy; however, over half of these individuals had eliminated themselves from the competition after receiving the list of solos and orchestral excerpts which were to be prepared. The roster included the first movement of either the Haydn or Hummel concerto, plus excerpts from the first trumpet parts of the following orchestral pieces: Bach's *Christmas Oratorio*, Mahler's *Symphony Number 1*, Strauss' *Don Juan*, Beethoven's *Leonore Overture Number 2* and *Number 3*, Bartok's *Concerto for Orchestra*, Britten's *Young Person's Guide to the Orchestra*, and Stravinsky's *Petrouchka*.

My particular time of trial was 1:00 P.M. on Saturday, November 11. During the course of my hour in Orchestra Hall that day (when I performed as Candidate Number 129), I witnessed the same dignified aspects of Chicago Symphony audition procedures that I had observed four years earlier: a total of only five candidates playing each hour, individual dressing rooms for each applicant to prepare and wait in, a heel-muffling carpeted walkway on the stage, a wall of screens across the front edge of the stage, fair voting by committee members with no conversations allowed, and hourly notification of the results. During the course of my audition, which lasted over fifteen minutes on stage, I played a major portion of the first movement of the Hummel concerto, plus all of the orchestral pieces on the list except the Beethoven *Leonore Overture Number 3* and the Britten *Guide*.

By the end of the following Monday, after the remaining preliminary auditions had been heard, a total of three candidates had been advanced to the final round, representing one percent of those individuals who had applied to audition. The finalists included George Vosburgh, who was a senior at the Eastman Conservatory, Steve Hendrickson, a good friend of mine who had spent two years training in the Civic Orchestra and was now free-lancing around Chicago, and Tim Kent.

Between then and the final audition, which was scheduled for Monday, January 15, I continued my training regimen of weekly solo programs for another two months. In addition, Steve Hendrickson and I got together at his apartment once each week to play mock auditions for each other. To make these experiences more valuable and real, the listener in each instance turned his back on the player. Thus, no visual distractions were involved for the listener, and the player attempted to make any changes between various horns imperceptible to the listener. Being good friends and wanting the audition preparation to be a healthy learning experience, we offered each other amiable but frank critiques. In the process of our weekly sessions over the course of these two months, Steve and I not only improved our trumpet playing skills, but we also became better friends. During this time, I also took a single lesson each from Dale Clevenger, the CSO's principal French horn, Ed

Kleinhammer, the Orchestra's bass trombone, and Arnold Jacobs, the CSO tuba. All of these latter coaching sessions were invaluable to me, with each of these men encouraging me, in his own particular way and from his own perspective, to play as confidently and musically as possible.

It was during this period that I was playing the long run of the musical *Cats* at the Shubert Theatre downtown. Thus, on a few occasions I ran through the Hummel concerto and the excerpts for my friend Johnny Howell on Saturdays, during the interval between the matinee and the evening show, in a large rehearsal room at the theatre. Johnny's long career as a big band and commercial player had not involved any legit music, yet he made some very observant comments about my playing in those sessions.

By the weekend before the scheduled final audition in ✓ January of 1979, twenty-nine inches of snow lay on the ground everywhere in the Chicago region, and huge piles loomed beside every street where plows had cleared partial pathways. The white crystals had been falling throughout December and the first two weeks of January, without any above-freezing days to cause any melting. This 29 inches of accumulated snow on the ground represented the greatest amount to have ever been recorded in Chicago. Over the weekend, the especially heavy amount of new snowfall resulted in the closing of O'Hare Airport, the shutting down of the elevated train system in the city and suburbs, and the blocking of virtually all streets in the entire metropolitan area.

Since the roadways of Oak Park were nearly impassible, I could not travel from our apartment to the church to practice as usual. So I practiced as best I could all weekend in the apartment, with a cup mute muffling the sound somewhat from the many neighbors but also interfering considerably with my last-minute preparation and maintenance. To make matters worse, both of our boys came down with chicken pox over the weekend; their misery accentuated the rather crowded conditions in our one-bedroom apartment. Ben, six months old, having outgrown the bassinet, slept in a crib in the long hallway, while Kevin, 27 months old, slept on an air mattress in the living room.

Early on Monday, January 15, Radi Lah, the CSO personnel manager, called to notify me that the auditions which had been scheduled for that afternoon had been postponed until Tuesday. With O'Hare Airport closed, George Vosburgh could not fly in from New York, and the blocked streets and shutdown trains prevented the two local candidates and the listeners from traveling to Orchestra Hall. So Doree, who could not reach her hospital on the impassible streets, tended the sick boys while I put in another day of practicing with a cup mute, singing through the Hummel concerto and the excerpts, and listening to CSO recordings to keep that sound clearly imprinted on my mind. The following day turned out to be an exact repetition of that same routine, with Radi's postponement phone call, crying babies, muted practice routines, singing of music, and listening to records and tapes. Finally, by Wednesday morning the airport had reopened, the elevated trains were moving again, and some streets had been plowed clear. This time, the call from the orchestra indicated that the audition was on.

Having been one of the five finalists when this same position had been open in 1974, when Phil Smith had won the job, I had had four long years to contemplate that former experience and learn from it. During those four years, I had applied two important precepts from the Dalai Lama: "When you lose, don't lose the lesson," and "Not getting what you want is sometimes a wonderful stroke of luck." This time around, I was much better equipped to both win the CSO position and meet the performance standards of the orchestra on a permanent daily basis. Before both the solo round and the later excerpts round of the audition, I maintained a very positive and upbeat attitude in my dressing room at Orchestra Hall, ready to do my very best presentation whenever the call came to go up on stage. Warming up only moderately on the horn, I sang aloud a few passages of the Hummel and the excerpts, and then silently ran through the rest in my head, keeping the mental picture of the music clear.

In the elevator on the way up to stage level, Mr. Williams, the gentle giant who was the head of security for Orchestra Hall, instructed me in his deep Southern drawl, "Do this one fo' yo' waff." Doree and I had gotten to know this kind and warm-hearted man during my days in the Civic Orchestra.

During both of the rounds on stage, I concentrated as fully as possible on only the music at hand, staring at the sheet on the stand and blocking out other input as much as I could. Without a screen blocking the view, I had to ignore the sensations of standing alone near the front of the stage, with Bud and Solti sitting together on the ground floor in front of me, a few rows back, and the nine members of the audition committee scattered among the other ground-floor seats. Before playing each passage, I visualized in my head exactly how I wanted it to come out of my bell: with a good sound, rhythmic, musically expressive, and in an appropriate style for that particular piece. If any given lick went less than exactly as planned, I did not dwell on it, but instead kept thinking only forward to the next passage.

After the solo round was finished, the round of orchestral excerpts was held, involving passages from each of the pieces that appeared on the list. In addition, the sight-reading capabilities of each finalist were tested on excerpts from the first trumpet part of Stravinsky's *Pulcinella Suite,* as well as on various third trumpet solo passages from Prokofiev's *Symphony Number 5.*

After we three candidates had completed the excerpts round, we waited in our respective dressing rooms downstairs for the final decision. When Radi Lah came down the stairway to deliver the results, he first went to George's door; I heard him say, "Sorry, George. You played well, but unfortunately you didn't get the job." Then I heard him deliver a very similar message to Steve. Apparently, Radi thought that I had heard these condolence messages, and thus understood their implications. Neither he nor anyone else came to my door to announce the good news, so I had to infer myself that I had become the newest member of the Chicago Symphony Orchestra. When Bud and the other members of the brass section who had been part of the audition committee came down to the locker room a few minutes later, they each congratulated me. These messages of warm welcome assured me that my assumptions of sweet success had been correct.

At this point in time, I had been working on my music-making skills for four months short of twenty years. In addition, I had first heard Bud and the Chicago brass section eleven years and three months earlier, at my introduction to live symphonic music on that October day back in 1967, at U of M. It had been a long haul up a rather zig-zag path, but each and every playing experience along the way had contributed to my total array of skills.

Upon arriving back at our small apartment in Oak Park, where Doree was waiting to hear the results, I headed directly for the bathroom without saying a word. There, I took down a little scrap of paper that had long been taped to the wall, handed it to two-year-old Kevin, and instructed him to deliver it to his mother. On the slip was printed a quote from Eddie Cantor: "It takes twenty years to become an overnight success."

Chapter Six

CSO Membership January of 1979– November of 1996

Within an hour of Doree's receiving the good news, Bud phoned her to express how pleased he was with the outcome of the audition. Also, he and Avis provided us with a pair of tickets for the Saturday evening concert. Bud indicated that I should take advantage of this last opportunity to hear the orchestra from the outside, since I would very soon be fully engrossed in it from the inside. When I called Cliff Lillya to deliver the news, he happily exclaimed, "Congratulations! You have made it to the top of the pile!"

On January 22, 1979, I officially started my employment with the Chicago Symphony. My tenure in Bud's section would span a period of ten weeks short of eighteen years. With my entry into the orchestra, the ensemble may have added to the list of nationalities that had been represented in its membership during the previous eighty-eight years, since my ancestors on the paternal side had hailed from Greece, Crete, and Egypt, while those on the maternal side had been French, French Canadian, Portuguese, English, and Scottish. (The family name Kent is a shortened Greek/Turkish name; my father, born Socrates Kapantais, meaning "Brave Black Man" in Turkish, changed his name to George Kent.) I joined a handful of young musicians in the ensemble who represented the early stages of a major wave of membership turnovers. Over the following decade, new players would replace a great many retiring members who had entered the orchestra during the early and mid-1950s, during the three years of Rafael Kubelik's tenure as Music Director and the first few years of Fritz Reiner's tenure. (Although Reiner is famous for having been a tyrant, Kubelik actually fired more CSO players during his first year on the job than Reiner did during his entire decade.) During Maestro Solti's era, between 1969 and 1990, a total of sixty new members, nearly all of them relatively young, would come aboard. At the time of my entry in 1979, at 29 $^2/_3$ years of age, Solti had been in charge for nearly a decade and Bud was 57 $^1/_2$ years old, *1979* with nearly 31 years of CSO experience already behind him. Even he did not imagine at this point that his record-breaking *Bud - 53 yrs.* tenure would extend for another 22 years. Among the 109 members at this time, some 45 of them had played in the Civic Orchestra in their youth; a few of these individuals had already *Almost 80 yrs old* been in the Symphony for 45 to 47 years. A total of thirty of the *when he finally retired* current members had joined the orchestra before my birth.

The remuneration package and working conditions protections of the CSO, which were the finest in the country, were the result of nearly two decades of organizing and negotiating by the members of the orchestra; further gains and improvements continued to be negotiated with the management every three years. The players in the other major orchestras throughout the U.S. sought to emulate the features of the Chicago contract as closely as possible. The base pay for all Chicago Symphony players in this particular year consisted of $500. for each of the 52 weeks, totaling $26,000. per year. To this amount was added generous extra pay for taping live concerts for radio broadcast thirty weeks a year, as well as for making recordings and playing televised concerts and extra concerts (by the time of the *over $100,000 a year* writing of this memoir in 2005, the 1979 salary had quadrupled and the pension had quintupled). The principal player in each section received considerably greater pay, through privately negotiated contracts. Starting three years earlier, in 1976, seniority pay had been eliminated for all new entering members, by the choice of the players, so that all of the members except the principals would eventually receive the same pay, and negotiated raises would apply equally across the board. Paid vacation time consisted of seven vacation weeks (usually two weeks in December, one week between the downtown season and the Ravinia season, and four weeks after Ravinia), two release weeks (which were arranged among the individual players within each section, as the work schedule and the literature allowed), and one split week (with about half of the members being off during one of the two weeks when pieces for moderate-sized ensembles were performed). In addition, the members received excellent health care coverage, sick leave, life insurance, travel insurance during tours, insurance for all instruments that were utilized on the job, a generous pension plan (for which a player qualified after ten years of service, with a maxiumum of thirty years counted), and half-pay retirement if a player became disabled. When on tour, management paid the hotel costs plus a considerable per-diem fee. Specific to the members of the trumpet section, the orchestra loaned each of them a Mount Vernon Bach C trumpet, and paid an extra fee for doubling on each concert when the printed parts specifically denoted cornets, piccolo trumpets, or flugelhorns.

The average number of services (rehearsals and concerts) per week was $7\frac{1}{2}$, typically involving four rehearsals and three or four concerts. The length of each rehearsal was limited to $2\frac{1}{2}$ hours and each concert to $2\frac{1}{4}$ hours ($2\frac{1}{2}$ hours for opera and choral concerts), with overtime fees paid for any extensions beyond these limits. The maximum amount of rehearsal time allowed on any given day was $4\frac{1}{2}$ hours. All recording sessions, televised concerts, and extra rehearsals and concerts were considered to be additions over and above the standard schedule, and were remunerated accordingly. The contract also specified a great number of protective limitations, such as no service beginning before noon if a service had been played the previous evening, a maximum of two services per day, a maximum length of 21 days and 34 days respectively for domestic and foreign tours, a maximum of six services (including five concerts) per week on tour, two days off guaranteed per week on tour, a limit of only one service allowed per runout trip, and at least twenty weeks with two days off guaranteed per year.

The typical weekly schedule consisted of a rehearsal on Tuesday morning, often a concert on Tuesday evening (presenting the same program as the previous week), two rehearsals on

Wednesday beginning at noon and ending at 7:00, a rehearsal on Thursday morning, and concerts on Thursday evening, Friday afternoon or evening, and Saturday evening, plus an extra concert occasionally on Sunday afternoon. Every few weeks, a runout by chartered train to play a concert in Milwaukee was scheduled on Monday, until this concert series was terminated in 1986. An additional rehearsal was also sometimes scheduled on Saturday morning, to look ahead to the following week's program. Each week during the downtown season, an entirely new program was presented, while each of the three concerts per week at Ravinia offered an entirely different program. Nearly every one of the Orchestra Hall concerts, plus a select few concerts at Ravinia, were taped for distribution to some five hundred radio stations across the U.S. and abroad for weekly broadcasts. The foreign recipients lived in Canada, Europe, Japan, Australia, and Russia. By the 1980s, these thirty annual broadcasts, which I had avidly devoured during my training years, were even beamed to my tiny hometown of Ossineke in northern Michigan, by National Public Radio in Mount Pleasant, Michigan.

Playing in the Symphony offered a vast number of improvements compared to my former life as a free-lance musician, both musically and logistically. The most obvious differences involved the immense upgrade in the musical abilities of the colleagues and conductors, and in the quality of the literature that was scheduled and the venue in which the services took place. Also, in addition to the massive increases in dependable salary, benefits, and working conditions protections, the feature of knowing in detail the daily work schedule far into the future was also a major improvement. Well before the nine-month Orchestra Hall season and the eight-week Ravinia season each commenced, the players would receive the detailed schedule for that particular season, indicating the times of each rehearsal and concert and the literature which was scheduled. This feature of knowing the long-term work plan was a rare treat, after the rather fluid lifestyle of a free-lancer, and allowed for long-range planning of outside performances, research trips, and vacation adventures. Another luxury of CSO membership was the regularity of working with the same colleagues and in the same hall each week, which was very conducive to developing consistency in musical styles and intonation, and blending together as a unified ensemble.

As I came to know in varying degrees my 108 colleagues over the following years, I discovered a very wide array of personalities among them. Within any group of highly intelligent, educated, and motivated individuals, such varieties always exist. However, the amount of time that each of these musicians (including me) had spent alone in a practice room while growing up, and the degree of persistence and effort that had been required to achieve and maintain this extreme level of musical proficiency, fostered an even greater degree of independence and, to a certain degree, more solitary behaviors than are usually found in the general populace. As one would expect, over the span of eighteen years I developed a close relationship with a number of my colleagues, moderate friendships with a great many of them, neutral relations with some of the colleagues, and downright hostilities with a few of them. However, a salient feature of the aggregate of the Chicago Symphony was that we all played together as a finely regulated and inspired ensemble regardless of our various interpersonal relationships. Our personal interactions with one another did not interfere in any way with our making music together as a solidly unified ensemble. In fact, the myriad experiences that we shared and endured together, both the inspired moments and the times of drudgery, tended to create closer bonds between many of the colleagues, much like the bonds that often grow between people who experience warfare or other traumas together. Various of the friendly and cooperative associations that developed between certain of the members were a joy to see. During the preparation time before each concert in Orchestra Hall, I had the opportunity to observe one such relationship directly across the locker room from my locker. One of our younger violinists, a tall and lanky gentleman, would reach up and plug the cord of an electric shaver into the ceiling light receptacle for his adjacent locker neighbor; the latter individual, our most elderly member, was a vertically challenged violinist who had already passed his 80th birthday.

In addition to their wide array of differing personalities, the CSO colleagues also exhibited an immense variety of personal interests. Besides those individuals who lived only to play their instruments in large and small ensembles and teach students, many others were involved in such activities as running long-distance races, turning wood on a lathe, grinding telescope lenses, raising orchids, mastering gourmet cooking, lifting weights, constructing or improving their home, gardening, photographing the heavens, fishing, constructing model train layouts, reading fiction and non-fiction, traveling, researching early musicians in U.S. orchestras, studying fine art and history, playing various sports, raising dogs, composing and arranging music, investing, attending Shakespearean plays, and collecting such varied items as Edison cylinder players, early prints, nomadic rugs, fossils, books, and early musical instruments.

Beginning with the third week of January, 1979 and extending over the next eighteen years on the job, I experienced and stored away a huge array of sublime and memorable moments, along with an even greater catalog of moments of slogging hard work. Our memories are simply a collection of particular moments, snapshots in time, that are preserved in our brains, some vividly and others indistinctly, which we sometimes bring to the surface and revisit. Certain memories, like various other items, can last forever if properly stored. Among the preserved mental images from my first week as a Chicago Symphony member was learning the manner in which symphonic musicans silently compliment one another during the course of a rehearsal or a concert: by shuffling one or both of their shoes against the floor, or by raising the toe end of one shoe and wiggling it back and forth. What a strange sight it must be for people in the audience to suddenly observe many shoes shuffling or wiggling back and forth on the stage after one of the musicians has executed a particularly beautiful or demanding passage or a solo. Another mental image from that first week was discovering how each of the members of the trumpet section kept one another on track on each page as the music progressed. Someone looking sideways across the section would see a finger-tap on the thigh by each member at the moment of passing of each rehearsal number or letter on every page. Over the years, each of us would occasionally experience moments of drifting attention, particularly during sleepy Friday afternoon concerts, and we would get back on track by noting our colleagues' finger-tappings.

A series of "firsts" for me took place during the following several months. My first week on the job, the program was notable in that one half of it consisted of a single Baroque choral piece, Handel *Dettingen Te Deum*; it was rather rare to find orchestral pieces from the Baroque era, calling for piccolo trumpets, on the Symphony's annual schedule. Another minor milestone, mostly appreciated by Doree, was the first listing of Timothy Kent as a member of the trumpet section in the printed program, which occurred during the second week on the job. The first recording sessions of my tenure, doing Mahler *Symphony Number Six* with Claudio Abbado, took place during the initial week of February, followed by the first nationwide radio broadcast, on March 13, of the first concert of my tenure (again, mostly significant to Doree). The first runout to Milwaukee, on February 5, introduced me to these enjoyable jaunts, which included a ride by car with Bud to the near-north train station and a trip on the chartered train during the afternoon, followed by a long break for dinner (I carried my own dinner to eat at the concert hall, and relished the several hours of quiet time for research), the concert performance, and finally a relaxing trip home by train and auto. On the return rail voyage, the regular conductor on these chartered rides would pass through the cars during the initial bumpy portion of the route and announce loudly, "We will be switching to the round wheels shortly." During the car rides home from the train station over the following years, Bud and I had some of our very best conversations, after a long but rather relaxed day of travel and performance. The CSO's Milwaukee concert series had begun on October 20, 1891, within a week of the initial founding of the ensemble. Unfortunately, the Symphony management would eventually discontinue these trips, after an uninterrupted run of ten concerts per season for ninety-five seasons, with the final one taking place on June 2, 1986. During that last memorable train ride north, our older son Kevin, age ten, would be taught to knit by Gizella Jacobs, the wife of our beloved tuba player Arnold Jacobs. The elimination of the Milwaukee runouts would immediately usher in the scheduling of a concert in Orchestra Hall virtually every Tuesday evening during the entire downtown season, which was more profitable for the management but much less enjoyable for the players.

A month after joining the orchestra, my biographical sketch first appeared in the program, in an article which introduced six new young members, including four violinists, a violist, and a trumpet player (since Doree particularly appreciated this article, I was obliged to collect a few of the programs for her, to send to family members). About this same time, the Symphony and Maestro Solti together won additional Grammy Awards, an annual occasion which had commenced with their first collaborative recording awards in February of 1972. In the spring, I thoroughly enjoyed my first trip to play in Carnegie Hall since becoming a member; the sensations were much deeper than they had been when I had performed there earlier as an extra player with the group. The March schedule brought recording sessions of Bruckner *Symphony Number Seven* with Barenboim, while the May recordings with Solti focused on the complete opera *Fidelio* by Beethoven (for which I played the offstage "Leonore" calls) and the *Symphony Number 4* of Tippet.

To carry out my duties in the section, I needed several additional horns in my arsenal, including a rotary valve trumpet, a cornet, and another Bach C trumpet. Bud provided me with a Yamaha rotary C trumpet, on a long-term loan until I eventually purchased an imported German version a few years later, while I found an old Martin C cornet hanging on the wall at the

Schilke Company downtown. I wished to leave one good Bach C trumpet at Orchestra Hall or Ravinia at all times and have another good one at home for practicing, so that I would not usually be carrying a horn when I commuted to and from work. I would just carry with me my mouthpiece, stored in a small leather pouch, in my pants pocket. So I arranged to travel on a day off to the Bach factory in Elkhart, Indiana to choose a new instrument, after a large group of C horns had been produced and were available for trying and selecting, before they would be shipped out to various dealers. Steve Hendrickson made this trip to the factory with me, so that we could play for each other and listen to the twenty or thirty horns that were laid out for us. Before this errand, Bud and I again discussed the most efficient manner of judging an array of horns, by tuning all of them to the same pitch, preferably with the aid of a tuning machine, and by carefully noting these features: the freedom and ease of blowing, as well as the responsiveness, in all registers; the tone; and the intonation, especially on the open tones and the second valve tones (the tones of the first and third valve combinations were less crucial, since they already required constant adjustments on a C trumpet, by means of moveable first and third valve slides). A tight, constricted horn often needed a valve alignment procedure to improve it; the constriction represented a blockage of the air flow, which was most commonly caused by misalignment of the valves, and sometimes by excess solder inside the tubes at the joints. He also reminded me that a horn would lose some of its brightness and acquire a rounder sound after about six months of playing, as it would gradually become broken in.

My customary routine before a morning rehearsal consisted of waking at 7:00, doing my exercise routine plus twenty minutes of running on a trampoline or a treadmill machine, eating a moderate breakfast of eggs, leaving the house at 8:20 to walk seven blocks to the train station, catching the 8:50 elevated train for a relaxed twenty-minute ride to downtown, walking a few blocks to Orchestra Hall, and arriving at about 9:20 for a 10:00 downbeat. Bud regularly commented, "No brass player should

have to play before noon," and I certainly seconded that sentiment. My morning regimen of exercises, running, and then
walking to the el, as well as the reading and research en route
and at the hall, all helped quite a bit to wake me up before a 10
A.M. downbeat. However, a morning start was definitely less
than ideal for brass players, for both the physical aspects and
the mental acuity.

During my morning procedure, I was able to do research
and writing while waiting on the train platform and during the
ride downtown, and during my easy warmup before the
rehearsal. In addition, my reading and writing continued
downstairs during the pieces on which I was not scheduled to
play, as well as during intermissions, the interval between two
rehearsals, and the interval between a rehearsal and a concert.
In my early years in the orchestra, I commuted back to Oak
Park between the morning rehearsal and the evening performance on such double-service days. Later, I found it to be more
beneficial to remain downtown and carry out research with the
materials that were available at the Newberry Library, or using
my own materials at the De Paul Library or at Orchestra Hall.
Whatever the locale of my afternoon activities, I took a 25
minute nap during the late afternoon and ate a light meal
shortly afterward. If I either omitted my short nap or ate too
much or too late, my concentration certainly suffered for it during the concert.

During my six years as a free-lance musician in Chicago
plus my eighteen years in the CSO, I traveled on the elevated
and subway trains to and from myriad locales throughout the
city, and at all times of the day and night. I carried my wallet in
a front pocket, kept a mace spray dispenser handy in my briefcase, and constantly wore on my chest a full size knife with a
homemade, rawhide-covered handle, in a neck sheath beneath
my shirt. (My friend and locker neighbor, tympanist Don Koss,
once commented, "I know many people wear a St. Christopher
medal to help protect them while traveling, but I see you have
a little something extra there.") However, I never had to resort
to either of my self-defense items, and only once did I witness

a criminal activity. Since there was a risk, to help avoid being involved in such incidents, I dressed down considerably, carried myself with an air that indicated I was not to be messed with, and tended to ride in the train car in which the conductor was working. As a free-lancer, I had always carried various horns with me, but once I began working in the Symphony, I tried to not transport any horns while commuting, whenever possible. I do realize that during any given day or evening, I may have been the scariest-looking individual on my particular train car, and that the other riders may have been wary of me. However, neither the plain-clothes Transit Authority police nor the uniformed Chicago Police with their muzzled attack dogs ever hindered me in the slightest on the trains, although they may have kept an eye on me (I know their dogs did). Ironically, during all of my years of commuting throughout the Chicago region, the solitary incident in which an attempt was made to prey upon me occurred one Friday afternoon when I accepted Bud's offer of a ride home from Orchestra Hall after the concert. As we were descending one of the below-ground Michigan Avenue stairways near the hall, to reach his car in the underground Grant Park Garage, a young man directly in front of us dramatically pretended to sprain his ankle on the stairs, as a distraction, while two of his confederates behind us reached into our back pockets seeking our wallets. Carrying one's wallet in a front pocket guarded against such a theft.

During my two years in the Civic Orchestra, I had discovered the advantages of warming up and practicing in the main basement storage room of Orchestra Hall, which was located directly beneath the stage, adjacent to the men's locker room. In this large area were stored the various grand pianos and many of the percussion instruments, as well as whatever chairs, stands, risers, and other items were not required on stage at a given time. Here, a brass player could do whatever preparation the job required without causing grief for the string and woodwind colleagues in the men's locker room. As soon as I joined the Symphony, I informally claimed the area in the storage room which was behind the stage cargo elevator. Since the stage crew changed clothes before concerts in this hidden, out-of-the-way area, there was a large florescent fixture brightly illuminating the area and their armoire. I mounted a couple of family portraits and scribbled crayon artworks by Kevin onto the wall with grey duct tape, and adopted the place. My friends Ed Kleinhammer on bass trombone and Gail Williams and Norm Schweikert on horn utilized the main portion of the storage room, on the opposite side of the cargo elevator from my "studio," for their warmup area. Ed, who referred to this under-stage area and its four inhabitants as "The Conservatory," supplied many of the jokes that brightened our routines before early-morning rehearsals. Gail, who had begun her membership with the CSO two weeks before I had come aboard, had the distinction of being the first female member of the Chicago brass section. Because she had broken the gender barrier, after eighty-eight years, the term that my U of M buddy Stan Szymko had coined years earlier for the section, "Bud and the Boys," could no longer apply. In our "Conservatory," Norm shared with me over the years his many discoveries as he researched the history of all the musicians who had played in the main symphonic ensembles of the U.S. When my three colleagues were not utilizing the main area and I was quietly ensconsed in my research and writing, hidden behind the elevator, the room appeared to be empty. For this reason, I was privy to a considerable number of fascinating private meetings and conversations in the room over the years, from my unobserved vantage point; however, the contents of these overheard conversations would always remain confidential.

Many of my colleagues in the orchestra completely filled their daily schedules by playing extra services outside of the regular CSO work schedule, both in Orchestra Hall and elsewhere, and also by teaching private lessons (Bud did the barest minimum of both of these activities). During the course of each downtown season, a considerable number of "Members of the Chicago Symphony" concerts were presented in the hall, utilizing non-members to fill out the ensemble as needed. These extra-paying rehearsals and performances, as well as the concerts which were presented by various chamber groups of CSO players in elementary schools throughout the city, were offered to each member of the orchestra by means of a system that ensured equitable earnings. It was only on the rarest of occasions that Bud agreed to play any of the "Members of" concerts, only when he was specifically asked by the conductor if he would please participate. During the first four months of my tenure, I played each of the extra "Members of" services. However, as soon as I learned that these gigs were entirely voluntarily, with no expectation of my playing them, I completely stopped accepting any of these extra services for the rest of my tenure. Younger free-lance players around town needed the chance to do these rehearsals and performances, to aid their development and bolster their incomes. In addition, I wished to spend as much time as possible on my non-musical activities.

I did play with a CSO brass quintet during my first 2 $^1/_3$ years in the orchestra. For the school concerts that we played throughout Chicago, which were usually presented on Friday mornings before the afternoon concerts, the personnel consisted of Will Scarlett and me on trumpet, Dan Gingrich on horn, Frank (Cris) Crisafulli on trombone, and the regular CSO substitute on tuba. When we occasionally played formal concerts, Arnold (Jake) Jacobs joined the group on tuba. It was certainly inspiring for me to play with Cris and Jake on these programs, since they had been the lower voices in the Chicago Symphony Brass Quintet with Bud ever since his arrival in 1948, the year before I was born. I had treasured for many years their quintet recordings from 1950 (a commercial platter) and 1966 (a tape made for WFMT radio broadcast).

Immediately upon joining the orchestra in January of 1979, I had curtailed all playing of outside free-lance jobs, even when called by bookers who had hired me for a number of years to do classy gigs. One of Bud's standard jokes when arriving in the locker room for Friday afternoon or evening concerts was to comment on how strenuous it had been to play the long parade down State Street earlier that day. Oddly enough, although I had never once been called to play a parade during all of my earlier times as a free-lancer, I received just such a call a few months after joining the CSO (and it was not a hoax, but a genuine booking call)! The one aspect of outside playing that I did maintain during my first five years on the job was my solo programs, with either piano or organ accompaniment. However, I now scaled back these concerts, which alternated trumpet and keyboard solo pieces, to about once every month. As before, I continued to tape these performances with my cassette machine, and utilized the playback sessions as training exercises. I also very occasionally played the Haydn and Hummel concertos and other solo pieces with suburban orchestras in the area.

The array of pieces from which I drew for my various solo programs included, but was not limited to, the following works: Balay *Petite Pièce Concertante*, Barat *Fantasie in E flat*, Buxtehude *Komm, Heiliger Geist, Herre Gott*, Clarke *Stars in a Velvety Sky*, Goedicke *Concert Etude*, Haydn *Concerto*, Hindemith *Sonata*, Hummel *Concerto*, Mendez *Clavelitos*, Purcell *Sonata*, Scarlatti *Sinfonia to "Il Giardino Di Amore,"* Telemann *Heroic Music*, Torelli *Concerto in D*, and Torelli *Sinfonia Avanti L'Opera*. Lyrical pieces which I found appropriate for church services and other events included the following: Arutyunian *Concerto in E flat* middle section (M to P), Buxtehude *Komm, Heiliger Geist, Herre Gott*, Colby song *Cross and Crown*, Gounod song *There is a Green Hill Far Away*, Haydn *Concerto* second movement, Hovhaness *Dawn Hymn* (playing the top voice on this atmospheric organ piece, which I found to be much better than both of his trumpet solos), Hummel *Concerto* second movement, Riisager *Concertino* second movement, Shelly song *Abide With Me*, Telemann *Concerto in D* second movement, and Telemann *La Grace* from *Heroic Music*.

In March of 1979, as soon as the huge piles of accumulated plowed snow had diminished and travel conditions had returned to nearly normal, Doree and I proceeded to shop for a house in Oak Park. Earlier, we had gathered enough savings to pay a 20 percent down payment on a home of medium price; however, we had held off from purchasing one, in case my

111

fortunes on the audition trail would lead us to another city. After I won the position in the CSO, we knew that we would purchase in Oak Park, since the logistics of traveling between this community and Orchestra Hall were so comfortable (for me on a daily basis via the el, and for both of us on those occasions when Doree attended the concerts by auto on the expressway, an easy drive each way after the rush hour traffic had dissipated). During the eight weeks of the Ravinia season each summer, in which the orchestra worked four or five days per week, the trip to Highland Park via carpool with colleagues took about 45 minutes. During the three days each week when the schedule included both an afternoon rehearsal and an evening concert, I found it very comfortable to carry my dinner to Ravinia, remain at the park during the interval between the two services, and utilize this span of several hours in the quiet, air-conditioned lounge for doing research and writing.

In our search for a home, Doree and I visited ten houses in Oak Park over the course of a single weekend, and chose the tenth one, which was coincidentally located directly across the street from the elegant stone church where I had been practicing for a number of years. We closed on it a few weeks later, and were happily settled in by mid-April. This move brought about an excellent improvement in my daily practicing regimen. While living in an apartment where trumpet playing was not permissible, I had been locked into a schedule of a single, extended practice session at the church each afternoon. Now, in our own home, I was able to spread my practicing out over the course of the entire day, with a relatively short session in the morning, a more extensive session in the afternoon, and a few ballads just before bedtime to end the day. By reducing the length of time between each playing session in this manner, I was now able to remain more warmed up throughout the entire span of waking hours, instead of having all of my practicing concentrated into a single, long session beginning in the early afternoon.

During my first five months on the job, the trumpet section was down one player, since Charley Geyer had departed from the second position before the September 1978 tour, to play lead in Houston. Ever since Bud had first established his own section in 1950 and 1951, each new member thereafter had joined by way of the fourth/utility trumpet position, and had later moved up within the section (except for Frank Kaderabek, who had entered as assistant first/third and remained in that slot). Due to this custom, even though both the second and fourth positions had been vacant in the fall of 1978, the audition had been held for the latter job, which I won the following January. Nearly all of the individuals who were members of Bud's section over the decades were highly developed players, able to play lead in virtually any of the other major U.S. orchestras. In fact, Frank Kaderabek left to play principal, first in Detroit and then in Philadelphia, Phil Smith departed for the lead slot in the New York Philharmonic, Charley Geyer moved on to play principal in Houston, and George Vosburgh would later vacate his slot to take the lead position in Pittsburgh. I had likewise trained nearly all my life to be a principal player, and had filled that role in most of the ensembles in which I had played before joining the CSO. However, I decided at this point to remain in the fourth/utility position of the Chicago section, rather than to either move up in the section or later leave to play lead elsewhere. I altered my career goals at this time, deciding to dedicate myself to raising the quality of section playing to a new level. Part of the attraction of the fourth/utility position for me was its great variety: during the course of a given season, I would play fourth, third, second, and first on various pieces, as well as playing the lead role in many of the offstage and onstage brass groups. I preferred spending my years playing in the finest trumpet section in the world, instead of playing principal trumpet in a brass section of less quality, as would have been the case even with the other four of the Big Five orchestras in the U.S.

Since I was not moving up to fill the second position, this was the slot for which auditions were held in the late spring of 1979. A great amount of time and energy had been expended by Bud and the audition committee in hearing 140 preliminary auditions during the previous fall, narrowing the field down to three finalists. Thus, George Vosburgh and Steve Hendrickson, the other two finalists in the audition which I had won in January, were invited to become automatic finalists in this new round. In addition, a number of preliminary candidates were also heard, from which one Civic-trained player was advanced to the finals. In the finals round, George won the CSO job; soon afterward, Steve won the position of principal trumpet in the National Symphony, where he happily spent the rest of his long and distinguished career. With the arrival of George at Ravinia in 1979, the Chicago Symphony trumpet section was again complete. Bud, George, Will, and I would remain together as a unit for thirteen years, until George would depart in the summer of 1992 and I would leave in November of 1996. This was by far the longest-running, unchanged section of trumpet players in the history of the CSO; the next two longest tenures each spanned only eight years, from 1892 to 1900 and from 1966 to 1974.

In June of 1979, I conducted the trumpet auditions for the summer session of the Civic Orchestra, as I would again in a couple of other years. Conducting these activities brought back memories of the auditions that I had played for Charley Geyer back in 1971 and 1972, when I had earned a slot in the Civic summer sessions during those two years. At this point, it was a fine feeling knowing that my own days of playing auditions to win a position had drawn to a close. However, each of us in the Chicago brass section actually played a number of very public auditions each week, at each of the performances (which were heard by both the live audience in the hall and the listeners of the radio broadcasts across the country), as well as during each studio recording session throughout the year.

Based on my years of studying with Bud and auditioning for professional positions, I drew up a list of the primary and secondary orchestral works which must be prepared by aspiring trumpet players who are intending to play auditions. To become fully trained, one must master not only the lead trumpet part but each of the parts for all of these pieces.

Primary works
(often found on lists of excerpts to be prepared):
Bach: *B Minor Mass, Christmas Oratorio, Magnificat,*
    Third Orchestral Suite
Bartok: *Concerto for Orchestra*
Beethoven: Offstage calls from *Leonore Overtures*
    Number 2 and 3
Berlioz: *Roman Carnival Overture, Symphony Fantastique*
Brahms: *Academic Festival Overture, Symphony Number 2*
Bruchner: *Symphonies Number 4 and 7*
Debussy: *Fetes* (from *Nocturnes*), *La Mer*
Dukas: *Sorcerer's Apprentice*
Franck: *Symphony in D Minor*
Gershwin: *Piano Concerto in F*
Mahler: *Symphonies Number 1, 2, 3, and 5*
Moussorgsky: *Night on Bald Mountain,*
    Pictures at an Exhibition
Prokofiev: *Lieutenant Kije, Scythian Suite*
Rachmaninov: *Piano Concerto Number 3*
Ravel: *Alborada del Gracioso, Daphnis and Chloe Suites,*
    La Valse, Piano Concerto, Rhapsodie Espagnole
Respighi: *Fountains of Rome, Pines of Rome*
Rimsky-Korsakov: *Capriccio Espagnol, Scheherazade*
Shostakovich: *Piano Concerto, Symphonies Number 1, 5, and 9*
Sibelius: *Symphony Number 2*
Strauss: *Also Sprach Zarathustra, Don Juan, Death and*
    Transfiguration, Don Quixote, Ein Heldenleben,
    Rosenkavelier Suite, Symphony Domestica,
    Till Eulenspiegel's Merry Pranks
Stravinsky: *Firebird Suite, Petrouchka, Rite of Spring*
Tchaikowsky: *Capriccio Italien, Nutcracker Suite,*
    Symphonies 4, 5, and 6
Wagner: *Götterdämmerung* Prelude, Funeral March,
    and Ride of the Walküres, *Lohengrin* Prelude,
    Meistersinger Prelude, *Parsifal* Prelude,
    Rienzi Overture, *Tannhäuser* Overture

Secondary Works
(occasionally found on lists of excerpts to be prepared):
Bach: *Brandenburg Concerto Number 2*
Beethoven: *Egmont Overture, Symphonies Number 5, 7, and 9*
Berg: *Wozzeck Suite*
Berlioz: *Harold in Italy*
Bizet: *Carmen Suites Number 1 and 2*
Brahms: *Symphony Number 1*
Britten: *Young Person's Guide to the Orchestra*
Copland: *El Salon Mexico, Rodeo*
Debussy: *Iberia*
Dvorak: *Symphony Number 4*
Gershwin: *An American in Paris*
Handel: *The Messiah, Water Music*
Hindemith: *Mathis der Maler, Symphonic Metamorphosis*
Ibert: *Escales*
Mahler: *Das Lied von der Erde, Symphonies Number 4 and 6*
Mozart: *Serenade Number 9* (Posthorn Serenade)
Prokofiev: *Symphony Number 5*
Ravel: *Bolero*
Rimsky-Korsakov: *Le Coq d'Or Suite*
Schuman: *Symphony Number 2*
Scriabin: *Poem of Ecstasy*
Stravinsky: *Fireworks Suite, L'Hisoire du Soldat, Pulcinella Suite, Song of the Nightingale*
Weber: *Oberon Overture* fanfares

At auditions for positions in German opera and symphony orchestras, one must be prepared to play the first movement of the Haydn concerto for the preliminary round, plus excerpts from the following operatic and symphonic works for the finals round:

Operas
(the bulk of the material that is heard in the finals round):
Beethoven: *Fidelio* (Leonore Number 2 and 3 offstage calls)
Bizet: *Carmen* (signal call, and low register lyric solo)
Nicolai: *Merry Wives of Windsor*
Strauss: *Rosenkavelier* (lyric solo in E flat, high lyric solo at
    Number 295)
Verdi: *Masked Ball* (solos at both Number 9 and Tempo I in
    Act 2), *Il Trovatore* (E flat solo at Number 44; conductors
    usually want the entire passage tongued, without slurs)
Wagner: *Meistersinger* (stage music at end of International
    series excerpts), *Parsifal* (lyric solos in Prelude), *Die
    Walküre* (excerpts from Prelude, and Scene 1 of Act 2)

Symphonic Works:
Moussorgsky: *Pictures at an Exhibition*
Ravel: *Piano Concerto*
Strauss: *Also Sprach Zarathustra, Symphony Domestica,
    Till Eulenspiegel's Merry Pranks*
Stravinsky: *Firebird Suite, Petrouchka*

My first Ravinia Festival season commenced in June of
1979. Ravinia Park, a beautiful array of trees, lawns, and
buildings in Highland Park, had been originally constructed as
an amusement park in 1902 by a railroad company, to promote
the use of the company's passenger trains. As early as 1906, a
summer season of symphonic music and some opera was introduced in the park, with the Chicago Symphony performing
there from that year on. After a number of years of being closed
during the Depression, the park and its musical offerings were
reinstated in the summer of 1936, with the CSO presenting the
first concert. The open-air wooden pavilion, destroyed by fire
just before the 1949 season, was replaced with a concrete version in 1950. During the following decade, theatre and ballet
productions, film showings, and art exhibits were also added to
the offerings. Seiji Ojawa became the Music Director of the

Ravinia Festival in 1964, followed by James Levine in 1972 and Christoph Eschenbach in 1997. Our work schedule during the eight-week Ravinia season consisted of one or two rehearsals on Wednesday and Thursday, followed by an afternoon rehearsal and an evening concert on Friday, Saturday, and Sunday. Each of the three concerts offered an entirely different program, with many of the Sunday performances devoted to pops concert fare. Due to the limited amount of rehearsal time per concert, the programming at Ravinia included a considerable number of pieces from the standard, well-known literature. Nearly every summer, it was a treat to accompany Doc Severinsen at one of the Sunday evening pops concerts. At each of his perfomances, he delighted in acknowledging Bud in the back row and announcing to the audience, "When I grow up, I want to play the trumpet like Bud Herseth!"

During the month-long vacation before beginning the 1979-80 downtown season, I made my first trip to study genealogy in eastern Canada. Some months later, expanding upon my Canadian discoveries, I spent the autumn, winter, and spring working out my entire French genealogy from the published parish records of Quebec Province at the Newberry Library in Chicago. In the process, I identified more than 725 direct ancestors, some extending back to the late 1400s, and mapped 120 specific locales in France and about sixty in Quebec where these individuals had lived.

The 1979-80 season began with a one-week strike, the first of my career, which was followed the next month by another unusual event: a performance of Bruchner *Symphony Number 5* in Holy Name Cathedral for the Pope during his U.S. visit. After the concert, when His Holiness stepped out onto the balcony of the cathedral, he quieted the cheering throngs by exclaiming cheerfully, "Please, I am not the Chicago Symphony!" Some of the highest points of this Orchestra Hall season, my first full one, included hearing Bud do the Haydn concerto on the subscription concerts, and my playing on the chamber music concert that was presented by the brass section. The lowest points included enduring a painful infected upper lip for two months during the fall, on which I had to play until the holiday vacation, and losing my friend Mr. Reynold Williams, the head of Orchestra Hall security, to a massive heart attack just offstage. Over the next few years, I came to know and respect his much younger replacement, Willie Yates, whom I always addressed as Mr. Yates, out of respect for his position. During this 1979-80 season, I taught the more advanced trumpet students of De Paul University at my home; however, since I was not impressed with their degree of dedication and preparation, I ceased teaching at the end of the second semester. Thereafter, except for one student who came from Germany, I did not teach again, either in association with a college or independently. Teaching helps one grow.

Some years later, after Michael Jordan had become the greatest all-around basketball player in the history of the sport, I found it particularly interesting to think back to what my activities had been while his youthful talents had been developing. At about the time that I became a CSO member, Michael was cut from his high school basketball team as a sophomore. The following year, during my first full season with the orchestra, he managed to make his high school team as a junior, after which he attended his first basketball summer camp. Even after his senior year, his first two choices for playing college ball turned him down; only during his college years did his immense talents blossom. In light of the long journey that had been required for my own training, I found the tale of his development to be heartening.

A survey of the CSO trumpet personnel during Bud's 53 yrs tenure (1948-2001) shows that he brought a total of thirteen players into the section during that span of time. After Bud joined the section in June of 1948, replacing Sydney Baker on first, the other three members remained constant for that season and the following year, with Gerald Huffman on second, Renold Schilke on third, and Frank Holz on fourth. For the 1950-51 season, Holz departed, Huffman and Schilke each moved down one position, and Rudy Nashan joined the group on second. For the following season, Huffman and Schilke left and Bill Babcock arrived on third and Bob Grocock on fourth. When the latter individual did not receive tenure after one season, Vince Cichowicz replaced him on fourth for the 1952-53 season. This personnel remained constant for six years, until Babcock left and was replaced for the 1958-59 season by Frank Kaderabek. Beginning with the 1960-61 season, the positions of Nashan and Cichowicz were exchanged; after 2 $^1/_2$ years, Nashan departed from fourth in January of 1963, to be eventually replaced by Will Scarlett in September of 1964. Two years later, Kaderabek left, Scarlett moved from fourth to third, and Charley Geyer entered on fourth. This section remained unchanged for eight years, between 1966 and 1974. When Cichowicz retired, Geyer moved from fourth to second and Phil Smith arrived on fourth in January of 1975. After the departure of both Geyer and Smith before the 1978-79 season, Tim Kent came in on fourth in January of 1979, followed by George Vosburgh on second in June. The personnel then remained constant over the span of thirteen seasons, until Vosburgh left in the summer of 1992, after which Scarlett moved from third to second and Mark Ridenour eventually joined the section on third in June of 1994. Kent retired in November of 1996, and was immediately replaced by John Hagstrom, who moved from fourth to second when Scarlett retired the following summer. Ben Wright played for two seasons on fourth, but did not receive tenure; he was eventually replaced by Tage Larsen in 2002. After Bud's retirement in June of 2001, Craig Morris played lead for two years, from 2001 to 2003, but was not tenured; he was eventually replaced by Chris Martin in June of 2005.

The following is a roster of each of the members of the section, in the order of their arrival, with the years of membership indicated for each individual:

Herseth: 53 (1948-2001)
Nashan: 13 (1950-1963)
Babcock: 7 (1951-1958)
Grocock: 1 (1951-1952)
Cichowicz: 22 (1952-1974)

Kaderabek: 8 (1958-1966)
Scarlett: 33 (1964-1997)
Geyer: 12 (1966-1978)
Smith: 4 (1975-1978)
Kent: 18 (1979-1996)
Vosburgh: 13 (1979-1992)
Ridenour (1994-   )
Hagstrom (1996-   )
Wright: 2 (1999-2001)
Morris: 2 (2001-2003)
Larsen (2002-   )
Martin (2005-   )

From the moment when Bud first established his own personnel in the section in 1950 and 1951, he sought to mold the
four players into the finest trumpet section in the country.
During the first years, the development of the four individuals
into a single cohesive unit was hastened by regular sectional
rehearsals led by Bud. Similarities in training facilitated this
process to a certain degree, since Nashan and Babcock had been
trained, like Bud, by members of the Boston Symphony at the
New England Conservatory (Grocock, however, who only lasted a single season in Chicago, had been trained at the Eastman
Conservatory). Once the unified traits of sound, intonation,
precise rhythms, correct styles, and expressive musicality had
been honed and deeply ingrained within the section, these elements were later emulated and adopted by each subsequent
member of the group, when changes in personnel gradually
occurred over the following decades. This adoption by each
new member of the pre-existing traits of the section was facilitated, in many cases, by previous training in the Chicago style
and quality of playing. Cichowicz, Kaderabek, Scarlett, Geyer,
and Kent had all been members of the Civic Orchestra of
Chicago, and had thus received sectional coaching and private
lessons from Bud, along with hearing the CSO live on a regular
basis, during their respective times in that training ensemble.
    Under Bud's guidance and leadership, not only the four

trumpets but also the six horns, four trombones, and one tuba of the Chicago Symphony together became the preeminent brass section in the world. These fifteen players became a cohesive, virtuosic unit, with Bud at its helm. His playing, for the most part, set the standards for the rich sound, the various styles, and the extreme level of quality, and he very seldom had to lead and guide by any other means than by his own example. Arnold (Jake) Jacobs, who developed his own tuba performance and teaching to a revered level of technical and musical mastery, regularly declared that Bud, by the musical and personal examples that he set, had been his greatest teacher. However, it would be incorrect to suggest that all of the musical standards of the brass section were established by Bud alone. He was an astute listener, and he picked up many traits from various of his colleagues.

The rehearsing and concertizing that the five members of the Chicago Symphony Brass Quintet carried out during Bud's initial years on the job played a considerable role in the progress and consolidation of the full brass section. Due to the small number of individuals who were involved in the chamber ensemble, communication between the players was more direct and intuitive; the musical principles that were developed within the quintet were then readily transferred to the full brass section. Besides Bud and Ren Schilke on trumpets, the other quintet members during the early years from 1948 on included Frank Crisafulli, the first trombone in the CSO since his arrival in 1938, Arnold Jacobs, the orchestra's tuba player since 1944, and Hugh Cowden on horn. (Later, Wayne Barrington, who spent the decade between 1954 and 1964 in the Symphony, played horn in the quintet. However, Phil Farkas, who served as the principal horn of the Symphony from 1947 to 1960, was not a member of this chamber ensemble). The 1950 commercial recording of the group, on the 33 r.p.m. Audiophile Platter Number AP-21, was recorded in Milwaukee. During this period, when the downtown CSO season ended in late April, the Brass Quintet toured for several weeks in May each year, before taking a vacation in advance of the Ravinia season. Since this platter represents the very earliest recording of Bud's playing, preceding by a year his first Chicago Symphony recordings, it is an invaluable demonstration of the attributes of his early music-making. His beautiful tone, absolute technical mastery, and very sophisticated musicianship were already very much in evidence (and he would continue to hone these various elements even further in the coming decades, and deepen his tone even more.) The recordings with the full orchestra the following year would also illustrate his amazing power and endurance.

The literature which was chosen for the CSO recordings of 1951-1953, under Music Director Rafael Kubelik, showcased the attributes of the full ensemble but particularly the brass section, which by this time had already developed its salient traits. The very first piece in this series on the Mercury label, which was also Bud's first recording with the orchestra, was Ravel's orchestration of the Moussorgsky composition *Pictures at an Exhibition*. This work had been premiered in Paris in May of 1923, and then in the U.S. in November of 1924 in Boston (when Bud was a three-year-old toddler), less than 27 years before the Chicago Symphony recording date. Over the four decades following the 1951 recording, *Pictures* would become one of the primary show-pieces for the playing of Bud and the Chicago brass, and it would be recorded by them five more times. The other works which were recorded under Kubelik in 1951 included Dvorak *New World Symphony* and Tchaikowsky *Symphony Number 4*. The following year, the ensemble continued the series of records with Tchaikowsky *Symphony Number 6* and Brahms *Symphony Number 1* (both of which Bud recorded without an assistant on April 21-22, just six weeks after his devastating auto accident); in early December, they recorded Schoenberg *Five Pieces for Orchestra* and the movements entitled *The Moldau* and *From Bohemia's Meadows and Forests* from Smetana's *Ma Vlast*. The recorded literature in 1953 included Hindemith *Symphonic Metamorphosis on Themes of Weber* and Mozart *Symphony Number 34* and *Symphony Number 38*.

The fifteen members of the brass section, making music together as a unified ensemble day in and day out, played a very wide variety of literature in a great array of situations over many years. In the process, they established a universal set of standards among themselves, and then continued to solidify and refine those standards over the following decades. Earlier recordings of the orchestra reveal that the sound of the Chicago brass players during the 1940s had not been at all dominant; the recordings also show that their performances had generally not been of particularly stellar quality. However, by the early 1950s, within three years of Bud's arrival, the overall brass sound had changed considerably and increased immensely, and numerous aspects of its musicality had soared. *what?*

By listening carefully to one another, the entire brass section had developed a homogeneous sound that extended from the bottom tones of the tuba to the top tones of the trumpets. Myriad earlier recordings of orchestras across the U.S. and Europe demonstrate that the tonal concept within the four different symphonic brass instruments had traditionally been quite disparate. Trumpets had tended to produce shrill and nasal sounds, with much emphasis on the higher overtones. In contrast, horns, trombones, and tubas had tended toward indistinct and diffused sounds, with emphasis on the lower overtones. The new distinctive sound of the Chicago brass choir was created by the trumpets playing with a deeper, richer, and more resonant sound than had been traditional, and by the lower brasses playing with sounds that had more crispness, sizzle, and projection than had been customary. This unique and attractive tonal continuity extended from Bud's trumpet at the top, down through each of the sections, to the anchors of Jake on tuba and Ed Kleinhammer (who had joined the orchestra in 1940) on bass trombone. It created an easily recognizable sound that was clear, intense, energetic, and exciting.

Part of this conversion of tonal concept was facilitated by Bud's usage of the C trumpet as his primary instrument. In virtually all orchestras throughout the world except those following French traditions, the B flat trumpet had been the standard instrument up to this time. In the U.S., only the Boston Symphony, replete with French players, utilized C trumpets. It was in the French orchestral tradition that Bud was trained between 1946 and 1948, by Georges Mager and Marcel Lafosse of the Boston orchestra (who also trained his first two CSO section replacements, Rudy Nashan and Bill Babcock). Thus, when Bud arrived in Chicago in 1948, he brought with him the more scintillating sound and crisper articulations of the C trumpet (which would eventually become the standard orchestral instrument virtually worldwide, following his stellar example).

Impeccable intonation was another salient trait of the Chicago brass, which was facilitated by the homogeneous sound of the fifteen players. Proper intonation resulted in support and reinforcement of one another's sound, instead of cancelling out each other; it also produced a clear and transparent choir sound, instead of a thick and muddy one. The overall result of combining well-meshed tonal concepts and good intonation was a grand, solid-cored sound which could be both powerful and delicate, as the literature required.

Other characteristics of the CSO brass section were the very disciplined correctness of rhythms and the attention to the smallest of details. Playing in approximately, but not exactly, the manner in which a composer had intended was not acceptable. A related trait was playing in the appropriate style for each piece, whatever the genre, and being very flexible in making the necessary adjustments for each of the different styles. Certain European orchestras, particularly in Berlin and Vienna, had their own traditional ways of playing: it was a style that was most appropriate for the music of Beethoven, Brahms, and Bruchner. However, their rather limited breadth of styles and adaptability made them much less flexible than the Chicago musicians, who could appropriately play a great array of compositions from the entire spectrum of musical periods. The adaptability of the Chicago Symphony brass players also enabled them to respond to the requests of a wide range of Music Directors and guest conductors, who each tended to elicit particular sounds and styles from the group.

Very expressive and dramatic musicality, coupled with a huge dynamic range, also became hallmarks of the CSO brass. One easily identifiable trait of this musicality was a very sustained manner of playing, without any decay of intensity on the longer tones. Other characteristics included a constant rhythmic pulse and constant forward movement of the music. In addition, the Chicago brass could play not only extremely powerfully but also very delicately. Their approach brought together both soloistic virtuosity and sensitive ensemble playing, reflecting the members' mastery of both the technical and the artistic aspects of music-making. Speaking of ensemble playing, another characteristic aspect of the CSO brass group was that all of the voices within it could be heard, instead of only hearing the lead voice in each section with background accompaniment being provided by the other colleagues. Overlaying all of these various musical attributes was a pervasive striving for the highest standards and a consummate professionalism, no matter the piece, the conductor, the venue, or the demands of the work schedule. In virtually every interview that Bud granted over his decades on the job, he credited the legendary attributes of the CSO brass choir to the excellent quality of the players in each position within that choir and their professional pride, as well as the many years in which the members had played together as a unit, which allowed them to mesh together musically. He once stated to an interviewer, "I'd bet that you could switch around the [positions of the] members of our brass section, and people in the audience wouldn't even know unless they looked. Everybody carries their weight, and that's why we sound the way we do." Over the span of a half-century, the Chicago style and quality of brass playing, with Bud at the forefront, would influence orchestral players all over the world.

It it particularly interesting to note the models of symphonic trumpet playing to which Bud Herseth had been exposed, first while he was growing up and later during his graduate-level training, and to observe how very much his own music-making eclipsed all those who had come before. Personally, Bud is much too gracious, modest, and self-effacing to suggest such a statement, but the recordings from that era clearly support this assertion. A great many of the characteristic traits of

1. Tim Kent at age 16, with his combo of fellow students called The Blue Notes (photo by Spring Photo).

2. Upper: Bud Herseth at U of M on October 1, 1967, the day Tim first met him and first heard symphonic music in a live performance.

3. Lower: Caricature of Tim after his freshman year of college (caricature by Tasco, photo by Herbert Vaughan).

4. Upper: Bud demonstrating a passage in his basement studio, during one of Tim's lessons ca. 1970.

5. Lower: Two very supportive spouses, Doree Kent (left) and Avis Herseth at the Herseth home in July of 1973, as the Kents were about to depart for their life in Germany.

6. Upper: Bud with Kevin Kent, 1976.

7. Lower: Tim prepared for a trip to his practice studio at a distant church, loaded with Kevin, four trumpets, and diaper bag.

8. The Chicago Symphony Orchestra, of which Tim was a member for nearly eighteen years (Rosenthal Archives, Chicago Symphony Orchestra).

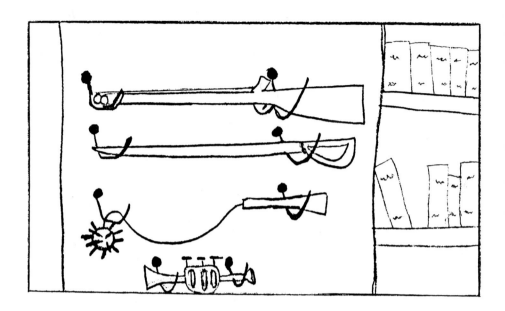

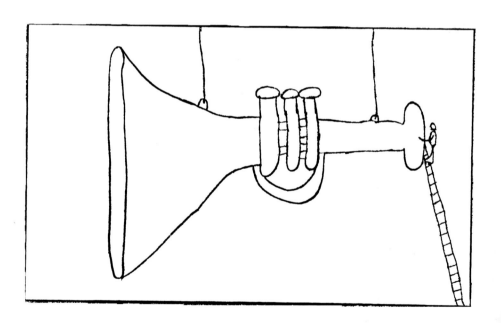

9-10. Upper and Lower: Two impressions by Richard Kanter, CSO oboist, after listening to 140 candidates audition for the trumpet position in the Symphony which Tim won in January of 1979.

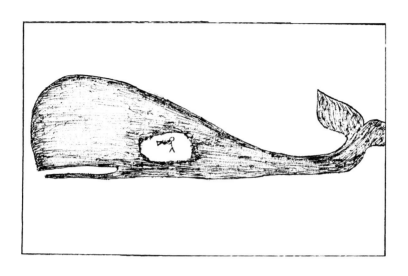

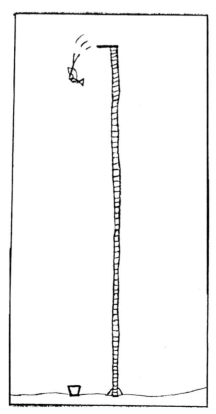

11-12. Upper and Lower: Two impressions by Richard Kanter, CSO oboist, after listening to 140 candidates audition for the trumpet position in the Symphony which Tim won in January of 1979.

13. Upper: The longest-running unchanged trumpet section in the history of the Chicago Symphony, together for thirteen years, from left to right: Bud Herseth, Tim Kent, George Vosburgh, and Will Scarlett (with former section member Phil Smith, visiting from New York), during summer of 1980.

14. Lower: Tim, George, and Phil paddling during the same summer gathering.

Trumpet Festival

Adolph Herseth

Timothy Kent

Organist
Carl Waldschmidt

Sunday, March 4, 1984
4 p.m.

UNITED LUTHERAN CHURCH
Ridgeland Avenue at Greenfield
Oak Park, Illinois

Information: 386-1576   *Freewill Offering*

15. Poster for program of trumpet duets and solos by Bud and Tim in 1984.

16. Upper: CSO brass section rehearsing in Orchestra Hall during fall of 1982, from foreground to background, trumpets Tim Kent, George Vosburgh, and Bud Herseth, trombones Jay Friedman, Frank Crisafulli, and Ed Kleinhammer, and tuba Arnold Jacobs. To right are horns Dick Oldberg, Norm Schweikert, and Dale Clevenger.

17. Lower: Tim keeping his chops in shape, while paddling the Mattawa River in Ontario with Doree and their sons Kevin and Ben, June of 1984.

18. Upper: Tim reading backstage amid CSO steamer trunks during a European tour, before a concert in Amsterdam in January of 1985.

19. Lower: Bud demonstrating for Doree how his chops feel after a concert, during 1986 tour of Japan.

20. Upper: Visiting Maestro Solti at his home in London at the conclusion of another European tour, September 19, 1989, from left to right, Tim, Solti, George Vosburgh, and Bud (photo by Sando Shia).

21. Lower: Colleagues enjoying brunch outside of the Maestro's poolside music room, left to right, Sando Shia, Betty Lambert, Frank Fiatarone, Sam Magad, and Tim (photo provided by Sando Shia).

22. Upper: Bud and Maestro Solti, at the farewell party hosted by the Maestro in Tokyo on April 18, 1990, at the end of another Japan tour.

23. Lower: Tim and Doree at the Chicago Symphony 100th anniversary festivities in October of 1991 (photo by Sando Shia).

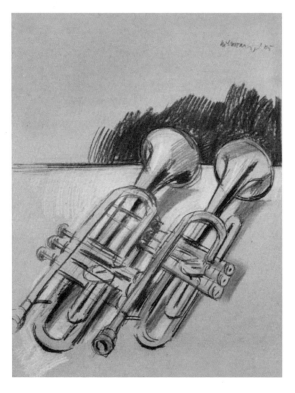

24. Upper: Arrival of the Kent family at Ft. Chipewyan in northern Alberta, at the north-western end of the 3,000 mile fur trade canoe route from Montreal, in August of 1995.

25. Lower: Artwork presented to Bud by Tim and Doree for his 75th birthday in July of 1996 (photo by Avis Herseth).

26. Upper: Bud preparing to drape Tim with the CSO Theodore Thomas Medallion for Distinguished Service, at the official retirement party for Tim in November of 1996 (photo by Sando Shia).

27. Lower: With Henry Fogel, President of the CSO, listening at left, Bud recounting his 27 years of association with Tim, including nine years of mentoring and then eighteen years as colleagues together in the section (photo by Sando Shia).

28. Upper: The CSO trumpet section at Tim's retirement festivities, from left to right: Mark Ridenour, John Hagstrom (who replaced Tim), Tim, and Bud. Doree was made an honorary section member for the day (photo by Avis Herseth).

29. Lower: Bud celebrating with Doree and the Kent sons Ben (left) and Kevin (photo by Sando Shia).

Bud's playing were not derived from his aural models, but were instead his own developments.

During his younger years, Bud heard radio broadcasts of the New York Philharmonic and later the NBC Symphony under the direction of Arturo Toscanini, as well as recordings of the Boston Symphony. In both of the first two orchestras, the principal trumpet position was held by Harry Glantz, who played in the Philharmonic from 1923 to 1942 (while Bud was ages 2 to 21) and in the NBC ensemble from 1942 on. In a 1977 interview, Bud made the following comments concerning this musician's playing: "Glantz was, I suppose, the biggest name in orchestral trumpet playing for many, many years. He was a big influence on all symphonic trumpet players...With Glantz, I think I was more impressed with the solidity of his playing. To my way of thinking, he was not as inspiring a player—in terms of [my] really getting turned on when he played—as Mager [the first trumpet in the Boston Symphony] was. But he was very reliable, with an excellent sound and style of playing, one that I think probably influenced more players than any other during that period." A telling comparison between Harry Glantz's music-making and the level of technical mastery and musicality which Bud developed may be made by listening to the recording that each of these musicians made of *Pictures at an Exhibition* within two years of each other in the early 1950s. Bud's version, recorded on April 23, 1951, represented his very first orchestral recording, after only three years on the job. Glantz recorded the work with the NBC Symphony under Toscanini in Carnegie Hall less than two years later, on January 26, 1953. (Interestingly, Bud performed this same piece in Carnegie Hall six weeks later, with the CSO under Kubelik on March 9, 1953.) In the opening *Promenade* movement, Bud's version presented a grand sound and an elegant and sustained style, which certainly cannot be said of the NBC recording. In the *Samuel Goldenberg and Schmuyle* movement, Bud played the extended muted solo effortlessly and musically; in contrast, the NBC version exhibited two players alternating with each other to play the single solo part, and in spite of sharing the burden, struggling considerably and being barely able to hold on until the end.

The other significant aural input during Bud's developmental years came from the Boston Symphony. In response to an interview question concerning which teachers had had an effect on his playing, Bud noted: "Marcel Lafosse and Georges Mager, at the New England Conservatory in Boston, where I went for two and a half years on the GI Bill after World War II. The first year and a half I studied with Lafosse [the second trumpet in Boston since 1926; first trumpet Mager's schedule was full], and with Mager for my final year. Mager was a very famous orchestral trumpet player in those days; he played in Boston under Koussevitsky, even Monteux, and must have played there thirty years or more [1919 to 1950]. He was a very exciting player and a very inspiring teacher. I owe a great deal to that man...[I received from him] primarily musical style, which was what I really wanted anyway. I could already play the trumpet...The thing I got from him was an understanding of the different styles you need to approach the wide variety of repertoire a symphony trumpet player is faced with...and that is the main thing he wanted to show me."

When one listens to Boston Symphony recordings from the specific period of these training years, it is very clear that Bud forged into new territory very early in his career, raising the level of technical mastery and musicianship immeasurably, compared to what he had heard during his time as a student. To support this statement, several examples of Boston recordings under Koussevitsky may be noted, beginning with Prokofiev *Symphony Number 5*, which was laid down on February 6, 1945; this was a few months before Bud applied for admission to the New England Conservatory. Equally telling is the recording of Shostakovich *Symphony Number Nine*, which was done on November 4, 1946 and April 2, 1947, while Bud was studying with Lafosse, the second trumpet in the ensemble. The group certainly must have rehearsed heavily for these particular sessions, since their recording was to be the very first one of this piece, which had been written in 1945. A third recording, which illustrates particularly clearly the musical abilities of both of Bud's teachers, was of the Stravinsky *Octet for Wind Instruments*. This latter session took place at Tanglewood, the summer home of the Boston Symphony, during the summer of 1948, just after Bud had completed his year of lessons with Mager and had begun his duties in the Chicago Symphony. The trumpet playing on the Boston recordings exhibits musicality that is somewhat emotional, but it definitely does not represent impeccable intonation, or precise rhythms, or superb technical mastery. The tone, although rather brilliant due to the use of C trumpets, is not deep and rich, and the styles of playing are certainly not characterized by long, sustained notes and phrases. In addition, the brass choir does not exhibit a unified single concept of sound or execution. Bud sometimes noted to me that he listened to the weekly Boston concerts during his training years with the goals of hearing how the trumpets played stylistically, and learning how their parts fit with the other parts in the orchestral whole, within various pieces and different genres. He also repeated to me several times the comment that Mager had made on various occasions: "There are no good teachers, only good students." Bud Herseth was certainly one of the very finest brass students of all time, taking in information from his predecessors and then advancing his art form to an entirely new, unprecedented level. As long as there have been symphony orchestras, the principal trumpet in various of the ensembles have each been considered by their local students and boosters to be very accomplished. However, ever since about 1950, anyone who has been aware of the worldwide trumpet scene has acknowledged that those individuals each represent a "big fish in a little pond." In comparison, Bud's legendary degree of artistry and technical prowess elevated him to the level of the alpha figure among the largest whales in the world's oceans.

The newly-developed sounds and styles of the CSO brass section from the early 1950s on matched well the qualities of the orchestra as a whole. The Symphony's Teutonic sound and manner of playing reflected very strong Germanic and central

European traditions, which had dominated the ensemble ever since its founding in 1891. (Very few of the orchestras in the world were older than the CSO: only New York [founded in 1842], Boston [1880], Berlin [1882], Concertgebouw in Amsterdam [1883], and the Metropolitan Opera in New York [1883].) The roster of Music Directors in Chicago, presented below with the nationality and years of tenure of each individual, reveals the Teutonic influences on the orchestra, which were tempered by French traditions in only two instances totaling nine years:

Theodore Thomas, German (1891-1905)
Frederick Stock, German (1905-1942)
Désiré Defauw, Belgian [French traditions] (1943-1947)
Artur Rodzinski, Austrian (1947-1948)
Various guest conductors (1948-1950)
Rafael Kubelik, Czechoslovakian (1950-1953)
Fritz Reiner, Hungarian (1953-1962)
Various guest conductors (1962-1963)
Jean Martinon, French (1963-1968)
Various guest conductors (1968-1969)
Georg Solti, Hungarian (1969-1991)
Daniel Barenboim, Argentinean/Israeli (1991-2006)

Germanic musical traditions had permeated the orchestra from its very beginning, since the personnel in the founding group had overwhelmingly been Germans. In addition, all rehearsals of the ensemble were conducted in the German language for nearly its first quarter-century, from 1891 until 1914. In the latter year, which marked the opening of World War I, Maestro Stock, himself German-born, instigated the new policy of conducting all rehearsals in English. The literature that was scheduled in Chicago also reflected a strong interest in Germanic and eastern European composers. In fact, a considerable number of pieces by prominent composers of these nationalities received their American premiere with the CSO. These works included Richard Strauss' tone poems *Till Eulenspiegel's Merry Pranks* (1895), *Also Sprach Zarathustra* (1897), *Don Quixote* (1899), *Ein Heldenleben* (1900, one year and seven days after its world premiere in Frankfurt), and *Macbeth* (1901); Bruchner's *Symphony Number 7* (1897); and Mahler's *Symphony Number 7* (1921). In addition, the very first guest conductor of the Chicago Symphony was Richard Strauss, who conducted the ensemble during the spring of 1904 in a program at the Auditorium Theatre, six months before Orchestra Hall was dedicated. This program included *Also Sprach Zarathustra, Till Eulenspiegel's Merry Pranks,* and *Death and Transfiguration,* plus numerous songs sung by the composer's wife, who was a prominent operatic performer. After the single rehearsal for this program, Strauss commented, "I have never led an orchestra that responded more quickly to my wishes than does this one. I had but one rehearsal with these men, and that one was hardly necessary."

This trait of responding to a conductor's wishes upon the first request, without needing to have it repeated later, was a sure sign of the members' musical integrity. This was just one of an entire array of traits which were passed down as the membership gradually evolved over many decades following the inception of the group in 1891. Due to the traditions and influences of the early players in the ensemble and its various Music Directors, the sound and style of the Chicago Symphony became brilliant, bold, and energetic, as well as very disciplined and precise. The orchestra's playing was also resonant and powerful, as well as dramatic, virtuosic, and expressive. Finally, the sound had a clarity of texture, and was greatly adaptable to a wide array of reportoire.

In many respects, Bud Herseth became the leader of not only the brass section of the CSO but also of the entire orchestra. As Maestro Barenboim noted, "Bud has been the artistic conscience of the orchestra for many, many years." This role of standard-setter and leader was accorded to him for a number of reasons, including his personality, his extreme degree of technical mastery and musicianship, and the fact that the sounds from his horn, projecting in a forward direction from the rear of the stage, could be easily heard by all of the members while they were playing.

The personality of Bud certainly reflected the fortitude and determination that he had inherited from his Viking ancestors. Affable and personable to the general public, he was extremely demanding of both himself and his colleagues when on the job. This eternal quest for the highest of standards was manifested by the personal example that he constantly set. Bud's manner of focusing on the smallest of details was reflected in the fact that he had earned a degree in mathematics during his undergraduate years (from Luther College in Decorah, Iowa), instead of a degree in music. As a testament to his personal standards, I never once heard him join in the critical and gossipy conversations that were prevalent in our corner of the locker room in Orchestra Hall and Ravinia. Likewise, he made it a point to never comment publicly on the negative qualities of any conductor or musician.

Bud's skills as a musician are legendary. Maestro Solti, one of the most prominent conductors on the globe, described Bud in his memoirs as "the *éminence grise* [supreme elder statesman] of the entire brass section, and perhaps the most revered and respected orchestral brass player in the world." Bud so mastered all of the technical aspects of brass playing that he could completely transcend the nuts-and-bolts features of playing, and could focus entirely on artful musicality. Due to the nature of the production of sound on brass instruments, the playing of these instruments is not entirely natural. In playing stringed instruments, including piano and harp, strings made of various materials are made to vibrate to produce the sounds; for all of the woodwinds except the flute, one or two wooden reeds are made to vibrate. In contrast, the sounds on brass instruments are produced by causing one's own lips to vibrate. Thus, the brass family of musical instruments involves the most physicality, and, note for note, the trumpet is the most physically strenuous instrument in the entire orchestra. Playing the brass instruments requires complete control of one's lips, facial muscles, tongue, and throat, as well as the breathing apparatus. For this reason, ever since the invention of their instruments, brass performers have been overly focused upon the physical aspects of playing. This incorrect focus often commences on the very first day of playing, when the lips are first formed into an embouchure and the mouthpiece is placed onto that embouchure. Over the centuries of brass playing, various performers have mastered certain components of the art: sound, intonation, range, power, articulation, delicate execution, endurance, lyrical singing, dynamic range, etc. However, highly advanced musicality has very rarely been reached, because no single individual ever achieved absolute mastery of every technical aspect of playing. It is no coincidence that, from the close of the Baroque era forward, brass players were generally perceived by performers on other symphonic instruments as less than truly sophisticated musicians. However, Bud Herseth did achieve absolute mastery of all features of the art of brass playing. Thus, he was able to rise above its physical components, and elevate the musical aspects of brass performance to previously unknown heights.

His immense musical abilities, coupled with the power of his personality, enabled Bud to securely lead the brass section, and often the entire orchestra, in conjunction with the wishes of each respective conductor. And unless the conductor indicated a specific way in which he wanted the orchestra to play a particular passage, Bud's long experience and musical integrity inspired his colleagues to follow his lead in interpreting the piece. Likewise, the greater the respect that Bud had for the musical concepts of a given conductor, the more he guided the band in acceding to the wishes of that conductor; to a certain degree, the opposite was also true when his measure of a conductor's talents and musical judgement was low. Over the span of many decades, Bud had performed all of the master works numerous times under many of the world's greatest conductors. His memory of those experiences was encyclopedic, and he brought those memories to the fore when a given piece was on the program.

In his role as the "conductor in the back row," Bud's responsibilites became all the more important the more insecure, unreliable, or unclear a given conductor was on the podium, and the more unwise were the conductor's judgements. In some cases, a conductor would insist upon an awkward tempo or an illogical and unnatural manner of playing a certain passage or an entire movement. In those cases, the members played in the requested way during the rehearsals and the first concert, in their usual cooperative manner. However, as that program progressed through its second, third, and fourth performances, those awkward tempos and poorly thought-out passages would very often gradually evolve into the orchestra's traditional manner of playing them in a more natural and musical way, without any verbal communication taking place between the players; this gradual progression was very often guided by Bud from the back row. In those instances when a conductor held firmly to his poor musical decisions, or when his leadership was simply not of high quality, Bud would comment in the locker room after a concert, "We wanted to play it better, but he wouldn't let us!" This phenomenon sometimes occurred when a conductor was inconsistent from performance to performance, particularly in reference to tempos and transitions. Certain conductors tried to defend this trait by explaining that it resulted from their inspired creativity, which enabled them to constantly invent new and exciting ideas. Such logic may apply when one is playing in a tiny chamber group, but it certainly does not apply to performances by a massive ensemble containing 109 players who are spread out on a large stage. Bud could only lead from the back row while he was actually playing; thus, he could not rectify every single mis-step that was made on the podium.

Bud's leadership role also became crucial when a conductor utilized nearly all of the rehearsal time to pick apart the individual components of a piece, and then did not give the group a chance to reassemble the work by playing it through with few or no stops during the dress rehearsal. This unwise approach placed a great burden on the orchestra as a whole and on Bud in particular, since we were then required to reassemble the piece into a unified whole during the first concert, while an audience was listening. For this reason, during the dress rehearsal on Thursday morning, Bud would sometimes growl to himself, "Just let us play it through!" Solti thoroughly understood this important principle of music-making, and invariably utilized the dress rehearsal as a complete run-through of each movement of every piece, with stops only for very serious reasons. In most instances, he remembered the points that he wished to mention, and noted those at the end of each movement instead of halting the forward flow during that movement. This very professional approach offered the orchestra members the chance to mesh their parts together as a unified whole before the first performance.

The problem of a conductor devoting nearly all of the available rehearsal time to individual details often applied when a new or unfamiliar piece was on the program with one or two of the more standard works. Not only would the conductor very often devote virtually all of our time and energies to the new piece, he would leave the more well-known works on the program for us to refresh and gel together during the first performance, when an audience was listening and the microphones were recording the concert for later radio broadcast. The conductors who picked apart every tiny detail had invariably been accustomed to working with second and third rate orchestras, whose players needed to be taught pieces from the bottom up. In the CSO, each of us responsibly learned our respective parts on our own, in advance of the rehearsals; thus, we mostly needed to play through each work one or several times, in order to coordinate and polish the details as an ensemble. By simply playing through most pieces, a great many of the elements would gel by themselves, due to the sensitive ears of the musicians. Then, a wise conductor would apply his own interpretations to the piece, and would work on the finer inner details which required particular attention. The approach of some conductors of "teaching" us pieces was actually a considerable show of disrespect to the orchestra, and reflected an ignorance of or disregard for our professionalism. The very best results were always achieved when there was mutual respect between the orchestra members and the conductor, a situation which was very much in evidence whenever we worked with Maestro Solti. Both he and the orchestra had extremely high musical standards, and our mutual goals and work methods meshed together extremely well.

In addition to ill-equipped conductors, Bud also strongly disliked any other situations in which the working conditions made fine playing more difficult. I remember one particular occasion in which I played second to him on an outdoor pops concert at a Chicago college campus, doing a program which was being broadcast live on the radio. To this day, I still remember how he dug in with determination on that low wooden stage beneath a canvas roof, when the wind picked up during the performance. First, the wind whistling across the microphones became part of our broadcast sonic product. Then, changing the pages on our stands and readjusting the long music-fastening clips became a major challenge. Finally, the gusts began toppling our music stands. I still have a clear mental image of Bud anchoring the base of his stand with one foot and moving clips and turning pages with his left hand, while determinedly playing the horn for the microphones and the radio audience with his right hand. He did not appreciate having to maintain his impeccable standards under such conditions.

The extremely high musical standards to which Bud dedicated his life caused him to develop a very strong work ethic, and to adopt strict and methodical measures to consistently maintain those levels of performance. In spite of his down-to-earth, unassuming demeanor, and his great ability to tell stories and crack jokes during relaxing times, Bud personally bore huge responsibilities. One cannot underestimate the pressures that came with being universally recognized as the premier orchestral trumpet player and brass performer in the world. This role entailed not only upholding the level of virtuosity that his colleagues and listeners everywhere had come to expect, but also shouldering the primary leadership position within the orchestra. But Bud was always up to both of these challenges, approaching his responsibilities with iron self-discipline and a seriousness of purpose that was infectious among his colleagues.

The intensity of Bud's fastidious preparations, during both his own private practice sessions and the orchestra's rehearsals, was surpassed only by his concentration during performances. Over his entire career of 53 years, he never shirked his personal practice duties, but instead constantly maintained and advanced his skills. To remain faithful to his practicing schedule, he taught students only very occasionally, and accepted extremely few engagements outside of the Symphony's schedule. The few gigs that he did accept, playing primarily solos and occasionally Baroque orchestral pieces, each contributed to the variety of his work, and thus provided him with even more incentives to keep practicing.

From his very first year on the job in Chicago, Bud developed many customs that enabled him to remain consistently solid and impeccable in his output. For rehearsals, he always arrived at the hall comfortably early, even if he did not play the first piece on the schedule, and shortly went up on stage to do most of his warmup and to carefully look over the parts. At the first rehearsal of a new program, he sometimes arrived on stage especially early, to check the sound and response of various horns and mouthpieces in the empty hall and decide which of them he would use on that particular program. By doing these tests before the other colleagues arrived, he could listen without distractions and interferences. When playing unfamiliar pieces, Bud always prepared his part in advance, by means of silent and vocal singing and some practicing. On each of the standard works, irregardless of how many times he had played them over the years, he still devoted plenty of time to mentally singing through his parts on stage beforehand, refreshing memories of earlier performances. In the process, he reviewed his former pencil markings on the parts, and added new ones as necessary to avoid mishaps. We in the section followed his example and, as needed, circled the keys of transposition, marked phrases and breathing places (as well as NB for "no breath here"), noted where mutes were put in and taken out, marked the beats in very complex rhythmic figures, inserted significant cues of other instruments, and marked fingerings on occasion. To avoid having to play immediately after counting a number of measures and then making a quick page-turn, we would write TURN at a certain place within the resting measures, and then rewrite the remaining bars of rests on the opposite side of the turned page. Bud would often jokingly announce in our corner of the locker room, "Well, I better go up and mark a few fingerings;" however, no pencil markings were considered too simplistic if they contributed to the quality of the performances. It was also a measure of the man that he always had a mute on his stand on stage, during every single rehearsal and concert, even if he was absolutely certain that no piece on the entire program would require a mute. During one of his early years on the job, having once found himself on stage at a rehearsal without a mute, he had vowed to himself that such an oversight would never happen again.

Before a concert, Bud's routine at the hall was much the same as before a rehearsal, except that he divided into two segments his time of warming up and mentally singing through his parts on stage. After the initial segment of time, he would suit up in his concert outfit downstairs and then return to the stage for further preparation, mostly involving silent singing. During his pre-concert routine, Bud very seldom played passages from the upcoming music; the most productive activity at this point was mental preparedness. Before and during a rehearsal, a concert, or a recording session, he was totally focused on producing the best possible performance. He was not nervous, but rather completely determined to play his best. To this end, he tuned out any and all distractions that might deter him from his firm goal, and focused only on the desired end product.

When the band toured, Bud invariably traveled to the first venue on the earliest day possible, to acclimate himself. If the itinerary took us overseas and involved jet lag, his early travel typically occurred in advance of the rest of the orchestra. Even while visiting interesting places and various friends and colleagues during a tour, he always structured these activities so that he could maintain his usual practice routines. During the days on which we had a rehearsal or a concert, he practiced according to his customary schedule at the concert hall, while on days off he did his usual routines either at the hall or in a room at the hotel, often in a banquet or conference room. Whatever the location in the world or the work schedule, Bud did whatever was necessary to maintain his playing in top form. Actually, he found the performances during tours to be especially satisfying and invigorating, even during those trips that involved a long and grueling itinerary. This extra degree of inspiration made the sacrifices of faithful practicing while on tour all the more worthwhile for him. To maintain his strenuous schedule of preparation and performance on the road, he tended to reserve the bulk of his socializing for the post-concert time, once the serious work of the day had been completed.

Due to Bud's extraordinary endurance and his very fast recovery time, the CSO management soon learned that they could plan extremely grueling programs and work schedules without collapsing the first trumpet player. And Bud always played with the full measure of his abilities at every rehearsal, concert, and recording session; he did not survive the unbelievably rigorous schedule by laying back. The recording sessions were fitted into the already-demanding work schedule of rehearsals and performances by holding them on Saturdays and Mondays; in most instances, the long Saturday sessions were followed by a concert that evening. Possibly the most grueling day of recording in Bud's long career took place on March 6, 1954, during which he and his colleagues, under Reiner's direction, laid down the two Strauss works *Ein Heldenleben* and *Dance of the Seven Veils*. The three rigorous sessions that day extended over a span of sixteen hours, from 9 A.M. to 1 A.M., with only a one-hour lunch break and a two-hour dinner break during that time.

The management and the Music Director very often selected works for both concerts and recordings that showcased the virtuosic playing of the orchestra, and especially pieces that featured the brass section. Typical examples of this programming may be noted in the Centennial Season of 1990-1991, which was also Solti's final season as Music Director. During the autumn of that year, at the age of 69, Bud played lead on Mahler *Symphony Number 5*, Shostakovich *Symphony Number 10*, Strauss *Don Juan, Till Eulenspiegel's Merry Pranks*, and *Ein Heldenleben* (all three of these latter works on a single concert!), Holst *The Planets*, Moussorgsky-Ravel *Pictures at an Exhibition*, and various other pieces before his four performances of the Hummel *Concerto* on December 6, 7, 8, and 11. He also record- ed *Till* and *Heldenleben* shortly after the all-Strauss concert, and played Mahler *Symphony Number 6* after his Hummel week, before taking a welcome holiday vacation. (Although he had myriad fond memories of playing each of these very significant works over many decades, he was particularly reminiscent during the week of *The Planets*, since that was the very first piece that he had heard the Boston Symphony play live when he had begun his studies at the New England Conservatory in January of 1946.) The second half of the 1990-91 season contin- ued nearly as heavily as its first half, containing Hindemith *Concert Music for Brass and Strings*, Bach *Orchestral Suite Number 3*, Bruckner *Symphony Number 2*, Mahler *Das Lied von der Erde*, Strauss *An Alpine Symphony*, Bruckner *Symphony Number 4*, and numerous other pieces that called for heavy-duty playing on Bud's part.

Mahler *Symphony Number 5*, which opened Solti's final sea- son as our boss and particularly featured Bud's talents, was the signature work of the Chicago-Solti combination during the Maestro's entire span of 22 seasons. This phenomenon had begun with performances of the piece in Chicago, Toledo, and Carnegie Hall in the spring of 1970, plus the production of a recording of the work at that time. Later, it had been featured as the show-piece during the orchestra's first European tour in the fall of 1971, the first tour of Japan in 1977, and on numer- ous other occasions. Solti also scheduled Mahler *Fifth* as the last piece on his final concert in Orchestra Hall as the CSO Music Director, on April 13, 1991, after which we repeated it in Carnegie Hall two days later. This work, which was premiered in Cologne, Germany on October 18, 1904, had been first performed by the Chicago Symphony under Stock 2 ¹/₂ years later, on March 22-23, 1907; it was the very first Mahler piece to have been played by the orchestra. Bud first performed it under Kubelik in December of 1950, 2 ¹/₂ years after arriving in Chicago.

Bud prided himself on being primarily an orchestral player, and within that context he regularly performed solos. However, he also played a number of solos each year while standing in front of an accompanying ensemble, which was sometimes the CSO and other times the Civic Orchestra or one of the many community and regional orchestras in the Chicago area. His first solo appearance as a stand-up soloist with the Chicago Symphony took place in February of 1953, when he played Copland *Quiet City* on a pops concert. Two years later, his first solo on subscription concerts in Orchestra Hall featured the Haydn *Concerto*, which he also played for his first solo appearance at the Ravinia Festival, in July of 1964. He was also featured on two occasions at the Mostly Mozart Festival in Lincoln Center in New York City. Most of Bud's solo presentations were of the Haydn and Hummel concertos, which had not been performed better by any other artist since they had been composed for the keyed trumpet in 1796 and 1803, respectively. However, he sometimes performed Baroque pieces for piccolo trumpet, including the Anonymous *Hollansk Kirkemarch*, Handel *Suite in D Major*, Purcell *Overture from "The Indian Queen,"* Purcell *Sonata*, Telemann *Concerto in D*, and Torelli *Sinfonia*, as well as the Bach *Brandenburg Concerto Number 2*, which was the most demanding piece in the entire trumpet repertoire. Sometimes these Baroque pieces featured one or more of his colleagues as well, such as the Anonymous *Three Sonatinas for Two Trumpets*, Manfredini *Sonata for Two Trumpets*, Telemann *Concerto for Three Trumpets and Two Oboes*, Torelli *Concerto for Four Trumpets and Two Oboes*, and Vivaldi *Concerto for Two Trumpets*. A number of these solo and multi-soloist pieces, along with the *Brandenburg Concerto*, were featured on the June Festival programs which were conducted by Jean

Martinon and Antonio Janigro in 1966 and 1967. In a rare and special event two decades later, Bud played the world premiere of the *Concerto for Trumpet and Orchestra* by the Czech composer Karel Husa on February 11-13, 1988. This work had been commissioned for Bud and Solti by the CSO management with funding from a private family foundation. After its premiere at the Chicago concerts, it was performed by Bud during the following month in each of the cities in which the orchestra played during our tour of Australia. Sitting in a backstage location to hear his solo performance in Melbourne, Doree had a special vantage point for seeing Bud, calm and composed, waiting to do his job. When he saw her, he greeted her with a broad smile and his two-eyed wink.

Every time Bud prepared and played a solo piece, he felt that the process improved his playing skills, and also injected variety into his work schedule. He loved all aspects of solo playing, and recorded the Haydn concerto with the Symphony accompaniment led by Abbado in 1985; the album also featured Mozart concertos played by Dale Clevenger on horn, Ray Still on oboe, and Willard Elliot on bassoon. Bud would have loved to have recorded an entire album of trumpet solo literature. However, he felt very strongly about his responsibilities to the Chicago Symphony, and he was not willing to siphon off time and energy from those duties during the course of an Orchestra Hall season or a Ravinia season, to rehearse and record a series of solos outside of the orchestra. His devoted fans all over the world would wish that he could have completed such a project during the various vacation weeks that occurred during the course of each year. However, Bud utilized these vacation periods to rest and refresh himself, both physically and mentally, so that he could return invigorated and continue to maintain his extremely high level of output during the orchestra's rigorous schedule.

As with many dedicated performers, Bud sometimes carried out his duties while ill or injured. In most instances, unless his symptoms were obvious, we colleagues were not usually even aware of the hinderances that he was enduring. In one case, he required serious dental work in the midst of a strenuous tour. In another instance, we did not learn until after returning from an extensive tour that he had played the entire tour with a detached retina in one eye! This was quite dangerous, since he could have become blind in that eye if the condition had worsened before receiving medical attention. These were just scattered examples of a great many instances in which Bud did not let his own health problems stand in the way of his fulfilling his obligations, due to the dedication that he held for his art. It was not his choice that emergency quadruple bypass surgery in the spring of 1995 kept him out the action for several months.

Part of his dedication involved seeking trumpets and mouthpieces that helped him deliver the desired musical product for each program. Bud possessed an encyclopedic knowledge of how various changes in equipment produced differences in sound quality, intonation, freedom of blowing, and responsiveness. In addition, he could judge the attributes of horns and mouthpieces extremely quickly. To produce the huge sound that was required in the CSO trumpet section, large bore instruments and large mouthpieces were a requirement. The composition and thickness of the metal of a horn, and whether it was left in its raw state or was plated with silver, effected its sound quality. Over the decades, Bud had the Schilke Company produce for him various bells in yellow brass, red brass, and beryllium, and in a variety of thicknesses and bore sizes. From his vast experience, he knew how myriad different bells and leadpipes produced varying musical results; how the sound became rounder and less bright as a horn became broken in over the course of its first six months of playing; how excessive wear of the valves caused the lower register to become fuzzy and unfocused and the upper register to become clearer; and how a horn lost some of its free-blowing characteristics as the valve pads, made of felt, were gradually crushed down over time, causing the valve ports to no longer line up exactly with the openings in the valve casings. Bud had taught me how the latter problem was rectified, by replacing the flattened pads with new ones of the correct thickness, and then checking the resulting alignment of the ports with the openings in the casings, by using a long-handled dental mirror.

Bud also discovered that the tuning slides of B flat and C trumpets were unintentionally all produced a little different from one another at the factory, due to slight variations in the diameter of the tubing, the amount of solder that was applied to the joints (especially if excess solder were present on the interior surface of the joints), and the snugness of the fit of the slide into the pipes of the horn. By experimentation, he also learned that, within the mouthpiece receiver at the outer end of a leadpipe, the amount of gap between the tip of the mouthpiece shank and the ledge (the end of the leadpipe within the receiver) was crucial. A space of about $^3/_{16}$ inch between shank and ledge was optimum on B flat and E flat horns, while a gap of slightly less than $^1/_8$ inch was best on C horns. A minimal space or no space at all, which was sometimes caused by a worn receiver allowing the mouthpiece to extend in too far, resulted in unclear articulations and poor response. Sometimes the location in which the receiver was mounted onto the leadpipe varied during assembly at the factory, and occasionally the interior diameter of the receiver was simply produced too large. In those cases in which the interior of the receiver was neither worn too large nor manufactured with too wide a diameter, it could be unsoldered and repositioned so that the gap became the proper size. If the interior of a receiver became too worn over time, the unit could be easily replaced by a skilled brass technician.

In spite of Bud's vast understanding of how various features of equipment altered the end product, he focused only lightly on this fact in his playing and teaching. For the most part, he relied on his own talents and efforts to produce the appropriate musical results from his horns and mouthpieces. This he clearly communicated on one occasion during a CSO east-coast tour, when the band played in one of the cities that had a Big Five Orchestra in permanent residence. The trumpet players in that particular ensemble were well-known for their constant quest for the ultimate instrument, regularly experimenting with alterations of various physical traits on their horns. When Bud exited from the hall after his performance there, an avid local student asked him what he did to his trumpets to be able to play like that; he responded: "I practice them!"

During the 1930s and 40s, the years of Bud's growing up and becoming trained, a very limited number of piccolo trumpets had been manufactured. After World War II, more of these high-pitched instruments began to be made. Thus, Bud was in the very first generation of adult trumpet players who had ready access to such horns, which caused an absolute explosion of interest in Baroque music. In addition, beginning in the early to mid-1960s, Bud and his section members began to utilize German trumpets with rotary valves for playing certain works of the Classical and Romantic periods, pieces by such composers as Mozart, Beethoven, Brahms, and Bruchner. Compared to the usual piston-valve instruments, the rotary-valve versions had a darker and less aggressive and penetrating sound, as well as a less concise intial articulation; these traits caused them to blend more with the horns and trombones. The Chicago trumpet section also utilized cornets in those instances in which the composer had specified these instruments.

During my eighteen years in the section, music critics would occasionally call me at home and approach me during tours, to ask what instrument Bud was using on a given piece. This particularly occurred when he was performing an offstage solo, and was thus not visible from the audience. I never supplied the requested information, since I knew that the writers would use it in their reviews to imply that their magnificent ears had been able to discern which horn he had used. As Bud occasionally muttered, "Critics—turn over any rock and five or six of them will crawl away!"

Relevent to the discussion of instruments is the fact that Bud was regularly troubled by recalcitrant valve action on most of his horns. Since I was not plagued by this particular problem, I surmised that it was caused by a constant gradual buildup of tobacco residues from one of his favorite relaxation activities, pipe smoking. As an antidote, he washed out his horns in the sinks of the locker room restroom every Thursday evening before the concert, and always had a bottle of valve oil handy in the mute rack of his stand on stage.

Whatever the instruments that were used, the Chicago trumpets and the entire brass section were noted for their big and brilliant sound and their exuberant and virtuosic manner of playing, and virtually all of the Music Directors and guest conductors who led the orchestra over the span of many decades liked to hear them in action. Sometimes the zeal of the conductors was accentuated by the fact that the position of the podium, at the very front edge of the stage, was the poorest location in Orchestra Hall to really judge the amount of sound that was being produced in those back two rows of the stage. Thus, from the early 1950s on, conductors in Chicago asked for lots of brass sound, which sometimes required the players to push their instruments beyond their normal limits. Bud sometimes explained the conductors' actions in this way, with his trademark broad grin: "When a person has a big Mercedes, he sometimes likes to take it out on the road and really open it up." One reviewer of a tour concert summed up the dramatic power of the Chicago brass sound in this manner: "The brass section pinned the ushers and late-comers to the back wall."

Based upon my long years of training and my observations of the Chicago Symphony in action, I perceived that my role in the trumpet section was to emulate Bud's playing as closely as I could from within the section. The fifteen members of the Chicago brass group were an assemblage of virtuoso musicians who played in an extroverted style, who could also work together as a tightly-knit and sensitive ensemble. One of the primary reasons that the group produced such exciting music together was that the members within each of the individual sections did not play in a totally subservient, accompanying manner in relation to their respective section leader, as is so common in most other orchestras. Instead, each member of the Chicago brass choir performed as if his or her part was important and deserved to be heard within the complete tonal picture. This approach actually represented a faithful attempt to fulfill a composer's wishes. When a composer wrote, for example, several individual trumpet voices within a certain passage, he did not consider any interpersonal relationships that might exist between the individuals who would be playing those parts in the future, or whether the lead player would be weak, unconfident, or intimidated by extroverted playing within the section. The composer simply wrote out the individual parts as he wanted them to be played and heard. If he had not wished the lower voices to be heard in the musical product, he would not have composed them. In an ensemble that had a weak or unconfident lead trumpet, the Chicago system would not function properly, since the section players would be obliged to limit themselves to providing mild background accompaniment to support their underachieving principal player. However, this was certainly not the case with Bud, who was definitely not daunted by my playing out within the section. In fact, he had personally trained me over many years, and had assisted me in learning to play all of the section parts in each of the works of the standard literature in the manner in which he would have played them himself. A second reason for playing out within the section was provided by the laws of acoustics. Higher pitches are more audible to the audience than are lower pitches; thus, if the lower members of the trumpet section played slightly louder than the players on the upper voices, the audience would perceive the various parts as all being equal in volume.

When Bud was not playing on a particular piece or an entire program, and the lead part was being performed by the assistant first/third player, my approach to playing did not change. In fact, I faithfully played my part exactly as I would have if Bud had been on the first part. Irregardless of the playing that was taking place above me in the section, I observed all rhythmic figures absolutely correctly as written, did not enter early, did not rush tempos or rhythmic figures, and did not proceed hesitantly on soft, ticklish entrances. Even if my playing did not match that of my colleague(s) in the first

rehearsals, I maintained it as firmly as if I had been performing beneath Bud's lead voice, and eventually it was noticed
and usually emulated by my section mate(s). In these
instances, I was actually carrying out the role of principal from
within the section. This unconventional approach was by no
means intended to be unsupportive, or to undermine the confidence of my colleague(s); quite the contrary, I was clearly
indicating that I could be counted on to play my part correctly
no matter the circumstances.

Likewise, when the orchestra presented pops concerts that
included big band and jazzy pieces, I switched to a heavy style
of articulation and played the rhythms in the appropriate manner for those genres, rather than playing them squarely like a
legit player typically does when attempting to swing. Bud performed such pieces in the appropriate style, and when he was
not on the lead part, my section playing continued to mirror his
approach, which was emulated in time by my section mate(s).
When we did such programs, I continued to use my usual large
and deep mouthpiece and large-bore horn, instead of switching
to a shallower mouthpiece to play the high and grueling parts.
To me, it was worth the additional abuse to my chops to maintain my usual full tone and clear articulations.

To fulfill my obligations to the orchestra in a responsible
and professional manner, I checked the rosters on the bulletin
board several weeks in advance of each given program, to note
which pieces I had been assigned by Bud to play on that program, and to observe the order in which the pieces were to be
played during each rehearsal and concert. (In general, the order
during rehearsals was scheduled so that the pieces involving
the largest ensemble were rehearsed first, while the works that
required the fewest musicians were played last. However, solo
pieces with a reduced accompaniment ensemble were often
scheduled first or early during a rehearsal, to enable the soloist
to leave as early as possible.) After noting my assignments, I
looked over my parts for each piece in the Symphony library.
Many of the parts could be prepared sufficiently by silent
singing and pencil-marking in the library, while the ones

requiring additional preparation could be checked out and taken home for more extensive attention. Within the brass section, disciplined homework in advance of the first rehearsal of each piece was an absolute necessity. We did not utilize the rehearsals to become familiar with our individual parts, but rather to work to make them mesh together as a unified ensemble. I always arrived at Orchestra Hall comfortably early for each rehearsal and concert, and kept close track of which piece was being rehearsed or performed at any given moment, so that my colleagues would never have to wait for me to begin, or start rehearsing a piece without me. In addition, in those occasional instances in which I was not scheduled to play a given program, I still traveled to the hall to check in well before each concert, to make certain that the other section members had arrived; I continued this custom for about the first five years on the job, after which I arranged with Bud to be available by the phone in those rare cases when I was not needed for a certain program. Because of my constant performing in the orchestra and my regimen of private practicing, my playing continued to improve each week during my entire tenure of nearly eighteen years in the Symphony. As the weeks, months, and years passed, I could note slight but constant refinements in such aspects as my sound, intonation, solidity of rhythms and tempos, musicality, consistency, and self-confidence. These steady improvements were the result of hearing day in and day out the music that was being produced by my masterful colleagues throughout the brass section, emulating them, and making my own contributions to that music.

During all of my years in the CSO trumpet section, I had a good working relationship with Bud. With his three fellow section members, Bud shared a great many jovial moments, both on and off the job. However, as the three colleagues who played the same instrument and were in the closest proximity, we were also the ones who sensed most clearly when he felt the burdens of the job, and when he was concentrating most deeply to fulfill his responsibilities. Also, as his section mates, we were the individuals who were obliged to continuously match his style and quality; we were likewise the ones who quickly received notification when our quest for that perfection occasionally lagged. Being the consummate musician that he was, focused on the smallest of details and the finest of nuances, Bud was acutely aware of the playing that was being done around him. He expected as much dedication to excellence from his colleagues as he did from himself. He did allow for occasional lapses by his section members during rehearsals; however, this degree of slack did not apply to the repetition of an error. A repeat of an error is what would bring a rebuke. In some instances, it was simply a tapping of his foot, to indicate that the solidity of rhythm or tempo had slipped momentarily. Occasionally, it was a verbal comment, which was not delivered in a cordial manner, but instead in a gruff style: "You're flat on that G —get it up,"or "You're pushing that quintuplet figure." This curt style of communication reflected not only the extreme standards that he maintained himself but also the pressures that he bore. Bud expected that the professionalism of each member of the trumpet section, as well as the entire brass section, would result in impeccable playing, both individually and as an ensemble. However, he understood that unity of style and execution in a given piece sometimes required time and familiarity to make it all congeal. Thus, he was focused primarily on his own playing, and expected that we three colleagues would match him fully; he only commented when one of us did not completely mesh with him after an appropriate amount of rehearsing had elapsed, or when one of us occasionally strayed in our concentration. We four trumpets did possess a considerable spirit of teamwork; however, it was based primarily upon the musicianship and personal standards that each of us brought to the section, rather than on any shared authority. The strong convictions of the boss were ascendant at all times.

Over the course of Bud's more than five decades as principal of the section, he sometimes struck serious sparks with certain of the individuals in the section. To a certain degree, these major frictions came about because Bud's iron self-discipline and dedication to the highest of musical standards took precedence over his interest in interpersonal relationships. We were all in the Symphony for one primary reason, to produce music of the very highest quality. Every other aspect of the job was to be secondary to that focus. Because I had trained privately with Bud for so many years before joining his section, and had assiduously emulated both his playing and his work habits for even a longer period, I knew exactly what his musical and personal expectations were. As a result, I was the recipient of extremely few of his not-so-gentle rebukes, actually only a handful of them, over the course of eighteen years. For the most part, our relationship could be character-ized as each of us quietly doing what was necessary to create the highest quality product. He would never once observe me arriving at a rehearsal less than fully prepared, or rushing on stage from the basement at the last minute after a card game or a cribbage tournament or a too-late commute, or doing private projects on stage during the rests or tacet movements in a rehearsal. Bud did not take kindly to any complacency, or to anything less than total commitment.

I managed rather well in this potentially volatile environment, with its constant quest for perfection coupled with virtually no personal expressions of approval from the section leader, for one primary reason. During my eight years of trumpet training with my father at home, from ages ten to eighteen, this was exactly the situation that I had experienced. As a result, I had learned at a very early age to work quietly and independently on projects that were of interest to me, without expecting much support or approval from others. This youthful training equipped me excellently for my eventual careers, both of which involved decades of steady, solitary effort toward a particular goal, with little reinforcement from others along the way. Bud did not respond particularly well to colleagues who sought support and affirmation from him; nor did he care for overly brash individuals in his section.

Because I nearly always measured up to his expectations, Bud and I had a cordial relationship at nearly all times during my tenure. This relationship fostered many good conversations, in the car while driving to and from the train during Milwaukee runouts and on the trip home after Tuesday evening concerts, as well as on stage when we both arrived early before rehearsals. He would occasionally express his concerns about whether certain new members of the brass section were learning to fit in. In one case, he was irked that a new member among the trombones was repeatedly holding on slightly longer than the rest of the brass section at cutoffs. In another instance, we had a very frank discussion about a new member of our own section, including specific traits of his playing and the slim likelihood that he would adapt appropriately and attain tenure. Sometimes while Bud was trying out various horns and mouthpieces before a rehearsal, he would ask me what I heard when he played the various pieces of equipment. Because of our cordial relations, Bud always approved of my requests for unpaid release weeks to conduct far-flung research trips across the U.S. and Canada. He knew that I kept practicing well during each of these trips, and that I always returned to the job in as good a playing condition as if I had been at home. He also had a tendency to generously schedule me off the entire concert, or at least the second half of the concert, on the final performance of the Ravinia season, just before Doree and I would drive thirty to forty hours around the clock to commence one of our canoe trips across northern Canada.

One particular subject that I brought up during one of our chats, after I had been in the band about four months, involved the other member of our section at that time, and the treatment that I was receiving from him. At the time, Bud responded, "Just disregard it." This issue is mentioned here not to be in any way vindictive, but only to illustrate the point that musicians do not need to be close buddies to function together in an ensemble. Even before becoming a member of the Symphony, I had not liked this man as a person or respected him as a player (open auditions had only been introduced during my era, some ten years after he had become a member), and my opinions of him did not improve during our eighteen years as colleagues within the same trumpet section. Without presenting any specific details, I will only state that certain individuals do not respond well when they have a bit of power (even if it is only a mistaken perception of power), especially when their own insecurity issues are involved. The Chicago Symphony applies a two-year probationary period to all of its new members, during which the colleagues and the Music Director can thoroughly observe how a new player fits into the ensemble, both musically and personally. In the trumpet section, Bud obviously made the decision himself regarding whether a player would receive tenure or not. However, as a new outsider unfamiliar with the inner workings of orchestra business, I was concerned that the other section member would also have some input into my tenure status. Thus, during the five months of my first downtown season and the two following year-round periods, I quietly bore all of his posturings of superiority, and his lectures and scoldings concerning subjects both musical and non-musical.

Before the Martinon era (1963-1968), the assistant first/third player in each brass and woodwind section of the CSO played lead only on concerts for students; otherwise, the principal players of the Symphony were expected to perform on every piece. Starting in the mid 1960s, the assistant first members began playing lead on concerto accompaniments and pieces of lesser importance on each program. In the trumpet section, the fourth/utility player typically performed the second part with him on those works, or the third part when three players were required. Thus, the assistant first/third player and I performed as a twosome during a considerable part of each concert, often during the entire first half of the program. In addition, we sat beside each other in the third and fourth positions during those works that called for all four members of the section. In other words, we sat shoulder-to-shoulder during the majority of our time on the job.

When I was finally certain that my personal relations with him would in no way interfere with my tenure, which had become finalized, I spoke my mind freely. Before the start of a rehearsal one day at Ravinia in the summer of 1981, with the entire trumpet section listening, I stood in front of the music stand of my adjacent colleague and expressed my feelings and opinions very clearly. Thereafter, I never again engaged in a conversation with the man. I would say hello to him upon arriving at the hall and goodbye when leaving the hall, and that was the full extent of our communications. Over the next fifteen years, he would sometimes try to engage me in some talk about the job at hand, but I would always answer in a monosyllable, look away, and continue keeping to myself. When we performed together as a twosome, which occurred very often, I played my part in the manner in which I would have played it had Bud been on the first part, and I left it up to him to match my playing. This is noted here only to emphasize and underscore the commitment that we members of the Chicago Symphony lived by, dedicated to producing the very highest possible quality of music even though some of us were definitely not fast friends.

My generally solitary approach led me to spend most of my offstage time in Orchestra Hall ensconced in my private "studio" area of the basement, behind the equipment elevator, or reading quietly by myself on stage during intermissions or when not playing a certain piece in rehearsals. On one particular occasion when someone was seeking me after a concert, Bud noted how little time I spent communing in the locker room or the musicans' lounge before and after rehearsals and concerts by saying, "He's a fast-exit kind of guy." On tours, I preferred dining solitarily in restaurants, reading quietly in my hotel room and at the concert halls, and studying on my own at places of interest. These moments by myself refueled me for the high-powered rehearsals and concerts. As a general rule, I packed one book for each day of touring in my steamer trunk (which the stage hands hauled for us), and on certain of the trips in the U.S., I made my way through the entire stock of books. Backstage before an evening concert somewhere in Europe, Bud found me off in a quiet corridor busily devouring a history book, and teasingly asked, "Have they cut 'em off at the pass yet?" During tours in both the U.S. and abroad, I visited sights by myself and studied the displayed and stored collections at many museums, and during our annual week-long stints in New York City, I studied the stored collections each day at the Museum of the American Indian and the Museum of Natural History. One year, when I was doing a detailed study of dugout canoes at the latter institution, a young Puerto Rican technician was assigned to assist me in hauling around the various canoes in the dusty storage rooms during the entire week. On about the third day, he asked me where I was staying during my time in the city. After I checked the itinerary in my pocket for the name of the hotel and answered "The Parker-Meridien" (a very upscale chain of French hotels), he quickly placed me in "the others" category, based on my hotel accommodations, and the collegial relationship that we had developed was never again quite as warm and cordial on his part.

The fact that I seldom hung out with my lighter-skinned colleagues, who were also generally less shaggy and bearded than me, caused a number of interesting incidents during my years in the Symphony, incidents which were usually humorous to me but also provided food for thought. These occurrences took place particularly during and after the summer of 1984, when I grew my goatee into a full beard during the June vacation and gradually let my hair grow longer, causing the friends of our sons, age six and eight, to dub me "The Wolfman." (Coincidentally, George shaved off his full beard during the very same vacation period; when we saw each other on stage at the first Ravinia rehearsal, we both laughed.) In the daily interval between the rehearsal and the concert at Ravinia, I often ate my home-packed meal and studied on a bench along one of the quiet, tree-shaded edges of the park grounds. After seeing me there on the bench for several afternoons in a row, one of the administrators of the Ravinia Festival asked me, "Do you work in one of the restaurants here?" When I responded in the negative, she noted, "Oh. Then you must be with security." Since those were the only two categories of employment that she could imagine for me at the Festival, she was at a total loss for words when I stated, "No, I'm a member of the Orchestra."

Six years later, when my photo and biographical sketch appeared in the program booklet during the downtown season, an irate subscriber was prompted to write to the management, and also to send a copy of the letter to me via Orchestra Hall:

"October 25, 1990

Dear Mr. Fogel:

I think the undignified and unkempt appearance of Timothy Kent is a great detriment to all the members of the C.S.O. Management must exercise control over such outrageous appearance.

If Mr. Kent wishes to look like an unkempt woodsman, then that is where he should stay.

Sincerely,

An unhappy subscriber"

Actually, I perceived my role in this situation as providing an object lesson for the roughly 10,000 ticket holders who heard and saw me in action each week. It ought to have been food for thought for each of them to note that a guy whose appearance might frighten them if they encountered him on the street or the train could also make music of sufficient quality to be a long-standing member of the Chicago Symphony brass section.

Incidents related to my ethnic appearance also took place when the orchestra was on tour, both in the States and abroad. On one occasion, we 109 musicians, along with the stage hands, librarians, administrators, and Mr. Yates as security, were all boarding our privately chartered jet at O'Hare Airport, destined for a runout concert in downstate Illinois. When I was partway down the enclosed ramp that led from the gate to the plane's entrance, walking among various of my colleagues, two plainclothes policemen suddenly shouldered me against the wall, flashed their badges, and asked me if I was with the group. In yet another instance, decked out in a blue dress shirt, white sweater, and black dress slacks, I attended a post-concert reception with my colleagues in the ballroom at our swank Mayflower Hotel in Washington, D.C. When one of the wealthy matrons noticed that a couple of the platters of hors d'oeuvres were running low, she suggested that I take care of the situation, clearly assuming that I was one of the waiters who were serving at the event. I replied, "I don't work here," which surprised her considerably. A third incident on tour took place when we orchestra members returned to our downtown hotel in Louisville after playing a concert there. When I asked the doorman, resplendant in brown tails and black top hat, if there was a Coke machine in the lobby, he haughtily announced, "Our Coke machines are only for our guests." When I explained that I was staying there as a member of the Chicago Symphony, he immediately replied, with a considerably changed attitude, "Oh. We have a Coke machine on every floor by the ice machine, **Sir**."

Even during our European tours, I was sometimes mistaken as an interloper. During the course of one of our week-long stays in Salzburg, as we were filing from our chartered buses into the concert hall for a rehearsal, one of the uniformed security guards challenged me at the door: "Chicago Symphonie?" I answered gruffly, "Ya, sicher, bin ich ein mitglied des Chicago Symphonie Orchester! Wo ist ihre chef?" Germanic employees usually back off very quickly when you ask to see their boss.

However, even in my own home suburb of Oak Park, I sometimes encountered a similar mindset, with people making judgements based upon my ethnic appearance. When our boys were in kindergarten and second grade, I often walked them to Ridgeland Avenue, the one busy street that they had to cross en route to their school, and supervised their crossing before heading off to catch the elevated train downtown for my rehearsal. One morning, while we three were standing on the corner saying our goodbyes, a woman pulled up to the curb, rolled down the passenger window of her car, and asked the boys, "Is that man bothering you?" I answered, "I'm their father, walking them to school." She persisted: "Is that really true, boys? Do you know this man?" For once, my sons had the good sense not to leave me hanging out to dry, and acknowledged that, yes indeed, I was their dad.

In spite of the above-mentioned incidents, very few of the negative aspects of life in the Chicago Symphony were related to personal appearance or ethnicity. For me, one of the most disturbing aspects concerned the amount and quality of the contemporary music that was scheduled by management. Granted, a certain amount of high quality modern literature should be played each year by the orchestra; however, the key phrase is "high quality." In the same way that the musicians were dedicated to performing at the highest of levels, the management and Music Director had a responsibility to choose contemporary works that were worthy of our efforts. For many of the modern pieces that we performed, the amount of time and energy that was invested in preparing them, including both private practicing and group rehearsing, would have been sufficient to prepare ten or fifteen excellent works from the more standard literature. It was clear that the composers of a great many of the new works were simply stringing together a series of novel effects, rather than writing comprehensible, meaningful pieces of music. However, some of the composers apparently did not even have aural features in mind when they wrote their works. Instead, they focused upon the visual features, the actual appearance of the pages of music, which were absolutely black with notes clumped into very exotic and difficult rhythmic figures. Within the circle of contemporary composers, how the music itself looked was apparently impressive; however, their mind-boggling pages often contained few shreds of music. The degree of effort that we expended in performing each and every figure on the page correctly, due to our professionalism and our good attitude, was very seldom reflected in the sounds of these pieces. To make matters worse, the number of modern pieces that were scheduled each year absolutely soared after Maestro Solti's era, with the arrival of the new Music Director and the new principal guest conductor, who was himself a composer of *avante garde* works. Audiences clearly expressed their opinions about this major shift in programming by staying away in droves.

My sentiments concerning such "music" were revealed during the dress rehearsal in my last week on the job, when we were putting the finishing touches on yet another premiere of an undeserving work. I announced to my brass and woodwind colleagues in the back few rows: "After I'm retired in northern Michigan, whenever I miss this kind of music, I'll just go over to my neighbor's barn and shovel for a while." At the end of that week, in honor of my musical tastes, my friend and CSO tuba player Gene Pokorny presented me with a special retirement gift: a beautifully bound book entitled "Kent's Finest, A Comprehensive List of the Best Orchestral Works of the Late 20th Century." Appropriately enough, every one of its one hundred pages was completely blank! Ironically, at the only subscription concert that I have heard my colleagues play during the nine years since my retirement, one of the three pieces on the program was a brand new work. The printed parts instructed my friends to play, in free-form style, whatever they would each choose to play, at those moments when the conductor would point at them. Afterward, in response to this quasi-organized cacophony, I booed loudly and repeatedly from the gallery, while most of the rest of the audience clapped politely and demurely. What a complete waste of the time, energy, and highly developed talents of 109 dedicated artists!

In spite of the degree of excellence that we constantly sought as players, both individually and as an ensemble, and the degree of our professionalism, there were moments of hilarity and irreverence that occasionally cropped up during rehearsals and recording sessions. Bud did not customarily instigate these incidents on stage himself, but he certainly enjoyed them with the rest of us. I have preserved the delightful mental image of Bud during those times when something tickled him: bending forward at the waist in his chair so that his face angled toward the floor, and raising his right hand to his brow as if shielding his eyes and face. This posture may have dated back to the early days of tyrannical conductors, when it was in one's best interest to shield any laughter and loss of composure from the view of the podium. During one of the recording sessions for the sound track of the Disney movie *Fantasia 2000*, at the end of a particular take, Maestro Levine asked Gene Pokorny what had happened at a certain spot, where the tuba part was supposed to have been very prominent and he had not even been playing at the time. Gene pointed down toward the valves on his horn and explained, "Technical malfunction." Sitting directly behind him, I chimed in, "Well, Gene, you're getting to that age when that happens sometimes." Levine was baffled by the sudden burst of laughter among the brass and woodwind sections, but noone let him in on the joke.

After a couple of rehearsals on a particularly lackluster piece, one of the colleagues would invariably comment, "It'll be better when the dancing girls are added." Another standard comment arose nearly every time we played a somber Sibelius piece: "He really ought to have hit the vodka a little more during those long Scandinavian winters." Sometimes in the locker room after a concert, one of the colleagues would say to another: "I don't care what anyone else says, I think you played great." During a rehearsal at Ravinia one summer, Kurt Mazur, the Music Director of the New York Philharmonic, held forth at length about a very touching letter that Tchaikowsky had written concerning the piece that we were rehearsing. He read to us certain passages in which the composer had described, in very poetic terms, how deeply he felt about his new work. When Mazur finished his tale, which was intended to inspire us to even greater passion in our playing, George quipped from our section (but not loud enough for the conductor to hear), "So, do you want us to play it louder or softer?" At the surprise 50th birthday party that the orchestra threw for Maestro Barenboim in the fall of 1992, the brass section presented him with a very special gift. The heavy steel baton was engraved with these words: "Now, when we're working our asses off, you will be, too!"

Sometimes, incidents that inadvertently took place during performances were humorous only in retrospect. One such incident occurred on February 17, 1994, after we had diligently rehearsed Elliot Carter's *Partita* for three days, expending plenty of time and energy to master this crazy and difficult piece. Finally, the evening of the world premiere arrived. Everything was flowing along fine for about sixteen minutes of the eighteen-minute work, and we trumpets were on our last page of music and beginning to go for the home stretch. Only a few strings and woodwinds were playing. Suddenly, every light in Orchestra Hall went out. Total blackness everywhere. The music stopped. At first, the audience thought that this was part of the dramatic ending of this extremely modern piece; but, when the lights did not come back on for about a minute, they began to wonder. Suddenly, the lights returned. Barenboim flipped back a few pages, and indicated that we should start at Number 514. (Most of us were relieved that we did not have to return to the very beginning.) We resumed playing, and had proceeded for only about ten measures when the lights again were extinguished. This time, the audience laughed, knowing that this was not part of the score. A minute or so passed before the lights again returned. After we had resumed a second time and were moving toward the final climax, Barenboim misread the score about twenty measures from the end, and continued to conduct in 4/4 although the music had switched to 3/4 time. He could not understand why the piece was completely disintegrating; each of us was guessing where to play, and wondering just how this disaster would ultimately end. Finally, the Maestro was conducting amid utter silence. The last measure of the piece, as Carter had composed it, required the third trumpet (me) to play one loud note on the downbeat, followed by the other two trumpets on the upbeat. So after Barenboim had conducted two measures of silence, I decided that this was as good an ending point as any, and loudly played my note on the downbeat. My two section mates then joined in with their note on the upbeat, and the Maestro stopped conducting. Finally, the world premiere of the Carter *Partita* was history. None of us could see the expression on the composer's face, out of sight offstage; however, by the time he emerged onto the stage to acknowldege the applause, he had assumed the expected smiling mask. According to the terrific reviews that appeared the next day, none of the critics had been able to discern, amid the electrical interruptions, the musical train wreck that had taken place before their very eyes.

Sometimes when we colleagues were downstairs in the locker room, no matter what instrument we played, the conversation would occasionally turn to our common recurring nightmare. There were myriad variants to it, but the central concept was always the same: we were in a situation in which it would be difficult or impossible to measure up to the expected standards of excellence. Depending upon the version of the dream, we were late, or unprepared, or we could not find our concert outfit or our instrument or the music, or we were downstairs and could hear our colleagues playing on the stage without us. However, since life sometimes imitates art, various of us had actually experienced a similar incident at one time or another. For example, when the orchestra was recording Prokofiev *Lieutenant Kije* during the Reiner era, Bud had been chatting with colleagues from a visiting orchestra downstairs during a break, and had not noticed that the session had resumed. With the Maestro holding his baton poised for the downbeat, Bud ran upstairs, retrieved his horn, hustled to the offstage position, and wrestled his thumping heart into submission enough to play the offstage solos.

On one occasion when I was playing lead on an entire Beethoven program during a split-orchestra week, while en route to the Saturday evening concert, I became too engrossed in my reading on the train. As a result, I missed my stop at Adams and Wabash, and was obliged to ride quite a distance to the next stop, at White Sox Stadium down on the south side. At that time of the evening, the trains were only running at widely spaced intervals, so it took considerable time to catch a return train to downtown and then hustle to the hall, where I arrived at 8:05 for an 8:00 performance. The Stage Manager continued to hold the concert while I suited up, played four notes of warmup, and rushed onto the stage to do my job with sweat running profusely. Some years later, during a Japan tour, John Hagstrom overslept in his hotel room during an afternoon nap, and missed all of the orchestra buses to the hall for the evening concert. When he awakened, he rushed downstairs and caught a cab to the hall; however, the hour-long ride prevented him from arriving in time for the downbeat, and one of his colleague had to play his part. In spite of our greatest efforts, circumstances sometimes simply conspired to do us in.

Making recordings represented a rather important activity for the Chicago Symphony; every Music Director (except the founder Theodore Thomas), as well as various guest conductors, led the group in creating permanent sonic records. The CSO had the distinction of being the first American orchestra to record commercially under the leadership of its regular Music Director, in sessions led by Maestro Stock in May of 1916. In certain years, the recorded output was prodigious. For example, during both the 1958-59 season under Reiner and the 1976-77 season under Solti, the band laid down 29 works each season. During my time in the ensemble, we produced more recordings than any other American orchestra, in addition to having the largest live-broadcast radio audience in the country. The majority of our permanent recordings during this time were created in a studio situation, in both Medinah Temple and Orchestra Hall. During the renovation of Orchestra Hall in 1966, a great deal of its natural reverberation had been lost, causing Solti to move the orchestra's recording venue to Medinah Temple, a large open building in Chicago with lively acoustics. Years later, after Orchestra Hall received a number of additional renovations and some of its acoustical properties were improved, Solti finally returned the ensemble there for recordings. However, during these latter sessions, much of the seating areas on the ground floor and in the first balcony were covered with large sheets of plywood, in order to increase the reverberation in the rather dry hall. Our first permanent recording to be done during a live concert took place in Orchestra Hall in June of 1988, with our performance of Shostakovich *Symphony Number 7* with Bernstein, followed by our live recording there of Shostakovich *Symphony Number 8* with Solti the next February. Thereafter, recording in Orchestra Hall in live concert situations became much more common.

Several major drawbacks were involved in our making

recordings in studio settings, compared to recording live performances. First, in studio settings the members of the group
did not sit in the same positions and alignments in which we
had rehearsed and played the concerts. When we transferred to
Medinah Temple to record, the stage area was much larger than
in Orchestra Hall, and we were spread out more and positioned
in different configurations to suit the recording engineers, with
the brass well separated from the rest of the orchestra; in
addition, the acoustics of the room were very different from our
usual downtown venue. For recording sessions in Orchestra
Hall, an extension was built at the front of the stage, projecting
out over some of the ground-floor seats, and the ensemble was
moved forward on the stage, spread out more, and reconfigured according to the wishes of the engineers. Thus, in the
sessions at both locations we were hearing one another very
differently than in our performances, and in many cases we
were hearing each other very little. Another negative feature of
studio recordings was the need to play multiple takes of each
movement. First, a number of sections were played to adjust
the levels of the microphones, after which a number of
complete takes were done of each movement, with certain
alterations made in each one. Thus, it was not possible for the
players to know which of the various takes would ultimately
make their way into the finished product. This was psychologically counter-productive in all instances, but particularly when
we were performing very demanding pieces. The members
were expected to sound as fresh and inspired on the fourth take
as we had been during the first one, which was not humanly
possible, particularly in works that were very strenuous for the
brass section. A third troubling feature of studio recordings was
the great increase that was afforded to the engineers and
producers in their abilities to manipulate the sounds that we
laid down. They could separate our sections widely, record us
separately with different microphones, and then alter, mix, and
reduce our sounds however they wished in creating the finished
product. An example of their manipulation became
obvious during one particular recording session that was led by

a conductor who was not overly enamored with the power of the Chicago brass. For this session, a single shared microphone was placed directly in front of Bud and Jay, so that there was little likelihood of picking up the sounds of the section players who were associated with the first trumpet and first trombone. After one of the takes, when the producer in the control room suggested that the brass section play a little softer during the next run-through, Jay facetiously suggested that they just turn down the microphone a bit. In the ensuing discussion, it was revealed that that particular microphone, the only one on the stage for all of the trumpets, trombones, and tuba, was a sham, not even plugged into the system, and during the next break it was removed from the stage! The producer and the engineers had intended from the beginning to record only whatever of our sounds seeped into the microphones of the woodwinds and the strings. Because of the many hindrances that we labored under while trying to reproduce our usual performances in a studio setting, Bud would occasionally mutter between takes, "I'll be sure to kick the dog when I get home tonight!" (although he did not really have a dog, and would not have kicked it even if he did have one). The outstanding level of quality that he was able to maintain from the beginning to the end of long, grueling sessions was unbelievable. His musical output did not diminish even during the course of an entire day of recording, through myriad retakes and under challenging circumstances.

In recordings that were carried out during our live concerts, we were at least positioned in our customary seating arrangements, and were thus hearing one another in a familiar way. In addition, we were fueled by the impetus of performing for a live listening audience, and we only played the piece one time through; also, the recording staff was more limited in their capabilities of manipulating our sonic product. However, in the final analysis, all of our commercial recordings were rather fraudulent, considering the fact that various other individuals besides the players and the conductor had a great deal of control over how the finished product would sound. In fact, the band did not sound nearly as good on the commercial record-ings as we did in person. A much more realistic sonic record was created by the staff of WFMT radio, who recorded our live performances each week during the Orchestra Hall season and at selected concerts at Ravinia, for delayed broadcasts on National Public Radio. Hearing us play live in our own hall every single week, they were very familiar with our sound, and captured it on tape very realistically. In contrast to the recording companies, the WFMT staff were not interested in manipulating our end product, just in recording it faithfully and truthfully.

During my tenure of eighteen years, the technology of recording gravitated from 33 r.p.m. platters to cassette tapes to compact discs. One year, when we finished a European tour in London and were enjoying a brunch gathering at Maestro Solti's home before flying back to the States, he showed us a CD that he had on the piano in his downstairs music studio. Holding it up, he excitedly announced in his Hungarian accent, "Thees, my dears, ees the thing of the future." That small plastic disc, recorded digitally, represented a substantial leap forward in sonic technology.

One of the provisions of our contract specified that all members of the orchestra would be paid, no matter how few players were utilized on a given recording session; thus, we tended to record full-ensemble works on which everyone played. During my era, recordings were produced under the direction of Maestros Solti, Barenboim, Abbado, Levine, Tilson-Thomas, Bernstein, Jarvi, Tennstedt, Boulez, and Schenk. Probably the most unusual album that we recorded was enti-tled *Bear Down, Chicago Bears,* led by Solti to commemmorate the football championship of the Bears in the 1986 Super Bowl game. The platter, which featured on its cover a photo of the Maestro wearing a comical hat with the nose, eyes, and ears of a bear, contained the title song plus the *Star-Spangled Banner* and *Stars and Stripes Forever.* That project was certainly a stellar addition to the career resume of each member of the CSO.

Nearly thirteen of my eighteen years in the Symphony took

place during the heyday of the Solti era, which had begun nearly a decade earlier. During the Maestro's 22 years as Music
Director, the orchestra's prestige was consolidated worldwide.
The ensemble produced more commercial recordings than any
other symphony in the country, and these recordings won
Grammy Awards virtually every year, finally totaling 58 of
these awards. The radio audience, tuning in weekly to more
than five hundred stations across the country, was the largest of
any U.S. orchestra, while at home in Orchestra Hall, ticket sales
averaged 97 to 98 percent for each concert. Domestic or foreign
tours were an annual event, including a week-long stint each
year at Carnegie Hall. Superb programming by the management and the Music Director, including a very limited number
of contemporary works, showcased the unique virtuosic abilities of both the ensemble and the individual players, who, during contract negotiations every three years, made excellent
advances in salary, pension, benefits, and working conditions.
Private and government philanthropy was generous and solid,
and relations were generally good between the players and
management. Except for our relations with management, all of
these aspects of CSO life would remain constant throughout the
Solti era. By good fortune, only the last five years of my tenure
took place during the following era, during which nearly all of
the listed features of the orchestra suffered considerably.
However, through all of the down-turns, the superb quality of
the music that the players created each week did not diminish.

I have a vast reservoir of memories, mental snapshots, from
the years of my tenure, concerning both musical and non-
musical activities. During my first two years in the band, until
the major falling-out with my adjacent section mate occurred,
Doree and I had the section members and their spouses over
each December for a Greek or French meal and a jovial evening.
During these festive occasions, over wine and conviviality, Bud
would relate many entertaining tales of his earlier musical
adventures. He enjoyed taking on the mannerisms and voice of
Reiner to flavor the rich soup of his memories.

In 1981, in order to bolster my non-musical activites, which indirectly improved my trumpet playing, I switched my serious studying and collecting of the archaeology of North America from the prehistoric era to the historic era. I also delved all the further into the rarely celebrated early French history of the U.S. and Canada, including the era of the fur trade. Over the next two decades, I would assemble a huge research library of books and site excavation reports on the history and archaeology of this era, and would amass a very extensive collection of historic period artifacts as well. During the month-long vacation in May and June of 1981, our family visited and studied at some sixty ancestral locales in Quebec Province. Over the following decade, as all of the ancient notary records of the province would be abstracted and made available, I would be able to determine which of my 725 French ancestors had worked at various occupations in the fur trade. These individuals were engaged in the occupations of fur trade company manager, clerk, trader, interpreter, guide, voyageur, merchant/outfitter/fur buyer, investor, laborer, tradesman (cutler, gunsmith, post carpenter, etc.), birchbark canoe builder, and trans-Atlantic shipping merchant. I located the original notary documents of these people, transcribed and translated them with Doree's help, and decided to eventually produce a book containing the detailed biographies of these various individuals.

In the course of the orchestra's twelve-city European tour in August and September of 1981, foggy conditions forced the plane carrying our instruments and wardrobe trunks to land not in London but in distant Birmingham. There, British customs officials carried out a long and close inspection, causing the downbeat of our London concert that evening to be delayed by fifteen minutes. This delay was a bit awkward, since the performance was being broadcast live on BBC radio, and was also being taped by television cameras for later broadcast. The following January, during a tour of the western U.S., our equipment trucks were delayed in a blizzard between Salt Lake City and Tucson, causing the Tucson concert to be cancelled. Later in this same tour, our Sunday evening concert in San

Francisco was preceded in the afternoon by the Super Bowl game, in which the San Francisco team was playing. As I walked the streets of the city that afternoon, taking in the sights, I had the place virtually to myself. At intervals, the roar of thousands of voices would erupt from inside many of the buildings, as the populace closely followed and reacted to the action in the televised game. That evening, our bus ride to the concert hall was a bit wild, dodging the deliriously happy football fans on the streets, few of whom were headed for our concert. When such major sporting events took place while we were back home, it was a common sight to see Bud in our corner of the Orchestra Hall locker room with a small transistor radio held close to his ear, avidly following the action.

During the summer and fall of 1982, I made nine studying and collecting trips through seven midwestern states, sometimes with the family; later, over the two weeks of vacation during the holidays, we visited New Orleans and various other historical locales in the South. That September, the opening of the season was delayed for three weeks during the orchestra's strike, which was instigated primarily by the frictious actions of the new President and CEO during his first three years on the job. In addition, our well-liked personnel manager and bass player, Radi Lah, was struck down by a car in downtown Chicago one morning while he was en route to a rehearsal. Thereafter, the position of personnel manager was no longer held by an orchestra member, but by an individual from management, which further altered the relationship between players and management. During the summer of 1983, when our two sons were ages four and six years, we began doing long-distance canoeing trips as a family, first in Kentucky, then in Illinois, and finally in northern Minnesota.

The next season was an action-packed one, both within the orchestra and on the outside. In January, we toured the eastern seaboard region from Washington, D.C. to Florida; this event was followed some weeks later by a Trumpet Festival that Bud and I played on March 4, at his United Lutheran Church in Oak Park. After Bud had invited me to join him in this solo-and-duet event back in the fall, we had decided upon the pieces for the program:

> Anonymous *Three Sonatinas for Two Trumpets* (Herseth and Kent)
> Böhm *Prelude and Fugue in C Major for Organ*
> Buxtehude *Komm, Heiliger Geist, Herre Gott* (Kent)
> Torelli *Sinfonia con Tromba* (Herseth)
> Felton *A Little Trio for Organ*
> Franceschini *Sonata for Two Trumpets* (Herseth and Kent)
> Hovhaness *Dawn Hymn* (Kent)
> Anonymous *Hollandsk Kirkemarch* (Herseth)
> Purcell *Sonata* (Kent)
> Vaughn Williams *Rhosymedre for Organ*
> Handel *Suite in D Major* (Herseth)
> Manfredini *Concerto Per Due Trombe* (Herseth and Kent)

During the two weeks before the event, Bud and I ran through the program on two occasions in his basement. This was certainly a novel and exciting experience for me, five years after joining the Symphony, to be preparing a series of solos and piccolo duets with Bud. Just as he had done years before in my lessons when we would play Baroque pieces together, he sometimes noted happily after we would finish a movement, "Did you hear those resultant tones?!" It was always intriguing to hear those ghostlike third pitches that would occasionally be magically produced by the combination of our two pitches. On the Friday evening before our Sunday Trumpet Festival, after a heavy CSO afternoon concert of Bruchner downtown and a light meal at home, we met at the church to rehearse with the organist. For this rehearsal, Bud brought his Walkman cassette recorder and taped each of the pieces, so that we would have a recording of the program for ourselves. That tape became one of my most prized possessions! After the Saturday evening Bruchner concert, our son Kevin, seven years old, became quite ill with a high fever and other flu symptoms. Some weeks earlier, Doree had completely severed one of her ankle tendons while playing volleyball, had undergone reconstructive surgery, and was now barely moving about with her awkward leg cast. Thus, I was the one who had to wake up at intervals during the night, check Kevin's temperature, and sponge him with cold water to keep his temperature from spiking. On Sunday morning, after the erratic night of interrupted sleep, I did my usual morning warmup and then took Kevin to the hospital emergency room, since his temperature still hovered near 104 degrees. Returning home, I arranged a babysitter to stay with him for the afternoon, after which Doree, Ben, and I headed off for the Trumpet Festival. Partway through the program, Ben, age five, abandoned his cast-ridden mother in the ground-floor seating, located Avis in the balcony, and sat with her for the remainder of the concert. After the program had ended and Bud and I had packed away our horns in the quiet front corner of the church by the organ, he delivered the best compliment of my entire career; peering over his glasses, he said quietly, "You played **very** well today!" This event represented the absolute high point in all of my years of playing trumpet. It doesn't get better than this!

After the downtown season ended in June of 1984, we four began our family project of paddling the 3,000 miles of the mainline fur trade canoe route across the U.S. and Canada, in a series of annual segments. We wanted to experience first-hand the exact terrain and travel conditions that various of our ancestors had encountered while they paddled this route westward from Montreal, from about 1620 onward. The first year, when our boys were only ages five and seven, we limited our voyage in eastern Canada to about forty miles; in other years over the fifteen-year project, some of the individual trips in northwestern Canada would each cover more than 300 miles. Because we kept ourselves in good physical condition year-round and were healthy, no special physical preparation was required for these adventures, just acquiring and studying topographical maps, researching the route and its history, gathering and drying the food, and arranging the shuttle driver for our van. Due to the nature of this preparation, the majority of the adventures took place between my ears, involving many months of research and detailed planning before each trip. I

171

also relished the remembering and replaying of the experiences with satisfaction for years afterward.

During the long series of canoe trips, we learned about exhaustion, fear, discomforts, dangers, and the great power of the wind, which the French called *La Vielle* (The Old Woman) because she was an unpredictable nuisance and was vengeful at times. However, we also experenced the outstanding scenery, the satisfaction of reaching our destinations, and the joys of working together as a unit. From these adventures, we learned that we very rarely ever reach our physical or mental limits. If the situation demands it, we can nearly always press ourselves harder and farther than we ever imagined possible. These hard-won lessons were valuable for us not only while on canoe expeditions, but also when we were back in "civilization." One of the attractions of our paddling voyages was that they required from us so much more self-reliance than is typically necessary in our daily lives at home, where we have so many other individuals providing the vast majority of our needs. These expeditions also expanded and deepened our family bonds, by allowing us to experience together so many incidents that would not have presented themselves in our contemporary world. To have literally saved one another's lives over the course of the various trips certainly deepened our personal ties to each other.

The month-long vacation in August and September of 1984 took our family on a study trip focused on ancestry and history through the St. Lawrence Valley and the Gaspé Peninsula of Quebec, as well as New Brunswick, Nova Scotia, and New England. During the following season's European tour in January and February of 1985, I expanded my understanding of our French and British ancestors by studying at various museums during the concert stops in Paris and London. We were able to build upon this information as a family when we spent the following August-September vacation traveling through New York State and New England, and during the December vacation throughout the southeastern states. This was also the first year in a span of about eight years in which our household was a beehive of activitiy as both Kevin and Ben made their way through the programs of Cub Scouts and Boy Scouts. With considerable guidance from their father, both boys completed the Eagle rank, the highest level, before turning age thirteen.

The orchestra's tour of ten concerts in Japan and five concerts in Hong Kong during March of 1986 was a wonderfully enriching and expanding cultural experience, which Doree also shared. There are probably no quieter concert audiences in the world than those in Japan, who listen in utter silence, without a rustle or a cough! It was also a real treat reuniting near Tokyo with our Japanese friends from our time together in Trier, Germany; we had first become good friends in August of 1973, exactly 28 years after the bombing of Hiroshima and Nagasaki, when they had been babies. It was a marvel to see that Sayaka, who had been our kimono-wearing, chopstick-wielding surrogate daughter at the age of one and two years, was now quite grown up. To participate in the Japanese custom of continual gift-giving, Bud carried with him on such tours a considerable supply of Bach mouthpieces. He and Avis were absolutely in their element while traveling in the Orient, since they were both deeply intrigued with the history, art, architecture, foods, scenery, and cultures of the Far East.

The CSO tour of Texas and California in January of 1987 involved a number of very rare misadventures. First, the cargo trucks carrying our instruments and wardrobe trunks were delayed by a flat tire and a snowstorm in Arizona, and thus did not arrive in time for the concert in San Francisco. This caused us to play our performance there in civilian clothing, using loaned music and either loaned instruments or the instruments that some of us carried in hand for practicing. Later, one of the trucks left the road and overturned in Texas, causing serious damage to four basses and lesser damage to certain other instruments; a replacement truck was dispatched to retrieve the contents of the disabled vehicle, and we proceeded with our itinerary on schedule.

In June of 1987, our family was finally prepared to do our first private living history research, recreating in great detail the lives of a French trader of the 1600s and his native or Métis (mixed heritage) family. I had already spent sixteen years first studying and then replicating the various items of daily life of the native populations of the midwest region, as well as the primary items that the French traders brought into the area; over the following decade, I would continually add to our seventeenth century gear. During the course of the decade in which we would carry out this research on ancient ways of life, we would annually spend a week or more in an isolated wilderness setting, without modern items to interfere with our learning. Each year, we would paddle in our birchbark canoe to a remote site on a lake or river, and there we would focus on a couple different aspects of wilderness living, such as hunting and trapping, woodworking, cooking, hide tanning, sewing, and recreation. First, we would learn by the hands-on approach how to do each of the tasks that were related to that particular area by using traditional native materials and techinques. Then, we would repeat each of those tasks using imported French implements and materials, to determine if the new imported items brought improvements over the traditional native methods, and if so, specifically why the improvements took place. In the process, we also became familiar with many of the native customs that the French adopted, such as methods of hunting and trapping, and traveling by snowshoes and toboggan in winter and by canoe during the unfrozen months. French colonists also adopted many native garments, learned to harvest a wide array of wild foods, and took up native methods of warfare. We came to realize that the exchanges that took place between the two cultures went in both directions during much of the French period. Carrying out this living history research was very thought-provoking for us, and an excellent learning experience as a family. We would do these reenactment activities during the shorter vacation period each year, which usually took place in June between the downtown season and the Ravinia season, and do our long-distance paddling jaunts and our extensive research trips during the longer vacation, which usually followed the Ravinia season in

August and September. We also made study trips during the two holiday weeks in December.

The Symphony's tour of Australia, spanning three weeks in February and March of 1988, was an outstanding experience, which Doree relished all the more since she had no concerts to play. Unusual and beautiful scenery, a zoo and nature preserves with distinctive Australian animals and plants, and high quality museums presenting the ancient culture of the Aborigines and the post-1788 settlement by Europeans, all made it a particularly interesting trip for all of the musicians and their family members. The particular highlights for me were two outstanding museums near Perth displaying artifacts from ancient shipwrecks that had been excavated off the coast, including four Dutch vessels dating from the 1600s and four British ships from the following century. Bud carried an especially heavy burden on this tour, since he performed the new *Concerto for Trumpet* by Husa in each of the four cities on the itinerary, in addition to his usual duties. Before one of the concerts in Perth, a "sculptor" who flew in from Chicago arranged 10,000 candle-filled paper bags made of white, red, or brown paper in patterns on the lawn and the exterior staircase of the concert hall. When the candles were all lit after the performance, they created quite an impressive sight from the outside balcony of the hall. In the evenings, Doree would return from such places as Rottnest Island and Kangaroo Creek and describe for me the many fascinating parts of Australia that I was missing by practicing, rehearsing, and performing.

Back at Orchestra Hall in June of 1988, Leonard Bernstein led us in two weeks of performances and recordings of Shostakovich *Symphony Number 1* and *Symphony Number 7*, celebrating his 70th birthday. During the summers of 1946 and 1947, when Bud had played at Tanglewood (the summer home of the Boston Symphony) during his student days at the New England Conservatory, Bernstein, three years his senior, had offered him the position of principal trumpet of the New York City Center Opera, of which he was the conductor (Bud did not accept the offer). In 1951, three years after Bud had become the principal of the Chicago Symphony, the Maestro had guest-conducted the CSO. Later, he had served as the Music Director of the New York Philharmonic for a decade, beginning in 1958, but he had not been back with the Chicago Symphony in 37 years, since his 1951 visit. During his first week with us in 1988, he coached three young conductors as they each took their turn on the podium over the course of a couple of days, in conjunction with the annual gathering of the American Symphony Orchestra League. On the first day while one of these protegés was conducting, the Maestro strolled to the back row to observe, and apparently noticed that I had on top of my briefcase a coin-collecting magazine that had been loaned to me, because it containing an article about peace medals that had been presented to native allies by the French, British, and American governments during previous centuries. The following day, as another of the young conductors was leading us in a busy piece, I suddenly noticed the silver-covered toes of Bernstein's boots on the stage floor beside me. He sat down on the vacant chair adjacent to mine and, as I tried to continue counting the measures of rests, he quietly asked, "Are you into numismatics?" At first I was rather taken aback, thinking that he was possibly proposing a "get-together" back at his hotel after the rehearsal. Then I glanced down, saw the loaned magazine with the article about peace medals sticking out of my briefcase, and noted that it was entitled *The Numismatic Journal*. I laughed, explained to him why I had that publication, and gave a capsule description of my fur trade studies. By now, I had completely lost my place in the music, and the Maestro did not help matters when he picked up one of my mutes and pretended to play it like it was a trumpet! That first week, we rehearsed and performed the Shostakovich *Symphony Number 1* and then recorded it in studio sessions. During the second week, we rehearsed and recorded in live performances the *Symphony Number 7*, on which I played lead among the brass band players who were perched on the elevated chorus banks at the right edge of the stage. At the conclusion of the second week's dress rehearsal, the Maestro proceeded to hug and kiss each of the principal players. This extra minute or two of activity caused the rehearsal to be extended into official overtime, for which management was obliged to pay out about $2,500. to the players.

In September of that year, I began my decades-long master study of dugout canoes across North America. During the previous March, after acquiring a mid-1800s example from Wisconsin, I had discovered that there was minimal literature on these watercraft carved from a single log, except some studies of dugouts in the southeastern U.S. and a narrow strip of land along the northwest coast, where they were quite common. Deciding to do a book about the dugouts in all of the other regions of North America except those two areas, I wrote to 4,900 museums in the U.S. and Canada, in an attempt to locate the majority of the surviving examples. From the various responses to my inquiries, I learned that I would have nearly five hundred specimens to work with for my major study. My goal in this research project was to record every attribute of all of the known surviving dugout canoes in the study area, in such minute detail that a woodworker could create a nearly exact replica of any of these originals while working with only my drawings, photos, and descriptions. I began the project by studying a number of canoes that September in Michigan, Wisconsin, Minnesota, and Iowa.

The Saturday evening concert on March 18, 1989 was unique for me. I had spent much of the day with Ben, enjoying the Pinewood Derby with him and his fellow Cub Scouts. Then, I learned that I had to leave home early enough so that I could first drive to a jail on the near north side of Chicago and bail Doree out, in order for her to hear the Janacek *Sinfonietta*, one of her favorite pieces. That afternoon, she had been arrested, along with a considerable number of nuns, priests, and other activists, for blocking traffic on North Michigan Avenue. This was done as part of a non-violent demonstration by about seven hundred concerned citizens against U.S. military aid to the oppressive government of El Salvador, a cause that was dear to Doree's heart. Although the customary procedures of the Chicago police department dictated that prisoners were to be released only in the order in which they had been brought in, the officers bent the rules a little in this case, so that she could make it downtown in time for the concert (she arrived at her gallery seat at 7:59). The Sunday issue of the *Chicago Tribune* featured a large color photo of my demure wife being dragged by two burly Chicago policemen to a waiting paddy wagon. On the *Sinfonietta*, I was playing lead trumpet in the separate brass group, which was arrayed on the elevated chorus banks at the right edge of the stage. Earlier in the week, I had been afflicted with conjunctivitis or pinkeye in both eyes, and had been unable to see well enough to play the dress rehearsal on Thursday morning. However, by that evening I was able to see at least enough to play the concert, by moving the music stand as close as possible, leaning forward, and blinking constantly.

In April, the extended tour to Washington, D.C. and New York City offered opportunities for me to study fourteen dugout canoes at the Smithsonian Institution and the Museum of the American Indian. That summer, during numerous runout trips within the Ravinia schedule, I focused on 41 additional dugouts in Minnesota, Wisconsin, Michigan, Illinois, and Indiana. Later, during the tour of nearly four weeks in Europe during August and September, I was able to again increase my understanding of the lives of various ancestors; my activities during the tour included many days of studying museum collections, as well as visiting about ten parishes in Paris where my forebears had lived during the 1500s and 1600s.

During the summer of 1989, Sando Shia, who had immigrated from mainland China nine years earlier, joined the violin forces of the Symphony, and eventually became a dear friend. Some five years later, it was a treat for me and the other colleagues to play the *Star Spangled Banner* for her as a surprise before the start of a rehearsal, on the day after she acquired her United States citizenship. Through Sando's father, who had been a very prominent brass instructor at the Central Conservatory in Beijing, it was an honor for me to convey a full set of etude books and orchestral excerpt books to the younger generation of trumpet players in China.

March of 1990 brought another fascinating three-week tour of Japan; however, this time, I was obliged to wear a back brace and spend much of my time lying on the floor in the hotel room with my legs elevated, due to continuing problems with L-5, the troublesome vertebra at the base of my spine that had caused problems ever since my serious auto accident more than two decades earlier. From this point on, both at home in Orchestra Hall and on tour, the stage hands would set out a special chair for me on stage, which, along with a block to elevate my feet, eased the pain somewhat. During our stay in Tokyo, it was again a pleasure for Doree and me to reunite with our Japanese friends from our days in Germany. It was a very moving experience for us to visit the area of the city in which Shoko had lived as a tiny baby near the end of World War II, where she and her family had survived the horrific fire bombings of the civilian population by U.S. forces. There she was, some 45 years later, wafting cleansing incense smoke over herself and us at the Asakusa Temple, which had been rebuilt above the ashes in her old neighborhood.

Our recording schedule in the spring of 1990 included a live performance of Mahler *Symphony Number 1* led by Tennstedt, which was both taped for audio release and filmed for home video distribution. That summer offered many opportunities for me to study dugout canoes: after our living history research adventures in June, I processed 34 dugouts in Michigan and Wisconsin, and then did a couple more on a runout to Kentucky and Tennessee during the Ravinia season. During the course of the month-long vacation at the end of the summer, following our canoe voyage in central Canada, I studied nineteen more canoes during a huge family trip through central and western Canada and in South Dakota and Nebraska while en route home. Immediately afterward, the orchestra toured Europe, playing fourteen concerts in eleven cities in eight countries.

On October 6, 1990, we launched the Centennial Season of the Chicago Symphony, with a gala concert that was conducted by Solti and his designated replacement, Daniel Barenboim. By this point, 41 new players had entered the ensemble since French hornist Gail Williams and I had joined the group in January of 1979, nearly twelve years earlier. During that time, the other new members within the brass section had included George Vosburgh in 1979 on trumpet, Charlie Vernon in 1986 and Mike Mulcahy in 1989 on trombone, and Gene Pokorny in 1989 on tuba. We 43 replacement members from the previous twelve years represented 40 percent of the total membership of the ensemble, as well as 40 percent of the brass section.

The following spring, we were approaching the finale of Solti's 22 seasons as Music Director. At a pause in the music during one of the rehearsals, he mused in his thick accent, "You know, we do not try to achieve this level of perfection for those ladies in the audience who jangle their bracelets and unwrap their candies during our concerts. We do it for ourselves, and for our art." His very last concerts as our boss took place during our week in Carnegie Hall on April 14-20, 1991, during festivities that also commemmorated the centennial of this famous and outstanding concert hall. A century earlier, Tchaikowsky had conducted the New York Philharmonic in a five-day music festival to inaugurate Carnegie Hall. Solti's final concert as Music Director, on Friday evening, April 19, was a live recorded performance of Verdi's opera *Othello*, in a concert presentation starring Luciano Pavarotti and Kiri Te Kanawa, who were positioned on stage near my chair. At the end of that afternoon, after returning from a long day of studying dugout canoes at the Museum of the American Indian, I was notified that one of the offstage trumpet players whom we had brought from Chicago had returned home when his wife had suddenly gone into labor. So I made my way to the hall especially early, looked over his part, and noted when I would have to leave the stage to play it for five minutes and then return to the stage to finish the piece on my own part. That evening, I received numerous shuffles from my colleagues for performing those extra duties. During the curtain calls, Bud led the orchestra in a "tusch" for Maestro Solti, to mark his official transition to the position of Music Director Laureate. This improvised fanfare in the key of E flat, intentionally raucous and blaring and dominated by the brass section, was the ultimate compliment that an orchestra could bestow upon an individual. In addition to my work that week with dugouts at the Museum of the American Indian, I also studied other examples at the American Museum of Natural History and the Brooklyn Museum. In June, I studied 34 more specimens during a strenuous trip of 6,500 miles by myself at thirty locations in Missouri, Iowa, Kansas, Nebraska, Colorado, Wyoming, Montana, Minnesota, central Ontario, and Michigan, as well as working on various others in Wisconsin and Minnesota later during runouts from Ravinia. After our August paddling adventures in central Canada, I spent three weeks researching 34 more craft in Idaho, Washington, Vancouver Island, Oregon, and California during our family trip.

In September of 1991, we went out on strike for seventeen days, during the time which would have included Barenboim's two weeks of inaugural concerts as the new Music Director. After the contract settlement, we played the gala Centennial Concert of the CSO on October 19, under the direction of Kubelik, Solti, and Barenboim. During the curtain calls, Bud again led the forces in a raucous "tusch" to honor these two former and one current Music Directors. During the ensuing fifteen years as the boss of the orchestra, Barenboim would help to choose the replacements for one-third of the members as the most elderly colleagues gradually retired.

Back to my other obsessions. At this time, noone in North America thought that there were any birchbark cargo canoes of the fur trade era still surviving. This even included Tappan Adney, who had dedicated his work between 1887 and 1950 to preserving all information about the bark canoes of North America. Then, in the fall of 1991, I heard a rumor that there was supposedly a large fur trade canoe somewhere in the area of Buffalo, New York. Through various connections, I finally tracked this mystery craft to the Buffalo Canoe Club during the following winter; but when I contacted them by phone, they thought that I was a prank caller. The Club had preserved for more than a century an original 25 foot specimen dating from 1860; however, it had been destroyed in an arsonist's fire ten weeks before my call! Luckily, a canoe restorer had taken a number of detailed photos and some basic measurements of it a few years earlier; thus, I would later be able to extrapolate and reconstruct most of the data about that canoe from his evidence. The historian at the Buffalo Canoe Club indicated that he thought there might be a similar canoe at the Royal Military College in London, England. After making several phone calls to London, I finally located the treasure at the National Maritime Museum in Greenwich, just outside of London: it was a 29 foot cargo canoe from Canada that had been in the possession of the British Royal Family for at least a century. At this point, I decided to write a book about the birchbark canoes of the fur trade. Over time, I would locate eight original specimens from the 1800s, including two more full size versions in Michigan and Ohio, a miniature model in the Canadian Museum of Civilisation, and three miniature models in the Smithsonian Institution.

During the Symphony's tour of Europe in the spring of 1992, which was preceded by concerts in Ann Arbor, New York, and Washington, we played in Madrid, London, Paris, and Cologne. During each of our several days in London, I spent most of my waking hours perched on long ladders and atop a tall wheeled platform at the National Maritime Museum, documenting in minute detail the huge cargo canoe, which was mounted upside down on a wall rack twelve feet above the floor. I had 24 hour access to both the museum building and the display gallery where the canoe was located. Thus, I would spend all day working on the craft, tear myself away from it each day around 5 P.M., take an hour's cab ride from the museum to Royal Albert Hall, suit up in my tails, play the concert, sleep in my hotel room for a couple hours, and then return to the museum in the wee hours of the night to continue my exciting studies. After one of the concerts, a colleague said, "Last night when I couldn't sleep, I looked out of my hotel window at about 3 A.M. and saw you catching a cab. Where were you going at that time of the night?" Even when I divulged to him what I had been involved in during my off hours, he probably doubted that any museum in London would allow an outsider access to their collections in the wee hours of the night. During this tour, our televised performances in Cologne included the Strauss tone poems *Don Juan*, *Till Eulenspiegel's Merry Pranks*, and *Ein Heldenleben*. This programming placed an especially heavy burden on Bud, both as an individual player and as the leader of the ensemble, since these performances were filmed for broadcast in both Europe and in the United States.

After returning to Chicago, I studied another 31 dugout canoes in southern Michigan during the final weeks of the Orchestra Hall season, a dozen more during the Ravinia weeks in runouts to Indiana, Ohio, Michigan, and West Virginia, and 27 additional examples at the Canadian Canoe Museum and in southern Ontario during our long vacation, following our family paddling trip in central Canada. Interspersed within this full schedule was the orchestra's week in Salzburg, Austria in June, playing the Easter Festival, of which Solti had become the director. It was during this summer that George Vosburgh left our CSO section to take the principal position in Pittsburgh; we then managed with subsitutes for two years, until the section was again complete by the summer of 1994, with the arrival of Mark Ridenour.

During the spring of 1993, the orchestra performed again at the Salzburg festival, as well as in four cities in Spain. It was particularly significant to visit Barcelona at this time, since this year marked the four hundredth anniversary of Columbus' return there, when he had reported back to Queen Isabella at the conclusion of his 1492-1493 first voyage to the New World. During the June vacation, after doing our family living history research for a week, I studied dugout canoes in Michigan and Wisconsin; later, I thoroughly documented the birchbark fur trade canoe that I had discovered in Ohio, during a long runout trip from Ravinia. I also took a couple of unpaid release weeks off from Ravinia to study 26 dugouts in Ontario and at the

Canadian Museum of Civilisation, where I also documented a miniature birchbark fur trade canoe; later, during the long vacation I worked on a number of dugouts in Minnesota, after our canoe trip in northwestern Canada. This was the summer in which the orchestra began the three-year project of recording the sound track for the Disney movie *Fantasia 2000*; after each segment of animation was completed in California, we would record the music to exactly match the film's action and timings. (Years later, the *Fantasia* film would become a great favorite of Amaya, our first grandchild.)

Before the orchestra departed for our European tour of May 13-June 4, 1994, we played for several days in New York City, during which time I studied a number of dugouts in the Bronx at the storage facility of the Museum of the American Indian. Then, en route to Berlin to commence the tour, I traveled on my own to London, where I spent several days of nearly around-the-clock action at the National Maritime Museum, completing my documentation of the huge cargo canoe there. After enjoying our family activities of living history research in northern Michigan in June and our paddling adventures in northwestern Canada in July, Doree and I spent nearly a month during the long vacation studying dugouts in Nova Scotia, New Brunswick, Quebec, and Ontario. At the conclusion of the latter trip, I had completed my detailed research on 355 dugout canoes over the span of seven years; however, I still had another 125 to do for my master project, at 75 locales in the Atlantic states ranging from Maine to North Carolina. When the Symphony returned to work in September of 1994, we celebrated during a series of concerts the 25th anniversary of Solti's having become the Music Director. In the span of time since that very significant occasion in September of 1969, sixty new members had joined during his tenure of 22 years, while another eleven members had come aboard since Barenboim had taken over the position; only 38 of the current players in 1994 (35 percent of the 109 members) had been present at the beginning of the Solti era.

In February of 1995, I took a couple of unpaid release weeks off to study three miniature birchbark fur trade canoes and several other watercraft at the storage facilities of the Smithsonian Institution. A number of weeks later, the runout concert that the orchestra performed at U of M in Ann Arbor was particularly significant for me. While I was playing lead on one of the pieces that evening, I reminisced about having heard live symphonic music for the very first time performed on that stage in Hill Auditorium, back in 1967 when I had been a brand new freshman, in a CSO program that had included Bud's performance of the Teleman Concerto. Cliff Lillya sent me a nice note the day after our concert, which inspired me to reflect on his significant input into my successes.

That spring and early summer, without warning, the pain in my troublesome lowest vertebra became especially severe. I finally had my orthopedic surgeon administer cortesone injections into the area of that vertebra, but they brought no relief. Later, his recommendation of spinal fusion surgery was not backed up by a second surgeon, so I was left with no real recourse but to live with the pain as best I could. The requirements of my occupation, involving long periods of holding relatively still without opportunities to vary my position or walk around, made this especially challenging as a long-term plan. Some of the most painful times occurred during concerts in the tacet movements for the trumpets, when I was not actively counting rests and making music and my concentrated focus on the playing of my colleagues was not a sufficient enough distraction. However, when I was able to successfully rearrange my mental focus during those inactive movements, I made some of my very best connections between pieces of historical data!

The Ravinia season of 1995 brought another kind of challenge to the entire orchestra, in the form of extreme heat over an extended period; during this summer, a new all-time high of 106 degrees was recorded in the Chicago region. During the course of this long heat wave, some five hundred people expired from its effects in the greater metropolitan area. On the very hottest days, even with the stage air conditioning unit at

Ravinia operating at full capacity, the onstage temperature still measured about 90 degrees or more. Unfortunately, the cooling unit, mounted on the roof of the building, was only able to reduce the temperature of the intake air by about 25 degrees, and the roof-level air that it was taking in measured about 115 or 120 degrees. In mid-August, we Kents escaped the heat by paddling to our furthest destination in northwestern Canada, to Fort Chipewyan in northern Alberta, where the temperatures were in the 60s most days. At the end of the voyage, we contacted the pilot of a float plane to fly north and transport us out, with our canoe lashed to one of the pontoons. During the following three years, we would paddle the fur trade route on Lakes Huron, Winnipeg, and Superior (which we had skipped during our annual westward progression), to eventually complete our goal of venturing over the entire 3,000 miles of the mainline canoe route between Montreal and Fort Chipewyan.

On January 1, 1996, I typed out a letter to Henry Fogel, the President and CEO of the Chicago Symphony, which bore a heading that was appropriate for the day of the year:

"New Year's Resolution 1996
Dear Henry,
I hereby give notice that I am resigning from my position
as a member of the trumpet section of the Chicago Symphony
as of the end of October, 1996.
Sincerely, Timothy Kent"

Eight years earlier, I had decided with Doree that I would retire from the orchestra at the earliest feasible time, so that I could devote myself full time to researching, writing, and publishing. I had already gathered enough original historical data to write about a dozen major books, and I was still avidly continuing my research. However, between the orchestra's heavy schedule of rehearsals and concerts and my own practicing schedule, there was simply not enough additional time available to actually bring to completion all of these extensive projects while working the CSO job. To reach our goals, Doree and I established an ambitious savings plan, which we carried out over an eight-year period. First, we paid off our Oak Park house, and then our Michigan retirement house (my boyhood home, which we purchased from my parents, who had lived there since 1948). We then amassed enough savings so that we could live comfortably without any other income for another 12 $^1/_2$ years after my retirement at the age of 47 $^1/_2$, until the orchestra pension would begin at age 60. Shortly after I had joined the Symphony, Doree had left her job as the director of an adolescent unit in a psychiatric hospital, and had earned a Master's degree in social work from the University of Illinois at Chicago. Then, after a number of years in private practice, she had returned to her former hospital as an outpatient social worker. Finally, after 23 years of assisting troubled teenagers and families, Doree decided to work as an adoptions counselor, facilitating mostly foreign adoptions. The major advantage that we held in reaching our financial goals was that, through our combined salaries, we had a very substantial income compared to our very modest material aspirations. We firmly believed in that old adage, "He who believes he has enough is rich." In many ways, the example set by Bud and Avis had inspired and bolstered our outlook on various subjects.

I had not divulged my specific retirement plans to any of my colleagues during the eight years of our financial preparations. On the first day back to work in January of 1996, before handing in a copy of my resignation letter to the personnel manager and posting a second copy on the bulletin board for my colleagues, I first showed it to Bud in our corner of the locker room. After reading it, he said quietly, "I'm sorry to hear this. I'm sorry to hear you're leaving." Four months later, when extensive auditions were held to fill my position in April and May, I was invited and welcomed by the audition committee to take part in the procedures; however, I left that task to my colleagues on the committee.

As soon as I posted my retirement notice on the bulletin board in January, nearly all of the colleagues approached me privately, wished me well, asked about my future plans, and made additional comments. Many of their statements revealed that I was certainly not alone in my sentiments about our job in the orchestra being "too much of a good thing:"

"You're living out everybody's fantasy!" "I see you're going to be getting a life soon. I will say, you've got guts!" "You posted it right on the board, mincing no words, before any rumors got started; way to go!" "So you're leaving us! It was quite a shock to read your note. It's so rare around here for someone to leave like you are." "I wish I had arranged something on the side like that." "I'm sorry to hear about your decision to go. I mean, it will be good for you, but bad for us. I could never do it; I don't have the guts." "That's great that you can just walk away. But we'll miss you." "You're not old enough to retire. But I understand you have all these other interests. All I have is this." "Finally somebody had the guts to cut himself free; it gives me goosebumps!" "You are courageous to do it. I trust you have psychological and financial backup. Won't you miss playing? I couldn't do it; I have only had music my whole life. I would be lost without it." "Your plans are good for you, but what about us? We need you." "I know you are interested in a lot of other activities besides playing. I wish you well." "I want to tell you what a loss this orchestra is going to have by your leaving." "So you're going to leave this place. I can tell that you are really broken up about it." "I know why you're smiling; leaving has been a fantasy of mine for a long time. But I can't see giving up a hundred grand a year." "It's great you've got something else to move right into." "We're going to miss you. I think you are the envy of all of your colleagues." "I really admire you for leaving as big a job as this to do what you really want to do and are good at." "I'm so locked in, I can't imagine any change like that for me in the near future." "What a big thing to do, to completely change careers in midlife. I really envy you." "I see you're leaving to do what you really want to do with your life. That's great!" "You suddenly gave us all the idea, 'I can end this all if I really want out.' That's great." "I'm glad to hear you're going to find a life away from this place. Congratulations. This is no way to spend a life!" "I'm green with envy." "We are all so happy for you and envious of you, too!" In addition to these heartfelt responses from my comrades in the trenches, Henry Fogel responded, *"I was shocked to get your letter. That's the most unusual New Year's resolution I've ever heard. We're really going to miss you, but I understand that you have other activities you want to do. But we're really going to miss you."*

From March 31 to April 7, the orchestra was once again out of the country, playing a series of concerts at the Berlin Festival. A couple weeks later, I spent a very frigid three days studying the final birchbark fur trade cargo canoe for my book. This specimen was displayed in the hold of the *S.S. Valley Camp*, an early Great Lakes freighter that was permanently docked at Sault Ste. Marie, Michigan, near the Soo Locks, where it had been converted into a maritime museum. Not only was the weather outside cold and snowy in that northern locale, but the bilge water of the ship, beneath the steel floor of the hold on which I stood for three days to study the canoe, was still frozen solid. The hand-held light that I used to study canoes in dimly lit corners of museums was my only source of heat during those three 18-hour days of communing with that historic craft. I loved the task!

On the occasion of Bud's 75th birthday in July of 1996, the orchestra held a festive private reception with a cake in his honor at Ravinia, for a gathering of the colleagues and Bud's family members. Doree and I privately presented him with a large charcoal drawing of a pair of trumpets, which we had commissioned from an artist in Germany. The theme of the work, which hangs in its black wooden frame on their living room wall, was inspired by Bud's teasing comment that he had married his childhood sweetheart Avis in order to get her trumpet. Over the years, he had occasionally admitted that he had coveted that horn ever since they had played together in the brass quartet of their school in Bertha, Minnesota in the sixth grade. We were never sure just how true that story was; however, it was indeed a very nice trumpet, and it had certainly resulted in a happy and long-lasting marriage.

My final weeks as a member of the Chicago Symphony trumpet section commenced in the autumn of 1996, with a September 4-14 tour of the British Isles that included concerts in Birmingham, Manchester, London, and Dublin. During the tour concerts, I was obliged to focus especially intently, since the pain medication tended to cause my attention to drift. After one of the concerts, when I was about to board the orchestra bus to return to the hotel, I could not recall having packed my horn in our trumpet trunk for transport to the next city on the itinerary. Making my way back into the empty hall, I located my instrument atop a wardrobe trunk in the backstage area, where I had aimlessly left it in my medicated stupor. That way of operating was certainly out of the ordinary for me. Before departing from Dublin for Chicago, Dick Kanter, our second oboe, arranged for another of the colleagues to take a photo of us together, to commemmorate the hundreds of hours that we two recluses had read in our adjacent hotel rooms while on myriad tours over the previous eighteen years. (My final domestic tour had taken place during the previous November, when the band had played at various East Coast venues. When we had performed in Boston's Symphony Hall, it had been interesting for me to reminisce about the cattle-call audition that I had played there 22 years earlier, when I had been bumped from the roster of finalists.)

John Hagstrom, who had won the audition for my position in the CSO, filled out the section during my final months on the job, since Will Scarlett was out with a head injury suffered in a backward fall of his chair off our stage risers. Working with John during those months was a special experience, since it offered both of us the rare opportunity to enjoy a historic transition, a musical hand-off. In addition, our personal chemistry led to some great bantering.

About three weeks before my official retirement date, during the last series of concerts that I would play with Maestro Barenboim, he and I were backstage between pieces, waiting to go on for the next work. He commented seriously, "I read about you in the program, and I was very surprised. I thought that you were just a simple musician like the rest of us." I responded, "All those activities are an antidote to this," and pointed at my horn. He looked at me with a quizzical expression as I stepped out onto the stage to take my seat. I suspect that making music had never created sensations within him that required an antidote.

The program for my final week as a trumpet player included Haydn *Symphony Number 92* played by Bud and me, a contemporary piece involving Mark, John, and me, and Beethoven *Symphony Number 7*, again with Bud and me on the trumpet parts. Christoph Eschenbach, who would shortly become the Music Director of the Ravinia Festival, was on the podium. As we had previously done during all of our years together on the job, Bud and I concurred about how refreshing it was to occasionally play pieces from the Classical period, which required such a different approach from the heavy Romantic works of Strauss, Mahler, Bruckner, and other composers. The Maestro had brought his own Haydn and Beethoven parts from the Houston Symphony library for the CSO to use; myriad notations on the first trumpet part of the Beethoven clearly indicated that, in that orchestra, two players shared the work of performing the single lead part. Beneath the first set of pencil markings which noted where each of the Houston players would spell each other off, Bud added his own notation: "Even at 75, I can still play this part by myself, without an assistant, as should any principal trumpet player worthy of the job."

Since management was generously hosting a retirement party for me and all of my colleagues after the Friday evening concert, they also provided complimentary tickets to Doree, Kevin, and Ben, so that they could hear that performance. The previous week, Carol Lee Iott, the personnel manager who was an efficient and friendly liason between management and players, had asked me whether I liked any foods particularly well; I had told her that olives of all sorts and dark chocolate (but not mixed together) were dear to my heart. With that meager information, she had arranged an astounding catered buffet, featuring olives in myriad preparations, many other goodies, and a chocolate cake decorated with a canoeing theme. As soon as I arrived in the Orchestra Hall ballroom after the concert, I rearranged the centerpiece of the cake, beneath the frosting message "Happy Canoeing, Tim" so that the chocolate canoe appeared to have crashed in mid-stream and had landed upside down atop the chocolate boulders.

Dumb

191

At the festivities, I received a handsome walnut plaque from my fellow musicians that read: "Presented by his colleagues to Tim Kent in recognition of 18 years as a member of the Chicago Symphony Orchestra, 1979-1996." Then, Henry Fogel presented me with the official Orchestral Association plaque commemorating my years of service, as well as a generous honorarium, after which he led my colleagues and the management team in a champagne toast. Finally, Bud presented to me the Theodore Thomas Medallion for Distinguished Service, a gold-plated medal of sterling silver engraved with my name and dates of membership. During the presentation, he managed to deftly drape the loop of red and black ribbon of the medal over my hairy head and around my neck. Then he reviewed our relationship of more than 29 years, starting with our initial meeting backstage after the CSO runout concert at Michigan in the fall of 1967, and extending through the many years of my training and finally our eighteen years as colleagues in the Symphony. When I had my turn at the microphone, I recalled some of the incidents during my orchestra tenure when I had been mistaken for kitchen and serving help, an intruder, and a suspected airline terrorist. I also aired my views on the quality of the contemporary music that we played, and the amount of it that management scheduled each year. During the discussion of the latter subject, my colleagues smiled knowingly. Then I wished them all the very best, after having spent eighteen years together "in the trenches."

After these formalities, we all happily dug into the buffet; anyone who has ever been on tour with the CSO is fully aware of just how lustily the members can demolish a free buffet spread! During the jovial chatting, Carol Lee Iott presented me with a trumpet lapel pin, Maestro Eschenbach offered his congratulations, and I received warm wishes from my individual colleagues. At one point, Bud, Mark, John, and I posed for our last section portrait, which also included Doree as an honorary member for the evening. (We have in our family album a photo of Avis taking this section portrait in one-handed fashion, while artfully juggling a plate, a napkin, and a full glass of champagne in her other hand.) In our discussions as a section at that time, I tried to pin Mark and John down as to which one of them would assume the serious responsibility of shouting "Play Ball!" at the conclusion of each performance of *The Star-Spangled Banner*, which the orchestra played each year at the opening of both the Orchestra Hall season and the Ravinia season. Unfortunately, neither of them would agree to assume this mantle of responsibility, which I had cheerfully shouldered for many years. Gene Pokorny, while chatting with Kevin and Ben, posed this quandary to them: "Now let me get this straight. Your dad made it all the way to the top in an occupation in which only the very slimmest percentage of players can even make a living. Now he's going to give it all up to write about canoes?"

Two days later, Sunday, November 3, marked my very last day as a trumpet player. I experienced various sensations, including happiness, relief, lightness, and a touch of sadness, as I went through all of the normal daily routines of a musician, knowing that each individual step represented the final morning warmup, the final commute to work, and the final suiting up to do a performance. In the basement "Conservatory" before the concert, Gail asked me how I was doing; when I responded, "Today is kind of an emotional roller coaster," we both sprouted a few unexpected tears. At the conclusion of the concert, I left my mutes in the mute rack on the stand, since I had always resented how they inhibited the free flow of sound out of my bell. I also left my overly-fancy white coat for Ravinia concerts in the locker, as a humorous legacy for John Hagstrom.

My career as a musician was now at its end. At the age of 47 ¹/₂, I had retired even before reaching the peak of my playing abilities, at a time when I was still improving slightly every single week. My age was also at least two decades younger than the typical age for retirement by Chicago Symphony members. During my earlier days, I had wholeheartedly devoted nearly twenty years of effort to preparing myself for a career as a high-level professional player. Then, I had spent a total of 6,500 days, nearly eighteen years, as Bud's colleague in the finest symphonic trumpet section, in the very best of the big-league orchestras. I could not have asked for better results from all of my years of preparation. I had experienced a wonderfully rich and satisfying array of musical adventures.

However, along the way, I had also become immersed in an entire series of historical activities in which I was doing original and pioneering independent work. As a result, I had a very interesting, enticing, and challenging new career ahead of me, an occupation that required my full time attention. Thus, the complete and permanent transition from musician to historian was very attractive and exciting to me, not in the least bit sad or daunting. Most of my adult years had been spent pushing beyond the comfort zone and forging into new and unfamiliar territory. This new chapter of my life was simply a continuation of that pattern.

Chapter Seven

Postlude, The After-Trumpet Years, November of 1996 Onward

During the summer before my retirement from playing, I had handed over to a suburban music store virtually all of my horns, mouthpieces, mutes, and music, to be advertised and sold by the store. I had retained only the Bach B flat that Bud had chosen for me back in 1970, my best Bach C, which I had selected at the factory and had played for nearly two decades of rehearsals and concerts, and two of my most often-used screw-rim Bach mouthpieces. I had also kept a few mutes, my etude books and orchestral excerpt books, and the sheet music from my favorite solo pieces. Occasionally during the summer and fall of 1996, I had been contacted by various individuals who had recently become the happy new owners of my pieces of musical equipment, which had served me well during both my training years and my professional career.

My intention in leaving the orchestra and entirely abandoning trumpet playing was to create sufficient time in my life so that I could complete all of the books for which I had already amassed the information, and also gather more data for additional books. Thus, on the day following my final Chicago Symphony concert, I washed, oiled, and greased my remaining two horns, and permanently stored them away with the other music-making items in a remote closet. From then on, whenever someone would bring up the subject of my playing, I would explain that my horns were safely secured in a place where they would cause no harm.

What a delicious luxury it was, to now have only one full time occupation, as a researcher and historian! I immediately launched into a morning-'til-night effort, seven days a week, to complete my first two-volume work, *Birchbark Canoes of the Fur*

Trade. In the first volume, I dealt with all aspects of the transporting of trade merchandise into the interior regions and furs and hides out to the eastern settlements in Quebec. Pertaining to the canoes themselves, I included chapters about their hull design and sizes, manufacture, decoration, repairs, and storage, and described how they were propelled (with paddles, pushing poles, a sail, and towing lines) and how they were carried on land across portages. Other chapters dealt with the equipment, shelters, cooking containers, and foods of the voyageurs who paddled these craft, the usual cargo items of the fur trade period, the containers of that cargo, and how they were loaded and unloaded offshore and carried across portages. Because of our family paddling adventures, I was able to better understand and incorporate all of the information about these various subjects from period documents. The second volume in the set described in minute detail every single component of each of the eight original surviving expedition canoes from the nineteenth century that I had located and documented, in the U.S., Canada, and England.

During my last week in the Symphony, a good friend and colleague had stated that all of my years of musical training, followed by nearly a quarter-century as a professional player, had equipped me beautifully for my new occupation. Now I could easily perceive the truth of her statement. High-level success as both a musician and a scholar entailed having a strong focus on the smallest of details and nuances, and also being able to both gather large amounts of information from various sources and organize and integrate that information. In addition, being willing to generate huge amounts of effort and perserverance, and having the mindset that there were few limits on the amount of effort that one could put out on any given day, were also traits of a musician that held true for a writer focused on historical research and personal experiences. As I delved into a full time writing schedule, I was amazed and pleased at how many hours were available within each day for scholarly work, after several decades of sandwiching it between all of my musical activities.

After I had the text and illustrations for *Birchbark Canoes* well under way, Doree and I prepared our Oak Park house for sale, sold it for the full assessed value within two days of putting it on the market, and quickly thinned out our belongings in anticipation of moving. In latter March, six days before closing the sale and moving to Michigan, we had the section members and their spouses over for a final festive celebration. On this occcasion, Bud and Avis presented me with a tiny trumpet in its case, accompanied by a perceptive note by Bud that said "This is just so you will never be without a trumpet," and a heartfelt one from Avis that read "We're sorry to see you go." They had been very much involved in our lives for nearly three decades, and Doree and I were deeply appreciative of all their inspiration, encouragement, and helpfulness over those many years.

After loading a large rental truck and our van with all of our belongings, including 42 cartons of my research materials and a large array of containers holding the artifact collection, and sedating our cat Pierre for the drive (Toby the dog and Claude the ferret had no qualms about highway travel), we permanently moved to Michigan on March 30. Upon our arrival up north, we learned that the area had received a record-breaking amount of snowfall that winter, totaling seventeen feet, while especially frigid temperatures had caused much of it to remain on the ground. The particularly cold spring weather that followed also postponed the thawing, so that by latter May, there were still deep drifts of snow in shaded areas of the woods.

We relished being immersed in semi- rural life, with deer, wild turkeys, porcupines, raccoons, and plenty of other wildlife just across the road near the Devil River, and many miles of untouched Lake Huron shoreline just a couple minutes away by car. During the course of our local travels, I discovered ancient artifacts at about a dozen prehistoric sites in the county.

It was very satisfying to move back into the log home in which I had grown up from infancy to adulthood, and to sit again in the family room where I had listened so avidly to recordings of exuberant commercial trumpet players in my youth, and later to recordings of Bud and the Chicago Symphony after my introduction to legit music as a freshman in college. As a retired CSO player, I again listened avidly in the same family room; however, the recordings were now often ones that my colleagues and I had produced, including the tape of the solo-and-duet concert that Bud and I had played five years after I had joined the band. To facilitate these enjoyable listening sessions, I burned onto CDs the extensive library of reel-to-reel tapes of live CSO concerts that I had captured from radio broadcasts over the years, from my student days onward. In addition to reliving myriad memories through recordings, replaying the soundtrack of my life, I also did my research and writing in the former bedrooms where I had practiced, received trumpet lessons from my father, studied, and formulated my dreams during my youthful days. The fallow field across the road, where I had played informal baseball games with my brother and a couple of friends as a boy, was now being plowed and planted annually. Thus, I was able to discover there on a regular basis artifacts of ancient occupations, dating back as far as 6,000 to 7,000 years. It was with considerable satisfaction that I settled into this second adulthood, since I had fully achieved my musical goals, and was well on my way toward fulfilling my aspirations as a historian, paddler, and living-history researcher.

Now that I was no longer an active performer, it was fascinating to follow the gradual progression of my dreams that concerned musical themes. At first, I was occasionally visited by the classic nightmare that had sometimes haunted each of us in the Symphony, the one in which we were unable to measure up qualitatively for various reasons. Over time, I could definitely note that daily trumpet playing had receded from my mental tracks: I began having dreams in which I was in the proper location for a performance, I was fully dressed in my concert clothes, I had both my horn and the appropriate music, and every note that I played came out of my bell as a magnificent pearl, with no effort! Possibly an additional explanation for this dramatic alteration of my dreams was the long English coach horn dating from the mid-nineteenth century that I had suspended on the wall above the head of our bed, along with its mouthpiece and the tubular leather case. Perhaps these items functioned much like a native dream-catcher, filtering out any less-than-positive dreams. Aside from the fantastic improvements in my trumpet-playing dreams, and their virtual disappearance over the course of several years, I also noticed that, by not experiencing the constant emotional outlet of playing, I tended to sprout tears much more readily, especially when listening to soulful music.

In July of 1997, we paddled the mainline route on Lake Winnipeg, which represented the penultimate segment in our 3,000 mile family project of covering the entire fur trade canoe route across the U.S. and Canada. This was also my very first paddling jaunt since retiring as a player. During nearly all of the previous years, while doing canoe voyages, living history re-enactments, and research trips, I had been obliged to keep in shape by practicing three times a day. However, during the month-long vacations, I had been able to take a complete break from playing for about two weeks, and then had gradually gotten back in shape in time to return to work. On this particular voyage, it was a great relief to not have a trumpet in its gig bag as part of our gear, and not to have any expectation of practicing!

In early September of 1997, we received word that Maestro Solti had passed away, six weeks before the planned gala CSO concert which would have celebrated both his birthday and the occasion of his thousandth concert with the orchestra. As soon as I heard the sad news, I mentally heard the *Air on a G String* movement from Bach's *Third Orchestral Suite*. The Symphony traditionally played this quiet, contemplative piece to open the first concert after a colleague had passed away. The Maestro's death inspired a considerable amount of reminiscing for Doree and me, as well as several listening sessions in his honor. It had always been very clear that Solti was as demanding of himself as he was of the players in the orchestra. He never conducted a program with us without having first prepared and studied the scores extensively. Even when we were scheduled to play pieces that he had been conducting for many decades, he continued to rethink many aspects of the works and to reconsider how to faithfully respect the wishes of the composers. The "secret" to the exceptional relationship between the Maestro and the Chicago Symphony was that both conductor and players had very high personal standards, an extreme degree of professionalism, and mutual respect for each other. The results were clearly reflected in the music that we made together.

Late in the fall of 1997, Doree and I traveled back to the Chicago region so that I could usher my two volumes of *Birchbark Canoes of the Fur Trade* through the printing process. I followed the procedure daily for six weeks, from November 15 through December 26, educating myself on all stages of book manufacturing. As a publisher, it was very important for me to understand all facets of the operation. Finally, after my many weeks of careful attention, the shipment of 6,000 volumes was delivered to Michigan.

In June of 1998, we again traveled to Chicago, this time to join in the festivities celebrating the astounding fact that Bud had completed fifty years as the principal trumpet of the CSO. Having been a non-player for a year and a half, I was not able to actively participate in the gala concert of "Gabriel's Trumpets", but I thoroughly enjoyed it as a listener in the audience. Although Bud was just six weeks short of 77 years old, he still played the Haydn concerto on the program with his signature confidence and musicality. Afterward, the gathering with former and current brass players of the orchestra and members of Bud and Avis' family was great fun. It was an honor to help celebrate his legacy of a half-century of supreme music-making, and the occasion evoked a cascade of special memories for Doree and me. During the course of this visit, John Hagstrom gave us a guided tour of both the newly renovated Orchestra Hall and the new buildings of the Symphony Center. As a direct result of this little tour, during the next year or so, I had recurring dreams of coming back to the hall to perform as an extra player on CSO concerts, and not being able to find my way onto the stage, due to the reconfigured layout of the downstairs rooms and the backstage areas, which were no longer familiar to me.

During July, we paddled the north shore of Lake Superior, thus completing our fifteen years of family adventures along the full length of the mainline fur trade canoe route, which stretched from Montreal to Fort Chipewyan in northern Alberta. This had been a demanding and very valuable project, one that had taught each of us a great many lessons about ourselves, the natural world, and the major challenges that our ancestors had faced.

Shortly after completing this voyage, we received from the printing plant several thousand copies of the book *Tahquamenon Tales*, which I had written during the previous year. In this volume, I described in detail what we had experienced and learned during my nearly two decades of preparation and the decade in which our family had carried out our living history research, as we had recreated the lifeways of a French trader of the 1600s and his native or Métis family. At this point, I was already well into the early stages of writing the two volumes entitled *Ft. Pontchartrain at Detroit, A Guide to the Daily Lives of Fur Trade and Military Personnel, Settlers, and Missionaries at French Posts*. I would labor ten to fourteen hours a day on this latter project for three years, without a day off, after having earlier spent nearly two decades gathering the information. These two volumes, describing virtually all of the objects of daily life of the colonial era and explaining how they were used by the French and native populations, were published in 2001, during the tricentennial of Ft. Pontchartrain and the city of Detroit.

During the same summer of 2001, Bud retired from the Chicago Symphony, after 53 years at the helm, just weeks short of his 80th birthday. Not only had he raised immensely the standard of excellence of brass playing all over the world, by his personal example, he had also set a record for longevity as a lead trumpet on the job, which is likely never to be matched or surpassed at any time in the future.

Frank Crisafulli passed away not long after Bud's 50th anniversary celebration in 1998, and Arnold Jacobs left this world six months after Bud's retirement in 2001. Cris and Jake had represented the bottom voices in the Chicago Symphony Brass Quintet ever since Bud had arrived in 1948. The esteemed instrumental voices that had helped to create the Chicago Symphony brass sound and style were being gradually stilled, one player at a time. However, the solid legacy that the CSO brass section had established over the course of a half-century of performances and recordings would live on, both in Chicago and across the globe, through new generations of players who had been inspired by their masterful example.

Although I was no longer an active player, my work in the research and writing career was still guided by the standards and precepts that Bud and my Symphony colleagues had instilled in me, and at regular intervals I continued to listen with special appreciation to the music that we had produced together, for both my recreation and inspiration. In 2003, I completed and published the book *Paddling Across the Peninsula, An Important Cross-Michigan Canoe Route During the French Regime*, which was followed the next year by the two-volume set entitled *Rendezvous at the Straits, Fur Trade and Military Activities at Fort De Buade and Fort Michilimackinac, 1669-1781*. The text on the dedication page in each of the latter two volumes reads: "For Adolph 'Bud' Herseth, my role model of impeccable standards, with respect, admiration, and appreciation."

At this point, eight years after having left the orchestra, I have written and published eight historical volumes, four of which have received the prestigious State History Award from the Historical Society of Michigan. Looking ahead, I still have at least a half-dozen more titles waiting to be completed. These works include an account of our family's paddling adventures along the mainline fur trade route across the U.S. and Canada, a study of the dugout canoes of North America, a series of biographies of some twenty French ancestors who were involved in the fur trade between about 1618 and 1758, a study of the birchbark canoes of the Great Lakes native populations, and a book on the protohistoric or earliest period of the French fur trade.

During my several decades of historical research and writing, my approach has been to quietly and independently do massive amounts of work of the very highest quality, with my own financing. When each product is finally completed, I publish it myself, to make the information available to others. I have always felt that when my work would be made public and would be studied by knowledgeable people, it would be appreciated for its real value. This has now been borne out, through distinguished awards, book reviews in important publications, and widespread national and international sales.

My ongoing research, writing, and publishing are truly independent. I am not burdened with any concerns about job security or the attendant politics and maneuverings. In addition, I have no pressures related to receiving grant monies, no fund-raising obligations, no administrator's demands concerning either the content of my work or the schedule of completion, no need to explain to editors or publishers the importance of including certain data in the product, and no manager's opinions about costs, sales, and profits. My efforts are focused entirely on the historical questions for which I want to discover answers and explanations. I have no concerns for the amount of time, energy, and funds that are expended in the quest; instead, I strive only for the authenticity and truthfulnesss of the end products. This is the primary reason why I have chosen to self-publish my works, in order to retain complete control of the quality and quantity of the contents.

My intention to publish each of my books myself also apparently has a genetic foundation! This supposition is based on that fact that I am descended from a long line of master printers and booksellers in Paris. Gutenburg pioneered the concept of moveable type in Germany, and began printing his Bible in about 1450. About ninety years later, my ancestor Louis Sevestre began his 41 year career as a master printer in Paris, which spanned the years from 1543 to 1584. He was followed by his son Thomas, who was a printer and book seller at the University of Paris from 1586 to 1605. His son Etienne likewise carried on the same tradition during his lifetime, working until about 1625. Finally, Charles Sevestre, the fourth generation of my printer-and-bookseller ancestors in Paris, left the Old World in 1636, and emigrated with his family to Quebec. There, he became the clerk of the fur trading company for all of New France, running the warehouse. So my genetic code seems to be rather heavily imprinted with producing books!

In most respects, my approach to historical work has been the very same as the approach that I utilized while training as a musician, which involved steady preparation and forward progress until I eventually reached a level which enabled me to play in the finest of the big-league orchestras. This gradual sequence was an exercise in patience and steadiness, advancing tenaciously forward in small increments, and appreciating the continual accumulation of abilities and knowledge along the way. The amount of time and effort that were required to reach the ultimate destination was of virtually no concern. The only goal was to keep the objective in sight and to disregard all obstacles and discomforts that appeared along the way. The long-term dream of becoming a high-level player had involved a considerable amount of determination, persistence, and optimism, as well as a great deal of dogged daily effort, which had gradually accumulated day by day and year by year until the desired end result was finally achieved.

From my years of preparation in two different occupations, I am very aware of the importance of our developing disciplined habits, so that we do not have to decide each hour of every day if we are going to strive to make progress. Instead, we simply labor steadily forward each hour, seeking to achieve the highest quality possible, not with the goal of recognition of our efforts by others, but simply for the personal joy of participating in high-quality activities. I found it rather sad and pathetic to read that the baseball superstar Ted Williams had expressed his goal as a young man in this way: "When I walk down the street, I want people to say, 'There goes the best hitter that ever lived.'" Unfortunately, he was intent upon not only achieving the highest quality in his particular profession;

he was also looking forward to basking in the recognition and adulation of others. My experiences as both a musician and a historian have taught me to be content with working quietly and steadily to achieve excellence, without expecting much acknowledgement or credit from others. The quality of the results will suffice as the personal reward for the efforts expended.

From my perspective as a successful long-term trumpet player and historian, I can readily understand the Dalai Lama's sentiment, "Great love and great achievements involve great risks." For virtually everything in life, there is a price to be paid. In most instances, it is not possible for us to know in advance the full price that will be exacted for any given goal, or choice, or forward stride, or achievement, or action. Likewise, the hoped-for rewards and results are never guaranteed, even if we pay the full price. This is one of the risks that are involved in seeking one's dreams.

During my decades of first preparing for and then working as a musician and a historian, I have paid numerous prices, first while laboring to achieve my goals and then while maintaining the quality of work in both of the occupations. Some of these prices have involved investing great amounts of time, effort, and money, as well as having to ignore myriad other activities which I could have enjoyed with that effort, time, and money. Another major price has involved my eschewing the security of more conventional areas of work, ones with a much higher likelihood of employment and steady income. Instead, I have taken the much riskier path, seeking two occupations that require mainly independent training and offer little likelihood of financial security. Having established my personal goals aimed toward each of these two areas of work, I am convinced that the prices that have been paid to reach and maintain an extreme level of quality in each of them have definitely been worth the results that have been achieved.

In the process of rejecting the comfortable, well-trodden path at the professional level, with job security and a solid, guaranteed income, I have avoided the university scene as both a musician and a historian. In the latter field, I am intent upon carrying out active and pioneering historical work. I am totally uninterested in spending a great deal of my time teaching standard courses of previously discovered information, preparing and grading exams, reading and critiquing papers, attending departmental meetings, and carrying out the other duties of a professor. I likewise have no interest in basking in the institutional attention of students, colleagues, and administrators.

In the discussion of the prices that one must pay to strive for and achieve one's goals and dreams, it is very appropriate to also acknowledge the myriad prices that are paid at all stages by one's spouse or significant other and one's children, and the importance of the support of these family members. In order for me to fulfill my aspirations and work in both of my occupations, Doree and our sons Kevin and Ben generously adapted to many aspects of daily life that created an atmosphere conducive to my maximum success. For my work as a trumpet player, these included dealing with such features as my napping and sleeping schedules (a 25 minute nap on concert days at about 4 P.M., and a bedtime of 10 P.M. before work mornings), the content and timing of meals (the main meal of the day at noon, and a light dinner at 4:30 on concert days), and letting old Dad practice uninterrupted in the basement (without boisterous activity or music upstairs, even when the boys' friends were visiting). In addition, our family activities had to be carried out according to unconventional schedules. When the majority of the population was off from work, or was celebrating such holidays as the Fourth of July, I was nearly always working, since our performances took place during evenings and weekends, when the public was off and thus available to partake of our offerings. In addition, even during those days in which I was free from the orchestra's schedule of rehearsals and concerts, I was still obliged to practice three times a day, interspersed throughout whatever activities we were doing as a family. These reconfigurations of daily life did not represent the family members catering to the wishes of a prima donna, but instead simply a practical arranging of daily life so that I could do my job successfully. For my work as a historian and living-history researcher, each of the family members enthusiastically joined me in taking myriad historical, genealogical, and archaeological study trips across the U.S. and Canada, in recreating the lifeways of the seventeenth century fur trade, and in doing long-distance paddling expeditions in the wilderness. In addition to my appreciation of all of this flexibility and support from my three family members, I must also acknowledge that the massive amounts of time, energy, and funds that were required for me to both master and then work professionally in two occupations could have instead been lavished on family and home. This latter issue likewise represented a substantial set of prices that my family members paid in order for me to attain various successes. However we gladly chose to live in a modest Oak Park home, like my mentor, and we generally chose a very simple lifestyle. At holidays, we most valued the presents that we made by hand for each other and the gifts of services that we presented to each other.

During the final week in which I was writing these informal memoirs, I received in a Chinese fortune cookie the following message: "You will be fortunate in the opportunities presented to you." My life has generally consisted of one long series of fortunate opportunities. Rarely have I felt much entitlement in this world: I consider it to be entirely an accident of fate that I was born into the dominant race in a country blessed with immense natural resources and food production potential, and generally lacking breeding conditions for many of the world's most devastating diseases, such as malaria. I feel that I bear deep obligations to appreciate, respect, and do my best to honor the myriad opportunities and abilities that I have been granted. By the way that I have tried to conduct my life and my work, I have sought to advance both the art of brass playing and the knowledge of life during previous eras of North American history. Along the way, my life has been greatly enriched by very many individuals, including Bud Herseth, and I am grateful for the inspiration, encouragement, and opportunities that he and others have offered to me. It has been one fantastic trip!

Chapter Eight

Trumpet Lessons with Adolph Herseth

Bud always felt a strong commitment to pass on to students his artistry and his vast store of knowledge. He considered the example that he set through his performances and recordings with the Chicago Symphony and his solo performances to be his most important method of teaching. In addition, he delivered his lessons in a more personal manner to a select few students. These lessons included regular private sessons plus sectional coaching with the four trumpet players of the Civic Orchestra each year, during the eight-month main season of that ensemble. In addition, he granted occasional private lessons to a limited number of professional and semi-professional players from both the United States and abroad, who would travel to him for assistance. Besides these one-on-one and sectional lessons, Bud also coached a much wider audience when he presented his esteemed master classes, in both the U.S. and around the world.

I had the extremely good fortune to receive very extensive training from Bud in each of the above categories, over an extended number of years. In my case, these tutoring sessions included his performances with the Symphony (which I absorbed both in person and via broadcasts and recordings), his numerous solo presentations in the Chicago region, the regularly scheduled private lessons that he granted to me on a year-round basis both before and during my two-year tenure in the Civic Orchestra, his sectional coaching while I was a member of the Civic, his private lessons during my early professional years, and my attendance at the master classes that he occasionally presented in the Chicago area. In addition, I later received intensive on-the-job training by working closely with him in the CSO trumpet section for eighteen years, and also by playing a program of solos and duets with him after I had been in the orchestra for five years. Through all of these combined avenues, an immense amount of guidance and direction in the art of brass playing and music making flowed into me from the master.

During my training years, Bud provided a great number of tips that assisted me in my development as a musician. Many of these gifts from him were overarching concepts, which defined and explained his various approaches to making music in an artistic manner. However, an even greater number of his pointers were specific to the individual pieces at hand. My etude books, my volumes of orchestral excerpts, and my sheet music of the standard solo pieces are replete with my pencil notations reflecting his coaching. In addition, the notebook in which I jotted down both his general concepts and his specific pointers concerning various aspects of playing and certain pieces gradually developed into a treasure trove of invaluable information.

It would be both burdensome and boring to the non-trumpet-playing readers for me to present here the myriad tips and pieces of advice that Bud offered over the years concerning specific etudes, orchestral works, and solos, as well as those concerning trumpets, mouthpieces, and mutes. It will suffice to convey the elation that I often felt when he made a number of suggestions concerning a given passage, since his pointers typically made the elements of that passage suddenly fall into place, and sound much like a recording of Bud Herseth and the CSO!

During each of my tutoring sessions with Bud, which usually ran for two to three hours, he regaled me with his vast store of anecdotes about various pieces, concert halls, and conductors, as well as the misadventures of offstage playing, plus other delightful and not-so-delightful incidents from his long career. It is not my role to present these myriad stories here, since that role is reserved for Bud. However, it may be of considerable interest to both musicians and other individuals for me to offer here a small selection of the concepts that were conveyed in his coaching sessions during the course of my many years of training.

I was an absolute greenhorn in the area of symphonic music and its performance when I commenced my lessons with Bud. As a result, many of the pointers that I needed were rudimentary ones (although they served me well throughout my entire career). On the other hand, I had received eight years of solid training in the fundamentals of trumpet playing from my father before my introduction to legit music. No aspects of this firm early foundation ever required alteration during my many years of music-making. What I did need were multiple layers of additional coaching. Thus, the tutoring that I received from Bud, beginning when I was nearly twenty years old, leaned very heavily toward musical concepts and the finer points of artistic performance, and much less toward the actual craft of playing the instrument. This is very much reflected in the notations that I recorded on my pages of music and in my lesson notebook. However, this also reflected Bud's own approach to playing as well, since he nearly always focused on the musical aspects of performance.

It is very important for readers to understand that the following musical concepts were just some of those that were passed on from Bud to me. A huge number of other facets of music-making were conveyed to me via his performances of orchestral pieces, brass ensemble works, and solos, as well as the passages that he played and sang while sitting beside me during my lessons in his basement studio. By emulating his aural model, I became infused with a huge body of musical principles that were seldom or never communicated verbally. Some of these non-verbal features included the appropriate styles in which to play a wide variety of music, as well as fine tone quality and accuracy of intonation and rhythm. He also conveyed, through the example of his playing, a manner of making music that was guided by the greatest degree of professionalism, dedication to excellence, and passion for the highest quality.

Musicality and Artistry

Music is a form of communication, the telling of a story. Since vocalizing is the most natural form of musical expression, an instrumentalist should approach playing as if he or she were singing a song with a text. Send a message to the listener every time you play, sometimes by imagining specific words for the music.

Do not just play the notes that are printed on the page; convey their meaning by imitating the human voice. Translate the instructions of the printed music into a story-line of sounds, so that you are concentrating on projecting thoughts and ideas. Tell a tale, express emotions, and utilize a very wide range of dynamics. Let it hang out a little, take some chances, do not hold back. Focus on sending a message, rather than on executing a passage.

The style of playing that is always mellow and mild is comparable to a story-teller who always speaks in a moderate monotone. Be authoritative and expressive with each note, thinking of the notes within each phrase as individual words within a sentence. The whole point of music-making is to convey a story clearly and effectively, not just to produce a steady stream of sounds.

The best approach is to mentally visualize exactly what you intend to come out of your bell: the sound, the melody, the phrasing, the emotional content, the message. Then, with a very positive attitude, focus on creating that mental product while you are playing, utilizing an expressive lyrical approach.

Do not sabotage yourself before or during your perform-ance by worrying about succeeding, or anticipating errors, or thinking about the physical processes that are involved. Likewise, ignore the physical sensations of playing and the situation in which you find yourself. Simply concentrate on the desired musical goals. Except in occasional instances, it is very important to avoid all thoughts about the physical, mechanical activities that are involved in performing, as well as the physical sensations that are produced by the act of playing. The process of making music must always be directed outward, not focused inward.

With the proper attitude and a strong focus on musician-ship and artistry, most of the technical and physical aspects of playing will evolve naturally. For this reason, always perform, never practice.

There are appropriate times for both beautiful and crude styles of playing, depending on the story line of the music. However, certain attributes contribute to the musicality of playing in nearly all styles and instances. These attributes include a round, natural tone in all registers (not an artificial squeak in the high range), a steady rhythmic pulsation, a constant forward directional flow of the musical line, and long phrases that represent vocalized sentences rather than fragmentary portions of sentences.

Give considerable thought to the appropriate performance style for each piece, including its historical period. Listen to live performances and recordings of excellent musicians for input. The considerations should include such features as the color of the tone, the type of articulations, the usage and qualities of vibrato and its degree of obviousness, etc. To broaden your repertoire of playing styles, it is important to perform a wide variety of different styles and genres of music, such as symphonic musicians playing dance band, jazz, and rock music. Whatever the type of music being performed, it is crucial to always play in a very musical manner. Familiarity with these various genres will contribute considerably to mastering the great array of different styles that a symphonic musician must perform in the repertoire today.

When you are performing in an ensemble, never play isolated notes or passages. Listen carefully to your colleagues, and study the score if possible, so that you know what your part is contributing to the sound of the ensemble at each given moment, and also so that you understand which musical elements in the group are important and which are secondary at each moment.

Singing

Singing your music, as an integral part of daily preparation and performing, is an invaluable aid in playing in a natural, vocal manner. It is equally beneficial no matter what piece of music you are preparing. The act of singing clarifies and reinforces the mental image of the end product that you want to produce on the instrument. However, vocalizing also allows you to solidify the mental images without any interference from the physical equipment of the mouthpiece, the horn, and the occasional mute, and without depleting your chops.

Utilize the syllables "ta" or "to" (pronounced like the word "toe") most of the time when you sing, since these sounds replicate the standard and staccato articulations that are produced on brass instruments. However, on legato tongued passages, sing the syllables "da" or "do" (pronounced like "doe"). Singing with these two syllables, whether they are initiated by a "t" or a "d," also causes the throat to remain habitually wide open, and the tongue to remain flat on the floor of the mouth. This facilitates the unobstructed outward flow of air while you are singing and playing, and the inward flow of air when you are breathing.

Ideally, you would sing all music in the correct concert pitch, as it would sound on the horn. However, the range of a piece very often eliminates this possibility. In any case, the correct relative pitches of the notes, in relation to each other, must be maintained at all times when singing. It is also important to be able to mentally visualize the exact concert pitch of the first tone of a passage. This should be occasionally checked by singing the first tone just before you are ready to start playing, and then checking your sung pitch against the pitch on the horn or a keyboard.

When you use singing to become familiar with a brand new piece, it allows you to work out most of the musical details before you first play the piece on the horn. Through vocalizing, you can master in advance the transposition, the steady rhythmic pulsations, the articulation patterns, the smooth slurs, the natural phrasing, the relaxed and steady flow of air, and the musical messages, and also firmly set the pitches and their intonation in your ear. All of this will take place while you are maintaining your mental concept of a beautiful tone in all registers. By using this approach, all of the associations with the piece are positive and musical, without any tension or apprehension, before you produce it on the instrument. Your focus is maintained on musicality and artistry, rather than on the technical, physical aspects of playing the horn.

Rhythmic pulsation, while both singing and playing, adds solidity and liveliness to all music, and helps all of the elements of the music fall into their proper places. This crucial pulsation is produced by adding a breath accent (not a tongued accent) on each of the primary beats in the music (on beats 1 and 3 in 4/4 meter, for example). This rhythmic pulsating, usually unobserved by the listener, provides you with guideposts for making all of the notes and the rhythmic figures fit naturally into the phrases and the melody lines. [When I would play for Bud during lessons, I was regularly amazed at the degree of obviousness of the pulsating breath accents that he would request; these accents seemed overly obvious to me as the producer, but they were either inaudible or barely audible to the listener. In addition, it was amazing just how effectively these accents functioned in giving the music a natural bounce, liveliness, and expressiveness.]

After becoming quite familiar with a piece through vocalizing, when you perform the piece on the horn, mimic your sung version and the mental images that your singing developed. After you have completed one or more passages on the instrument, replay them in your head, compare them to your ideal mental image, sing them again, and then play them again on the horn. By this method, your attitude will remain positive, your focus will stay fixed on the mental product that you want to recreate on the horn, your playing will become as natural as singing, and your chops will rest appropriately between each of the short performances.

Singing also is very effective for burnishing pieces that are already familiar to you. It allows you to refresh and clarify all of the elements of the music in your head before you play a piece. This approach is applicable at all times, as preparation for such activities as practicing privately, rehearsing with an accompanist or an ensemble, performing, and auditioning. It is invaluable for maintaining a positive and artistic approach to music-making. When a given situation is not conducive to vocalizing out loud, silent mental singing can be nearly as useful in burnishing your mental tracks.

Vocalizing of your music should be done for about a half-hour each day, in addition to the singing that you intersperse with playing during a practice session. These separate vocalizing sessions can be done at other times than the practice sessions that involve the horn.

Mouthpiece Buzzing

Buzzing on the mouthpiece is also an integral tool for performing well on brass instruments. Like singing, buzzing promotes a clear mental image of the desired musical product; however, it also involves many of the physical processes of playing, but without the interferences of the instrument.

On the mouthpiece, the individual pitches are in no way regulated and delineated, like they are when the horn is added. This lack of definition forces you to solidly fix the desired pitches and intervals in your ear, without the aid of the instrument. In addition, the lack of defined pitches also provides you with completely unrestricted freedom. The sense of uninhibited freedom that you experience while playing on only the mouthpiece is one of its greatest benifits, since the natural, vocal-style mannerisms that come with this freedom later transfer to the horn when it is added to the mouthpiece.

The mouthpiece is best played by being held with the thumb and one or two fingers near its outer tip, and angled in such a way that there is equal pressure on the embouchure from all areas of the rim. To emphasize the completely free, unrestricted aspects of mouthpiece buzzing (due to the missing horn), walk around casually, swing your free arm, bend your knees, and move you body around considerably while buzzing; however, for the most part, keep your trunk straight upright, since leaning will squeeze one of the lungs. Produce the biggest and richest sound possible, and play jazzy, showy, technical music rather than careful melodies. At the beginning of the buzzing session, do not be concerned with the initial articulation of a passage and the clarity of the articulations within the passage. Just get the lips vibrating and the air flowing first (which is easiest in low-register, slurred passages); then the clarity of the initial articulation and the tongueing within a passage will fall into place. Buzz both articulated lyrical tunes and technical passages. Like singing, mouthpiece buzzing can be very beneficial as preparation for playing difficult pieces. First buzz a passage on the mouthpiece, and then repeat it on the horn while retaining the free, uninhibited approach that you used while buzzing.

It is important to always buzz with your mouthpiece rather than with your lips alone. Buzzing without the mouthpiece develops an embouchure that has the width of the entire mouth, rather than the width of the mouthpiece rim.

Sound/Tone

Think of the sound at all times while you are playing. Clearly establish in your mind the sound that you want to produce, by doing plenty of listening and singing. Then, when you play, relay this mental concept through the horn to the listener, since the trumpet is simply a mirror of the sound that is in your head.

Play by sound, not by feel. Ignore all of the physical sensations of playing, and only focus on the product that is coming out of the bell.

The sound must always be the criterion for how to approach any element of playing, such as the appropriate amount of air, the degree of mouthpiece pressure to use, etc. However, a generous flow of air is absolutely crucial in producing a good sound.

❧

The greater the number of lip vibrations, the bigger and richer will be the tone. Thus, by practicing pedal tones a little each day, your lips will tend to adopt the vibrant quality of pedal tone production when playing in all registers, and increase the overall richness and fullness of your sound. [I played a few pedal tones at the very end of each private practice session, and also sometimes after particularly demanding rehearsals and recording sessions, since they refreshed my chops somewhat. I did them in downward octave slurs from each of the notes from low C downward (slurring down an octave from the note to the pedal tone and then back up an octave to the note), as well as sometimes playing simple melodies entirely in pedal tones. Since the pedal tones tend to be rather flat in pitch on the Bach C trumpet, I used these alternate fingerings for them: C-0 lipped up to the correct pitch, B-0 lipped up to the correct pitch, B flat-2, A-2, A flat-1, G-12, G flat-23, F-13, E-123.]

❧

To develop and maintain a good sound, practice long tones in all registers and at all volumes, concentrating on excellent quality.

❧

To produce a lively, focused tone in the low register, from low C down, pretend to say the syllable "tay" when playing in this register.

❧

When you play soft passages or short notes, produce as full and rich a sound as when you play at loud volume or on a long note.

❧

Start with a big, ringing sound on the first note of each phrase, rather than starting with less than a full tone and then increasing it to full size. To emphasize this concept, sometimes practice the first note of a lick in the middle or at the end of a passage, to clearly establish the full, fat, and relaxed sound of that first note in your mind. Then play the lick as written, while maintaining the mental image of that rich, healthy sound.

Likewise, always maintain the tone through the end of the final note of a phrase or a lick; especially concentrate on this when playing long phrases. To emphasize this aspect, sometimes practice just the end portion of a phrase or a lick alone, when you have a full breath, to remind yourself of just how it should sound when it appears at the end of the full-length phrase.

Vibrato often makes the tone appear to be fuller, partly by relaxing the player. However, the use of vibrato, as well as its speed, width, and obviousness to the listener, must be musically appropriate for the particular style of music that you are performing. In some instances, when a discrete amount of vibrato is appropriate, thinking of using virtually no vibrato will reduce the width and speed of your vibrato to the appropriate levels to fit the particular style of music.

In general, Bud used lip vibrato, except in those instances when he wanted to have an obvious, strong vibrato (such as when playing the offstage lyric solo in *The Pines of Rome*); then he used hand vibrato [I used hand vibrato at all times]. In some instances, he used vibrato instinctively, rather than intentionally; he was sometimes surprised to hear in a recording that he had used it, since he had not been aware of it while he had been playing.

Air and Breathing

The steady movement of flowing air, not the pressure of the air, is what produces and sustains the sound, by causing the lips to vibrate. The concept of "breath support" is not at all air pressure produced by a tight abdomen, but instead a steady stream of air flowing freely. This is the same as the action of the bow on a violin: it is the movement of the bow across the strings that produces the sound, not the pressure of the bow upon the strings.

Think of a big, thick column of flowing air while you play, and use a generous flow rate of air at all times. (It is physically possible to over-blow the amount of air, creating a whoofy, airy sound in the high register, for example; however, this very seldom happens. Use the quality of the tone as the deciding factor, so that you are focused more on the song and less on the wind.) Know exactly how long you are going to hold a note, and keep flowing the air right through to the end of it. By doing this, the final note will retain its rich quality of sound and will not fall off at its end.

When you play soft passages, flow the air as if you are playing loudly. Likewise, when playing short notes, especially on high pitches, flow the air as if you plan to hold them out long. Move the air, rather than allowing it to remain static, and mentally aim the air flow straight out, especially while playing in the high register.

Air flow is the key to endurance. By freely flowing plenty of air, the air bears the bulk of the work, rather than your embouchure. Thus, when your chops are tired, they are able to continue producing sound if you flow the air well. During heavy blowing passages, reduce the mouthpiece pressure somewhat if you can; imagine that you are blowing the mouthpiece away from your face.

To maximize the amount of air and its free flow, your throat must remain as open and motionless as possible while you are playing, and your tongue must remain flat on the bottom of your mouth, out of the way. When you sing the music with a big, open vocal sound and with the syllables "ta" or "to" and "da" or "do," you are continually practicing keeping these features of your airway open and unconstricted. By vocalizing, you are practicing this while focusing on the musical elements of performing, not on the physical aspects.

When you take in a breath, in order to maximize the amount of air brought in and minimize the amount of time required, imagine that you are silently pronouncing the syllable "ho." This silent syllable removes all obstructions in the airway that might be caused by the tongue and the throat. The sound of the air flowing in quickly and freely will indicate that your airway is open and unconstricted.

Practice breathing without the instrument, using the same maximum speed of inhale and exhale, flowing the air freely, without any pressure on the air. Also practice breathing while holding the horn and mouthpiece in position, but without playing, taking in a large volume of air in a minimal amount of time. By using the silent syllable "ho" for breathing, the size of the opening for taking in air at each side of the mouthpiece is maximized.

As you breathe, the lungs expand and push down the diaphragm, which in turn pushes out the stomach. Thus, a full, deep, relaxed breath causes the stomach to expand outward. Breathe deeply from the bottom of your lungs, not from high in your chest. However, after the lower area of your trunk has filled, let your chest and collarbone area rise naturally; do not restrict any natural movement of your trunk.

For a wind instrument player, the most valuable air is from the point when the lungs are about three-quarters full to a little below the "at rest" level. Above and below these two points, the effort to flow the air is greater, and the speed of its flow reduces. Thus, it is not of value to try to completely fill every available space in the top of your lungs when you take in a breath, or to utilize every bit of air at the bottom of your lungs when you play.

Take in a large amount of air in a very short period of time, so that the act of breathing is as quick as possible. By doing this, you will not disrupt the tempo at breathing points, and you will minimize the breaks in the musical line at those points. In some cases, when the upcoming phrase or lick after a phrasing point is rather short, and less than a maximum breath is needed to play it with a good sound, taking a shorter breath will keep the melodic line flowing well with a minimal interruption.

While you are playing, allow your trunk to collapse as your air flows out. Do not keep your chest and collarbone area in the raised position. If you are reaching the near-empty stage but still have more of the phrase to play, think of an easy outward flowing of the air, rather than of squeezing out the last of the air. Keep your elbows away from your sides, and imagine that your lungs are expanding, rather than contracting, as you approach the bottom of your supply of air.

Starting the Tone

It is crucial that you have a clear mental picture of the entire phrase that you are about to play, rather than having an image in your mind of only the beginning of the first note. In this way, you will be focused on an entire segment of music, rather than on just the initial tone.

For starting a soft passage, "set" the mouthpiece firmly on the embouchure with the full usual pressure that you use for playing the pitch that begins the passage. Do not wait to increase the mouthpiece pressure until after you have commenced playing.

Mentally visualize a big, beautiful sound, rather than a thin sound. Sometimes practice melodies around the initial entrance note, to establish a relaxed and singing sound in your mind.

Take in a big, relaxed "ho" breath, with no tension in your entire body. This is the only point at which you think at all of the mechanics. From the end of the breath intake onward, think only from the musical and artistic viewpoint, focusing only on the message that you wish to send to the listener.

Know exactly when you want the phrase to begin, and at that instant immediately commence singing the rich tone and flowing the air. For high entrances, this will entail using a fast, clean articulation. Do not start the tone with explosiveness, except when you are instructed to do so by written instructions on the page.

The above series of steps for commencing playing are to be done in a natural, relaxed, rhythmic sequence. Whatever the quality of the initial articulation of the entrance, concentrate on sustaining a good sound and producing the musical product that you envisioned.

Tongueing

Execute all articulations cleanly and clearly at all times, whether you are playing standard, staccato, or legato tongueing. This entails a fast tongue movement no matter the speed of the tempo; note this especially when you are playing slow tempos and legato articulations. Do not allow the tongue to work slowly and interfere with the air flow. Keep the tongue flat on the floor of the mouth while articulating, which you practice each time that you vocalize your music with "ta" or "to" and "da" or "do" syllables.

※

It is crucial that you maintain the fullness and the fine quality of your sound while articulating, whether in standard, staccato, or legato style, and in both single and multiple tongueing. When preparing to play an articulated passage, in order to maintain your focus on the tone, first vocalize the passage as written, then play it all slurred, and finally add the tongueing to the playing.

※

Note that playing tongued passages requires more air than playing slurred passages. To keep the air flowing freely, articulations should consist of only about five percent consonant (t or d) and ninety-five percent vowel (a or o). Too much emphasis on the consonants inhibits the flow of air; there should be no greater emphasis on the consonants while tongueing than there is in our normal speech.

※

When you want to accent an articulation, this is usually done by flowing more air at the beginning of that particular note, rather than by adding more tongue to that note.

※

To develop and maintain good articulations, you should practice solos and orchestral excerpts as much as tongueing exercises and etudes. Whatever the music you are performing for polishing articulations, keep your focus entirely on the musical features, rather than on any mechanical aspects. To avoid falling into habitual ruts, vary the styles of the articulations from time to time in the various etudes that emphasize tongueing. When practicing interval exercises, mix up the articulation styles.

When you are perfecting a staccato passage, first acquire the desired sound while playing it with standard tongueing, connecting all of the notes. Then gradually add the spaces between the notes, all the while maintaining the same fine quality of sound.

While you are practicing single, double, and triple tongueing, overlap the range of speeds of the three styles. This will equip you fully for any musical demands that you may encounter, and it will also facilitate the production of identical sounds within the three different styles.

There are instances when you should use the multiple tongueing patterns of ta-ka and ta-ta-ka not only for articulating at high speeds, but also for their musical effect. The configuration of ta-ka-ta is also useful in certain instances, particularly for producing clarity in each note when you are playing fanfare figures.

When playing cornet solos, the multiple tongueing passages should be smooth and legato. In most other instances, legato versions of double and triple tongueing are usually used only to facilitate very fast articulations.

High Range

When you play in the upper register, as in all other performing, first clearly imagine the fine tone and the musical message of the passage. Then vocalize it to firmly set the images in your head, and finally sing out the passage on the horn with plenty of air flow and without forcing. To encourage a generous movement of air in the upper register, crescendo as a passage ascends to its high notes. Do not back off from the high pitches; instead give them an extra amount of air. Also, to play in the upper range in a relaxed fashion, sometimes practice by glissando-ing up to the high pitches, to clearly fix their sound in your mind, and then play them without the glissando approach.

❧

To play with ease in the high register, practice a passage in the low range, then the middle range, and finally in the high range. Maintain the same generous flow of air, good quality of sound, and clear musical message in each of the registers.

❧

To maintain your focus on a rich tone in the high range, practice starting a melody on various upper pitches in a relaxed fashion without an initial articulation; sustain the good sound no matter the quality of the initial entrance. Later, add the initial articulation to the entrance, while maintaining your focus on the tone. Also sometimes practice entering on a high pitch and playing it as an isolated note, concentrating on the quality of the sound and the movement of the air.

❧

Sometimes practice a certain passage on one of your high horns, and then mimic the relaxed playing of the passage in the same concert pitches on the lower horns.

Miscellaneous Concepts

Know exactly how you think each passage in a piece should be played, and perform it that way unless the conductor instructs you otherwise. Do not wait to be told how to interpret a passage.

❧

When you are performing a particularly difficult lick, broaden the notes slightly and sing them out especially clearly, to make them all speak well.

Emphasize the short notes within a passage, with broadness and breath accents, in order to make them sound equally clear in relation to the long notes. *Primarily Orchestral Music Style*

✓ Every note within a line must have forward direction.

Sustain the dynamic level throughout a passage; do not lapse into a comfortable mezzoforte volume and coast along. Likewise, sustain the full sound of each note over its full length, rather than carelessly allowing the individual notes to decay.

Think of all the tones in a passage as being level, on the same plane, no matter how high or low the pitches are, and how wide the intervals are. This will be reinforced by your daily vocalizing, in which range and intervals are not challenging.

Keep the tempo moving steadily forward at all times; do not drag the tempo.

There is a natural tendency to be late when entering after a rest, especially if the rest is at the beginning of a measure. Listen closely to your colleagues, and join in without disrupting their pre-established tempo.

When you insert rubato into the rhythm, retain the basic steady pulse, the continuity of the phrase, and the larger musical units, rather than creating a series of separate, unrelated figures. Use very little rubato in Baroque solos.

❧

To play very soft passages, lean forward and point your bell into the music stand, to decrease the projection of your sound.

❧

Never back off when you play; have no inhibitions.

❧

Do not plan to project your musical ideas with your body language; instead, channel those ideas through your horn. Completely relax your body when you play, and if a certain amount of discreet body language happens to occur, let it happen.

❧

Never work harder than necessary to get the desired result.

❧

Your fingers and tongue must move as quickly in slow passages as in fast ones.

❧

In French literature, a dot over or under each note within a slurred group indicates that you are to lightly articulate each of those notes.

❧

In Mahler's works, a marcato marking (an inverted V symbol) over a note indicates that you are to add a broad breath accent to that note, not a hard tongued accent.

❧

It is not a question of being better than someone. How can you love trying to be better than another person? It is a matter of doing it for yourself, and also for the joy that you can bring to others.

༺

In a symphony orchestra, the desired sound of the French horns is produced by having their bells aimed backward, causing the sound to first bounce off the rear wall and then project out to the audience. In small brass groups, the horn sound should be more closely matched to the other instruments, which produce sounds from bells that are facing forward or upward. Thus, the members of chamber ensembles should be seated accordingly, so that the audience hears side-facing or forward-facing French horn bells.

Cornet Versus Trumpet

Originally, the cornet was generally conical over most of its length, expanding in bore diameter from the mouthpiece receiver to the beginning of the flare of the bell; in contrast, the trumpet was generally cylindrical, with much less expansion of the bore from the receiver to the beginning of the flare of the bell. As a result, the sounds and the characteristics of blowing of the two instruments differed accordingly. However, modern cornets and trumpets have very few differences between them. Trumpets are now more conical than before, and cornets are more cylindrical than before. As a result, they are very similar in their type of sound, smoothness and ease of blowing, projection, etc. Today, their differences are mostly just a matter of how the tubing is wound and curved. Stravinsky and Monteux (who premiered many of Stravinsky's works) both stated that the players did not have to use cornets on the parts that Stravinsky had labeled as cornet parts; these two distinguished maestros could not discern any differences between the sounds of the two instruments.

High Horns

Always relate your playing on the high horns to that on your big horns.

❧

Do not over-breathe or over-blow on the piccolo trumpet.

❧

Because of the lesser amount of air that is required on the piccolo, a great deal of piccolo playing will naturally cause you to breathe too shallowly when you are playing on the big horns, if you do not watch for this.

❧

Usually practice the piccolo at the end of your practice session, after you have finished all of your work on the big horns. However, it is useful to sometimes alternate back and forth between the piccolo with its smaller mouthpiece and the big horns with their larger mouthpieces, since you may occasionally be required to alternate in this manner in the performance of a piece.

❧

Keep in mind that piccolo playing is an extra specialty, not a major part of playing. The vast majority of your basic work takes place on the big horns, so these are the ones that ought to receive the most attention.

Practicing

Never practice; always perform. *NoT ALwnys.*

❧

yes In your daily practice sessions, balance the time spent on so-called "exercises" with time spent on real music. However, at all times, no matter the kind of piece, perform musically and artistically.

❧

When you are mastering a new piece, first become very

familiar with it by singing; then work it up slowly on the horn before finally bringing it up to full tempo.

❧

Melodic playing is very important, since it emphasizes good sound and musicality, and keeps your focus off the mechanics of playing. This vocal approach to music-making, even sometimes thinking of a specific text for the music, carries over when you perform technical pieces.

❧

Rest often during a practice session, whenever necessary to try to keep feeling fresh at all times. However, it is also important to play full-page, challenging etudes, to develop your endurance. Vocalizing during a practice session is excellent, since it allows your chops to rest while keeping your mind focused on artistic music-making and a beautiful sound. With this approach, you can be resting nearly as much as you are actually playing, making your practice sessions very productive and encouraging. When you reach the point where you are really forcing and the notes are not speaking, either take a long break or end the session.

❧

In general, practicing etudes offers many more benefits compared to practicing orchestral excerpts, since the etudes were composed to offer challenges, develop certain aspects of your playing, and keep your performing flexible.

❧

It is important that you maintain the entire range of technical skills and familiarity with all of the horns at all times, so that you are always ready for the demands of any piece. Do not focus too much on any particular aspect of performing in your daily practicing just because it is especially easy and pleasant for you; likewise, do not avoid any element of playing in your practicing because it is especially challenging for you.

To keep from falling into ruts of routine, and to develop a better understanding of the music that you play, vary the styles of articulation, the locations of the slurs and the tongued sections, the keys of transposition, and the volume level of pieces when you practice them on different days. Also, sometimes play them on trumpets with a different pitch. Improvise your own practice pieces, and invent variations on pieces that have already been written. In addition, vary the order of your practice session on different days. All of these approaches will keep your mind fresh, interested, and focused on artistry, rather than simply running through the same standard routine every day.

One of the major drawbacks of thinking of "the warm-up" as a separate part of daily playing is that this fosters the idea that you first warm up and then you perform. We must be performing from the first note of the day until the last one of the day. Approaching "the warm-up" as a set, prescribed preparation before performing easily leads to the idea in the player's mind that he or she cannot perform well, or sometimes not even perform at all, without going through "the warm-up" routine. From the very first note that you play in the morning, think of performing, but in an easy manner at first. We do have to acknowledge that we are using many muscles in playing, and, as with any strenuous muscular activity, these muscles have to be "awakened," so to speak, before they can operate at maximum efficiency. At the same time, the first portion of our daily playing is the time when our brain "wakes up," too. The speed at which this happens is related to how much is expected of the brain. That is why we should vary our daily playing routine, so the brain is not on automatic pilot. Instead, it needs to be very interested, and focused on producing artistic music with a fine sound from the first note to the last note throughout the day. Starting each session with mouthpiece buzzing is excellent, since it activates and engages the mind, the playing muscles, and the breathing apparatus.

❧

On days off in the schedule of rehearsals and concerts, starting the day with a half-hour session (with a break of about ten minutes in the middle), and then doing two more sessions during the course of the day and evening, each one about 45 minutes, is excellent for maintainance and progress. On days with an evening concert, doing the morning session plus a light session in the afternoon (with its content varying according to the demands of the program that particular week) puts you in good condition for the evening performance.

❧

yes

Practice the elements of playing that are not on that week's program. During heavy-blowing weeks, practice light lyrical pieces and delicate articulations. Likewise, on light weeks, practice demanding etudes and upper register pieces.

❧

Take advantage of the input of both a tape recorder and friendly listeners. They can be objective, and they sometimes hear what you cannot hear, while you are occupied being the producer of the music.

❧

When it is necessary to practice with a mute, such as when you have to play in a hotel room while on tour, the cup mute is best for these sessions. [Johnny Howell warmed up before each commercial show entirely with a cup mute. This was similar to a runner practicing while wearing ankle weights, and feeling very fleet of foot when the weights were finally removed. For Johnny, taking the cup mute out for playing the performance gave him the sensations of unfettered freedom.]

❧

Taking about two weeks off from playing once each year is excellent, for both refreshing your attitude and sharpening your musical approach to performing. Each time you return to the horn after this long annual break, your playing improves a little, since you return to music-making thinking slightly more clearly and artistically. After the long respite, start back by buzzing the mouthpiece three times a day, in ten to fifteen minute sessions, for two or three days. Then, a week of playing increasingly strenuous music should put you back into nearly full condition.

Transposing

Transposition, which involves playing different notes and in a different key than the music that appears on the printed page, is a constant requirement for symphonic trumpet players, due to the history of the instrument. A natural trumpet, without valves, could only produce the notes in its single overtone series. These harmonic notes were spaced in rather wide intervals, except in the upper register of the instrument. For example, on a trumpet pitched in the key of C, the ascending notes in the overtone series, from pedal C upward, would include C, C, G, C, E, G, B flat, C, D, E, F, and G. Thus, scale-like passages were available to the player only in the extreme upper range of the instrument.

To offset this major limitation on the number of available notes, crooks were invented. One of these U-shaped sections of tubing, when inserted into the instrument, changed its overall length and thus its key. Various crooks of different lengths would change the trumpet into various different keys, each with its own respective overtone series. After the development of crooks, composers could write for the trumpet in many different keys. During a performance, the player would change crooks as needed, to change keys and thus make the required notes available to him. For example, during the course of Mozart's opera *Don Giovanni*, the trumpet players changed crooks thirty-five times. By the early nineteenth century, the trumpet in low F (a perfect fifth below the modern C trumpet) had become the standard orchestral instrument. Supplied with a full array of crooks, the player could alter his F-pitched instrument to play in the keys of E, E flat, D, D flat, C, and B, and when the crooks were coupled together, also in B flat and A.

Finally, the Prussians Stölzel and Blühmel invented the valve in 1815, which was perfected within the following two decades. This development allowed the length of the trumpet, and thus its key, to be changed instantaneously. The seven valve combinations that were possible with three valves offered the player the equivalent of having the harmonic notes of seven natural trumpets, or one trumpet with six crooks, available at all times.

Early composers wrote trumpet parts in the keys of the various natural instruments that were available, and later in the various crook-derived keys. After the invention of valves, the B flat trumpet (a perfect fourth higher than the low F trumpet) became the standard orchestral instrument during the course of the nineteenth century, as the parts that were being written became more and more demanding. Later, during the second half of the twentieth century, the C trumpet supplanted the B flat in the role of the standard orchestral trumpet in most locales in the world. This long and convoluted history has led to the present situation, in which most orchestral parts require transposing, often involving a number of different transpositions within the course of a single piece. In addition, players sometimes choose to use another instrument than the C trumpet on a given piece, in order to facilitate its performance or to achieve a particular type of sound; these instances also require various transpositions.

The following list presents the methods that are commonly used for the various transpositions:

*Up a half step: read a half step higher, and add seven sharps
　　to the key
*Down a half step: read a half step lower, and add five sharps
　　to the key

*Up a whole step: read a whole step higher, and add two sharps to the key

*Down a whole step: read a whole step lower, and add two flats to the key

*Up a minor third: read in bass clef, and add three flats to the key

*Down a minor third: read in soprano clef, and add three sharps to the key

*Up a major third: read in bass clef, and add four sharps to the key

*Down a major third: read a major third lower, and add four flats to the key

*Up a perfect fourth: read a fourth higher, and add one flat to the key

*Down a perfect fourth: read a fourth lower, and add one sharp to the key

*Up a tritone: read in bass clef and one step higher, and add six sharps to the key

*Down a tritone: read in bass clef and one step higher and down an octave, and add six sharps to the key

*Up a perfect fifth: read a fifth higher, and add one sharp to the key

*Down a perfect fifth: read a fourth higher and down an octave, and add one flat to the key

These various transpositions must be mastered and maintained to such a degree that you can sight-read music in all of them with facility; this particularly applies to the most commonly encountered keys. When playing a C trumpet on the standard orchestral literature, this includes transposing trumpet parts written in A, B flat, D, E flat, E, and F.

Playing Auditions

Do not think of auditioning "for something," or "against someone." Just enjoy yourself, and present what music you have to offer. Apply the extra amount of adrenelin-driven energy that you have from the audition situation toward your music-making and artistry, rather than focusing on the situation. If the listeners like your offerings, fine; if not, that is fine too. You are no less of a musician just because the audition-ers did not happen to like your playing, or thought that it was not appropriate for their ensemble.

√While you are playing the audition, think positive, happy thoughts. You know that you have utilized the audition preparation period to considerably advance your musical skills, and that is the most important goal. Toss the passages off almost carelessly, taking appropriate musical risks.

While standing alone on the stage, if you perform the very loud orchestral passages at the full volume that would be appropriate within a full orchestra, your playing will tend to sound too loud and crass. To a certain degree, moderate all of the loudest passages during auditions, except when you are requested to play at full orchestral volume. Instead of maximum volume, project a very large, rich sound.

During the course of my many years of training with Bud, I developed a number of personal insights and perspectives. Certain of these outlooks, particularly those that pertained to my own progress and advancement as a player, would serve other aspiring musicians as well. One of these points involves the issue of assessing one's own progress. On many occasions during my younger years, when certain aspects of my playing would come out ideally, I would say to myself, "Someday, those good things that you now do occasionally will become habitual and regular." This is a kind of healthy and realistic encouragement that each of us can give to ourselves. The incre-ments of our forward progress are always very small, but as long as they accumulate steadily, the end goals will eventually be reached. Likewise, it is not appropriate to worry about and focus on "problems" in our playing. We must mentally reframe the situation, and simply acknowledge that not all of the elements of our music-making are fully developed yet. However, with serious dedication and constant effort, all of the various aspects of our playing will eventually develop as they should. Pertaining to our end goals, as we advance, our perspective on the level of quality that we want to achieve also changes. It is human nature that, as our skills become more developed, we automatically and continually raise the bar of our expectations of ourselves.

To developing and aspiring players, I would recommend focusing on these activities: listen frequently and intently to fine players in many different genres of music; practice in moderation and do plenty of vocalizing; and play various different styles and genres of music, always as musically and artistically as possible. In addition, I would urge them to seek out a teacher who focuses very much on the artistic approach, with only a light focus on the technical and physical aspects of playing, and only when absolutely necessary. I would also encourage young players to master the art of being both a style-setting, secure lead player and a sensitive section player, and learn to listen to and follow directives well. Finally, I would urge them to be hard on themselves and push forward with full dedication, yet I would also encourage them to avidly engage in a number of non-musical activities that they enjoy.

Success does not come easily or quickly, in spite of the quest for instant fame that pervades our culture. As encouragement to those who are seeking steady and solid forward progress, I would offer this well-known adage: "To attain excellence, you must care more than others think wise, risk more than others think safe, and dream more than others think practical."

The Author

   Growing up in the north woods of Michigan, Tim Kent was not introduced to symphonic music until the age of eighteen, when he entered the University of Michigan School of Music. At that point, he had received eight years of solid training in the fundamentals of trumpet playing from his father at home. After four months of trumpet lessons from Clifford Lillya at the University, when Tim was still an absolute novice in symphonic music, he began his many years of training with Adolph Herseth. This period of intensive instruction from the master spanned Tim's remaining college years, his two-year stint in the Civic Orchestra of Chicago, two years of playing in Germany, and nearly four years of free-lancing in Chicago. During the latter period, Tim played long-running shows and musicals, recorded sound tracks for films and television and radio commercials, and continued to hone his symphonic skills. Then, shortly before his thirtieth birthday, he was chosen by nationwide auditions to join the trumpet section of the Chicago Symphony Orchestra, where he spent the next eighteen years as a colleague of Bud Herseth. Thus, he is probably the only trumpet player who was taught and transformed by the master from an absolute greenhorn in symphonic music into a high-level performer over a very extended, long-term period. In addition, he worked closely with Bud on a daily basis as a colleague in his section for nearly two decades. These two experiences have given Tim a unique double perspective on the artistry of Adolph Herseth, as well as a deep insider's view of the entire brass section of the Chicago Symphony and its inner workings.

Before turning age 48, Tim retired from the Symphony, to devote himself fulltime to his other career, as a historical researcher and writer focusing on the colonial and fur trade era of North America. During the nine years since leaving the life of a musician, he has produced nine volumes, for which he has received the prestigious State History Award from the Historical Society of Michigan. His works that have been competed to date, besides his musical memoirs, include the following:

Birchbark Canoes of the Fur Trade, Volumes I and II.

Tahquamenon Tales; Experiences of an Early French Trader and His Native Family.

Ft. Pontchartrain at Detroit; A Guide to the Daily Lives of Fur Trade and Military Personnel, Settlers, and Missionaries at French Posts, Volumes I and II.

Paddling Across the Peninsula; An Important Cross-Michigan Canoe Route During the French Regime.

Rendezvous at the Straits; Fur Trade and Military Activities at Fort de Buade and Fort Michilimackinac, 1669-1781, Volumes I and II.

Books that are currently in the production stage include an account of the many adventures that Tim and his family experienced during their fifteen years of paddling the 3,000 mile length of the mainline fur trade canoe route across the U.S. and Canada; a highly detailed study of some five hundred surviving early dugout canoes scattered across North America; a series of biographies of about twenty of his direct French Canadian ancestors who were involved in the fur trade of North America from about 1618 to at least 1758 (he has deeply researched over 725 of his direct French ancestors, who came from over 120 communities in France); a study of the traditional birchbark canoes of the native populations of the Great Lakes region; and a treatise on the earliest protohistoric fur trade between the French and the native populations of North America. In addition to his immersion in research and writing, Tim is also active as a lecturer and a presenter of living history.

He is pictured below authentically dressed and equipped as a French trader of the 1600s, on East Moran Bay at St. Ignace, Michigan, at the Straits of Mackinac. Along this shoreline, his direct ancestor François Brunet dit Le Bourbonnais landed in the summer of 1685, having traveled here from Montreal to trade over the following fall, winter, and spring. Another direct ancestor, Jean-Baptiste Lalonde dit L'Espérance, arrived here from Montreal in the autumn of 1696, hired to carry out trading for Cadillac, the commandant of Ft. de Buade at St. Ignace.

In the photograph, the author is armed with an original wheellock pistol dating from about 1615 to 1640, which is accompanied by an original gunpowder belt flask which also dates from the seventeenth century. From the waist down, he is dressed in native fashion, with moccasins, leggings, knee garters, and a breechclout, along with a *sac à feu* or belt bag which was fashioned from a complete skunk skin. From the waist up, he is wearing a mixture of native and French articles, including a linen chemise, a shooting bag and sheathed tomahawk, a shoulder-suspended pistol holster, a knife in its neck sheath, a necklace of fox leg bones and black bear canines, a conch shell moon ornament, and a nose ring and ear ring made of copper rod. His black felt hat is decorated around its crown with a string of whitefish vertebrae, and on its upturned brim with the wing of a male mallard and two deer dew claws. This admixture of cultures was very typical for Frenchmen living in the interior regions of North America during the fur trade era.